Philosophy in a Time of Terror

PHILOSOPHY

IN A TIME OF TERROR

~~~~~~~~~~~~~~~~~~~~~~~~~~~~~~

DIALOGUES WITH
JÜRGEN HABERMAS AND
JACQUES DERRIDA

~~~~~~~~~~~~~~~~~~~~~~~~~~~~~~

Giovanna Borradori

THE UNIVERSITY OF CHICAGO PRESS

CHICAGO AND LONDON

GIOVANNA BORRADORI is associate professor of philosophy at Vassar College. She is the author of *The American Philosopher: Conversations with Quine, Davidson, Putnam, Nozick, Danto, Rorty, Cavell, MacIntyre, Kuhn,* published by the University of Chicago Press, and the editor of *Recoding Metaphysics: The New Italian Philosophy.*

The University of Chicago Press, Chicago 60637
The University of Chicago Press, Ltd., London
© 2003 by The University of Chicago
All rights reserved. Published 2003
Printed in the United States of America
12 11 10 09 08 07 06 05 04 03   1 2 3 4 5
ISBN: 0–226–06664–9 (cloth)

Library of Congress Cataloging-in-Publication Data

Habermas, Jürgen.
    Philosophy in a time of terror : dialogues with Jürgen Habermas and Jacques Derrida / [interviewed by] Giovanna Borradori.
      p. cm.
    Includes bibliographical references.
    ISBN 0–226–06664–9 (cloth : alk. paper)
      1. September 11 Terrorist Attacks, 2001. 2. Terrorism—Philosophy. 3. Political science—Philosophy. 4. Habermas, Jürgen—Interviews. 5. Derrida, Jacques—Interviews. I. Derrida, Jacques. II. Borradori, Giovanna. III. Title.

HV6432.7 .H32 2003
303.6′25—dc21   2002043559

♾ The paper used in this publication meets the minimum requirements of the American National Standard for Information Sciences—Permanence of Paper for Printed Library Materials, ANSI Z39.48–1992.

FOR

GERARDO AND LUCIA ZAMPAGLIONE

MY PRIVATE LITTLE HEROES

CONTENTS

PREFACE

~~~~~~~~~~~~~~~~~~~~~~~~~~~~~~~~~~~~~

Philosophy in a Time of Terror

~~~~~~~~~~~~~~~~~~~~~~~~~~~~~~~~~~~~~

Philosophy books are seldom conceived at a precise point in time or in a specific place. Kant mulled over *The Critique of Pure Reason* for eleven years: he called it the "silent decade." Spinoza worked most of his life at the *Ethics,* which was published posthumously. Socrates never wrote a single line. The case of this book is different, for it was conceived in the span of a few hours, in New York City, during the morning of September 11, 2001.

I lived 9/11 firsthand: I was separated from my children, who were stranded in their schools at the opposite ends of town, and from my husband, a reporter, who ran for his life covering the attack on the Twin Towers. From my perspective, the unthinkable broke out of a glorious late summer morning, which inexplicably turned into something close to apocalypse. All communication was suddenly cut: the phone and the Internet were down, no public transportation was available, the airports were closed and so were railway stations and bridges. Like the rest of the world, I watched the tragedy unfold on television; unlike the rest of the world, I knew that some fifty blocks from my home scores of people were jumping ninety floors to their death, some holding hands and some by themselves. As the World Trade Center collapsed, the escalation of events looked thoroughly open-ended: the Pentagon was in flames, the president displaced in the air, the vice-president hidden in a secret location, the White House evacuated, and reports of an explosion at the Capitol had just created a stampede of senators and congressmen. Until the fourth hijacked plane was confirmed to have gone down in Pennsylvania, like many I was convinced that the worst was still to come.

Even though the degree of personal involvement varied from case to case, virtually every New Yorker remembers in detail what they were doing when they learned that two commercial airliners, full of passengers and jet fuel, had crashed into the tallest buildings of the Manhattan skyline. Wall Street lawyers and cabdrivers, shopkeepers and Broadway actors, doormen and academics—all have a story to tell. Even children have their own special stories, usually tinted with disbelief, fear, and loneliness.

Mine is the story of a philosopher in a time of terror. Like every other story, it is uniquely woven into the life of its narrator. So, inevitably, my story concerns Europe and the European philosophical tradition, of which Jürgen Habermas and Jacques Derrida are arguably the two greatest living voices. Deafened by the myriad of sirens rushing downtown and alone in my East Side apartment, I remember trying to focus on the reality of my life beyond the immediate moment. Among many other thoughts that chaotically amassed in my mind, I was reminded that both Habermas and Derrida were scheduled to come to New York, separately and through unrelated channels, in just a few weeks' time. I wondered: Will they still be able to come? What will they make of this tragedy? Will I ever be able to ask them?

Habermas and Derrida ended up coming to New York according to their original plans, and I had the privilege of collecting their responses to the most devastating terrorist attack in history: they are the focus of *Philosophy in a Time of Terror*. Despite many references to current events, the guiding thread of the dialogues is to submit to philosophical analysis the most urgent questions regarding terror and terrorism. Has classical international law become obsolete in the face of the new subnational and crossnational threats? Who is sovereign over whom? Is it useful to evaluate globalization through the notions of cos-mopolitanism and world citizenry? Is the political and philosophical notion of dialogue, so crucial to every diplomatic strategy, a universal tool of communication? Or is dialogue a culturally specific practice, which might sometimes be simply inadequate? And finally, under what conditions is dialogue a feasible option?

The explicit ideology of the terrorists responsible for the attacks of 9/11 rejects modernity and secularization. Since these concepts were first articulated by the philosophers of the Enlightenment, philosophy is called to arms, for it is clear that it can offer a unique contribution at this delicate geopolitical junction. In my introductory essay, "Terror-ism and the Legacy of the Enlightenment: Habermas and Derrida," I defend this thesis from the angle opened by Habermas's and Derrida's sharply distinct readings of the Enlightenment. I also discuss the rela-tionship between philosophy and history and identify different models of political commitment. This will enable the reader to place the inter-ventions of Habermas and Derrida in a larger context.

The dialogues not only express Habermas's and Derrida's unique styles of thinking but bring into play the very core of their philosophi-cal theories. Each dialogue is accompanied by a critical essay in which my purpose is both to highlight the main arguments on terror and ter-rorism that Habermas and Derrida advance on this occasion and to show how they fit in the larger context of their respective theoretical frameworks.

This book is the first occasion in which Habermas and Derrida have agreed to appear side by side, responding to a similar sequence of questions in a parallel manner. I greatly appreciate their willingness to do so on the subject of 9/11 and the threat of global terrorism.

On 9/11 Habermas was at his home in Stamberg, in southern Ger-many, where he has lived for many years. Derrida was in Shanghai, China, for a series of lectures. The news found him sitting in a café with a friend. This book tells their stories, too. In their two dialogues with me, they recount what it meant for them to be in New York, a city that they both love, during the immediate aftermath of 9/11. Both were deeply affected by the fright produced by the anthrax attacks and the emotional devastation that one picked up just by walking on the street. Theirs, however, is also the story of what it took them, as philosophers, to expose the frameworks of their thought to the hardest of all tasks:

the evaluation of a single historical event. Because of the enormous self-confidence and risk that such exposure entails, for a philosopher this *is* a very personal story to tell.

The encounter with perhaps the most destructive day in their adult lives has stimulated, in both Habermas and Derrida, very authentic responses: responses, that is, that reflect the highly original ways in which each of them shapes, combines, and creates ideas.

Habermas's dialogue is dense, very compact, and elegantly traditional. His rather Spartan use of language allows his thinking to progress from concept to concept, with the steady and lucid pace that has made classical German philosophy so distinctive.

By contrast, Derrida's dialogue takes the reader on a longer and winding road that opens unpredictably onto large vistas and narrow canyons, some so deep that the bottom remains out of sight. His extreme sensitivity for subtle facts of language makes Derrida's thought virtually inseparable from the words in which it is expressed. The magic of this dialogue is to present, in an accessible and concentrated manner, his unmatched ability to combine inventiveness and rigor, circumvention and affirmation. Another great French philosopher, Blaise Pascal, spoke of these pairs as the two registers of philosophy: *esprit de finesse* and *esprit de géométrie*.

Despite the marked differences in their approaches, both of them hold that terrorism is an elusive concept that exposes the global political arena to imminent dangers as well as future challenges. It is unclear, for example, on what basis terrorism can claim a political content and thus be separated from ordinary criminal activity. Also, it is an open question whether there can be state terrorism, whether terrorism can be sharply distinguished from war, and finally, whether a state or coalition of states can declare war on something other than a political entity. This elusiveness is all too often overlooked by the Western media and the U.S. State Department, which use the term *terrorism* as a self-evident concept.

Habermas reconstructs the political content of terrorism as a function of the realism of its goals so that terrorism acquires political content only retrospectively. In national liberation movements it is quite common for those who are considered to be terrorists, and possibly even convicted as terrorists, to become, in a sudden turn of events, the new political leaders. Since the type of terrorism brought into focus by

9/11 does not seem to have politically realistic goals, Habermas disqualifies its political content. On this basis, he is quite alarmed by the decision to declare war against terrorism, which gives it political legitimation. Also, he is worried about the potential loss of legitimacy on the part of the liberal democratic governments, which he sees systematically exposed to the danger of overreacting against an unknown enemy. This is a considerable one both domestically, where the militarization of ordinary life could undermine the workings of the constitutional state and restrict the possibilities of democratic participation, and internationally, where the use of military resources may turn out to be disproportionate or ineffective.

Derrida claims that the deconstruction of the notion of terrorism is the only politically responsible course of action because the public use of it, as if it were a self-evident notion, perversely helps the terrorist cause. Such deconstruction consists, as if it were a self-evident notion, in showing that the sets of distinctions within which we understand the meaning of the term *terrorism* are problem-ridden. In his mind, not only does war entail the intimidation of civilians, and thus elements of terrorism, but no rigorous separation can be drawn between different kinds of terrorism, such as national and international, local and global. By rejecting the possibility of attaching any predicates to the supposed substance of terrorism, we obviously deny that terrorism has any stable meaning, agenda, and political content.

In addition, Derrida exhorts us to be vigilant about the relationship between terrorism and the globalized system of communication. It is a fact that, since the attacks of 9/11, the media have been bombarding the world with images and stories about terrorism. Derrida feels that this calls for critical reflection. By dwelling on the traumatic memory, victims typically try to reassure themselves that they can withstand the impact of what may repeat itself. Since 9/11, we have all been forced to reassure ourselves, with the result that terror appears less a past event than a future possibility. Indeed, Derrida is stunned at how naively the media contributed to multiplying the force of this traumatic experience. Yet, at the same time, he is also disconcerted at how real is the threat that terrorism might exploit the technological and information networks. Despite all the horror that we witnessed, he told me, it is not unfeasible that one day we will look back at 9/11 as the last example of a link between terror and territory, as the last eruption of an archaic the-

ater of violence destined to strike the imagination. For future attacks—
as would be the case with chemical and biological weapons or simply
major digital communication disruptions—may be silent, invisible, and
ultimately unimaginable.

In the face of these devastating perils, both Habermas and Derrida
call for a planetary response involving the transition from classical international law, still anchored in the nineteenth-century model of the
nation-state, to a new cosmopolitan order in which multilateral institutions and continental alliances would become the chief political actors.

Practically, this transition may require the creation of new institutions. Yet, and without a doubt, the first step is to strengthen the existing ones, to implement their diplomatic reach, and to respect their deliberations. On the theoretical front, the empowerment of international
actors demands a critical reassessment of the meaning of sovereignty.
In this respect, both Habermas and Derrida affirm the value of the Enlightenment ideals of world citizenry and cosmopolitan right. As Kant
put it, this is the state of a universal community in which all members
are entitled "to present themselves in the society of others by virtue of
their right to the communal possession of the earth's surface." As soon
as such a community is in place, a violation of rights in one part of the
world would be felt everywhere. Only under this condition will we be
able, Kant wrote, to flatter ourselves with the certainty "that we are
continually advancing towards a perpetual peace."

ACKNOWLEDGMENTS

I wish to express all my gratitude to Jürgen Habermas and Jacques Derrida for taking up the challenge of this book. I grew up on their texts, often wondering what sorts of persons could be bound to such astounding minds. This occasion gave me the opportunity not only to get a sense of their minds at work, which was for me a life-transforming experience, but also to know them as the unforgettable individuals that they are: two very different and yet unmistakably European gentlemen who have experienced much in their lives and whose fantastic intellectual power never obscures a very palpable human sensibility.

I also would like to thank my dearest friend and colleague, Michael Murray, without whom this book would not be what it is and, perhaps, would not even have reached completion. I can hardly find words to express what his support meant to me. He has read and critiqued every single page of this book, at each stage of refinement, giving me the gift of his inexhaustible philosophical knowledge and analytical sharpness. I know how much I owe him and I hold it very dear to my heart.

This project has a tragic birth date: September 11, 2001. During that very day, and in the months that followed, my brother, Pietro Borradori, was close to me, as was my friend Mariangela Zappia-Caillaux, who encouraged me both emotionally and professionally: as a career diplomat, she kept reassuring me that this project was a unique and very useful contribution. My thanks also go to Dr. Alvin Mesnikoff, who did not let me sink in the darkest moments.

I am very grateful to three wonderful friends. Richard J. Bernstein, for me a great source of philosophical and human inspiration throughout the years. James Traub, whose acute mind and implacable sense of humor made me laugh when laughter was really all I needed. And Brooke Kroeger, the strongest woman I know, whose affection and belief in me I will simply never forget.

Among the people to whom I feel most indebted are my editor at the University of Chicago Press, David Brent, and Giuseppe Laterza from Editori Laterza. Their confidence in this book as well as their kindness and friendship have been precious. At the University of Chicago Press I would like to thank Maia Melissa Rigas for her excellent copyediting of the manuscript under extreme circumstances.

I owe a lot to Luis Guzman, who did a wonderful job translating my dialogue with Habermas, and Michael Naas and Pascale-Anne Brault, whose rendering of my exchange with Derrida into English is nothing short of a work of art.

This book made me realize how important it is to feel valued and supported by one's home institution. I am very grateful to Vassar College and its president, Francis Fergusson; the chair of my department, Douglas Winblad; and Kathy Magurno, the department's administrative assistant. I also wish to thank all my students at Vassar College, who cheered for me and kept up my spirit. Special thanks go to Max Shmookler, my marvelous research assistant, and Zachary Allen, whose passion for philosophy and dedication to my project were really unforgettable.

My two children, Gerardo and Lucia Zampaglione, have been fabulous supporters of this book. They understood that it meant a lot to me and endured my extended absences from home and their lives. For this, I wish to thank them.

Finally, last on this list but first in my heart is my husband, Arturo Zampaglione. As we lived hand in hand through the tragedy and the trauma of 9/11, this is his book, too. That day, and every other day until today, he has offered me nothing less than his unconditional love.

INTRODUCTION
TERRORISM AND
THE LEGACY OF THE
ENLIGHTENMENT

~~~~~~

Habermas and Derrida

~~~~~~

One might wonder whether the discussion of 9/11 and global terrorism needs to reach as far as a critical reassessment of the political ideals of the Enlightenment. The thesis of this book is that it does. Both the attacks of 9/11 and the range of diplomatic and military reactions they have provoked require a reassessment of the validity of the Enlightenment project and ideals.

Habermas and Derrida agree that the juridical and political system structuring international law and existing multilateral institutions grows out of the Western philosophical heritage grounded in the Enlightenment, understood as a general intellectual orientation anchored on a number of key texts. If this is true, who else but a philosopher has the tools to critically examine the adequacy of the existing framework against its historical precedents? Also, I might add, the battle against terrorism and terror is not a chess game. There are no preset rules: in principle, there is no distinction between legal and illegal moves and no basis on which the best move can be decided. There are no identifiable pieces. And the chessboard is not self-contained, because it coincides with what Kant defined as the "communal possession of the earth's surface." Ever since its Greek dawn, philosophy has been the home of conceptual mazes of this sort. Carving out its field of competence as it moves along, philosophy should know better than any other discipline how to reorient itself even as the familiar points of reference seem to have been pulverized. This is the case with both the elusive concept of terrorism and the experience of terror that radiates from it.

In these dialogues, Habermas and Derrida clearly lay out the risks entailed by the pragmatic approach that purposefully avoids facing the conceptual complexity underlying the notion of terrorism. I will present the reasons they offer for such a warning in the last section of this essay. However, I believe the reader will be able to fully appreciate Habermas's and Derrida's arguments only by gaining a perspective on the unique position in which philosophy finds itself in the face of a single historical event of worldwide significance. After briefly exploring this question in the next section, I will then turn to the description of two alternative models of political commitment, which will provide a context for Habermas's and Derrida's interventions. This will frame the discussion for how both Habermas's and Derrida's approaches to philosophy have been molded by the traumas of twentieth-century history, including colonialism, totalitarianism, and the Holocaust. My suggestion is that if global terrorism is the opening trauma of the new millennium, philosophy may yet be unaware of the extent of its involvement with it.

Does Philosophy Have Anything to Say about History?

Aristotle famously declared that since philosophy studies universal principles and history, singular events, "even poetry is more philosophical than history."[1] His case hinges on the poetic genre of tragedy. From the *Oresteia* to *Antigone*, any of the Greek tragedies exhibits, in his reading, the fundamentally rational aspiration to understand, and possibly even explain, the feelings and internal conflicts of the protagonists. In trying to make rational and universal sense of the bundle of emotions that drive human existence, tragedy walks down a path parallel to philosophy. By contrast, since history does not revolve around universal principles, it remains opaque to philosophical analysis. In line with Aristotle's argument, since there is no obvious universal principle in light of which Napoleon had to send five hundred thousand soldiers to conquer Russia in 1812, causing the death of four hundred and seventy thousand of them, philosophy does not have much to say about it. In the same way that philosophy cannot contribute to the understanding of Napoleon's Russian campaign, it could be argued that it does not have anything interesting to add on 9/11, which, according to this interpretation, would have the status of an isolated contingent event.

After Aristotle, philosophy's indifference to history dominated the Western tradition until the middle of the eighteenth century,[2] when the French and American Revolutions disclosed that the present may host the possibility of a radical break from the past. Only then did philosophy begin to ponder whether reason might have an intrinsic moral and social responsibility and whether, on that ground, philosophy ought to develop a more active relationship with history. Despite his conservative disposition, Kant admired the revolutionary spirit for having given individuals a sense of their own independence in the face of authority, including the authority of the past. For Kant and other Enlightenment philosophers it became clear that the self-affirmation of reason has a historical impact, for only reason can indicate how to reshape the present into a better future. Yet, reason remained for them a mental faculty with which every individual is endowed simply by belonging to the human species and whose force is entirely independent of the contingencies of history.

Just one generation after Kant, Hegel took the final step in narrowing the distance between history and philosophy when he declared that reason itself is bound up with history. Reason, for him, is not an abstract mental faculty that all human beings come equipped with and can affirm on autonomous grounds; rather, it grows out of the way in which the individual understands herself as part of a community. If the ability to think is indelibly shaped by time and culture, only the study of history can disclose our nature and place in the world. From Hegel's perspective, since reason itself is history-dependent, the Aristotelian dictum is to be reversed: apart from philosophy, there is nothing more philosophical than history.

The relationship between history and philosophy has a direct impact on the meaning of responsibility and freedom. If reason is conceived of as preceding history, there is space for the rational agent to experience herself as an autonomous unit, whose choices result from her unique will and singular needs. In the middle of the nineteenth century, the liberalist tradition developed this sense of individual autonomy into a notion of negative freedom, according to which I am free when I am left alone, not interfered with, and able to choose as I please.[3] Hegel's response to this position, as well as the response of those who followed Hegel, including Marx and Freud, was that this is an illusory conception, for it does not probe beneath the surface and ask why individuals make the choices they do. Since these choices are limited by one's access to all kinds of resources—economic, cultural, educational, psychological, religious, technological—the idea that people can be left alone to make their own choices without interference by others does not make them free; on the contrary, it leaves them at the mercy of the dominant forces of their time.

Believing that there is nothing more philosophical than history implies that real freedom begins with the realization that individual choices are formed in permanent negotiation with external forces. Freedom is thus measured by the degree to which we become able to gain control over these forces, which otherwise would control us. In this perspective, philosophy not only is allowed but has the responsibility to contribute to the public discussion on the significance of 9/11, which emerges as an event with an impact on our understanding of the world and ourselves.

Two Models of Public Participation: Political Activism and Social Critique

In the twentieth century, the evaluation of the relation between philosophy and the present has had a crucial impact on how philosophers have interpreted their responsibility to society and politics. I would like to distinguish between two different models of social and political commitment, roughly aligned with the liberal approach and the

Hegelian lineage: I will call them *political activism* and *social critique*. British philosopher Bertrand Russell and German émigré to the United States Hannah Arendt, respectively, embody them. Both of these figures have engaged politics to the point of becoming public intellectuals. However, I suggest, each of them understood the relation between philosophy and politics from opposite ends. While Russell took political involvement as a matter of personal choice on the ground that philosophy is committed to the pursuit of timeless truth, for Arendt philosophy was always historically bound, so that any engagement with it carries a political import. The distinction between political activism and social critique that I will now articulate clarifies the intellectual scope of Habermas and Derrida's contributions to 9/11 and global terrorism.[4]

A monumental philosophical figure in the fields of logic, philosophy of mathematics, and metaphysics, Russell has also been one of the most visible political activists ever to operate on the international scene. The history of his political engagement covers the whole expanse of the twentieth century, from World War I to the late stages of the Cold War. A committed pacifist, he spent six months in jail in 1918. During the 1920s and 1930s, he wrote books that stirred controversy on sexual liberation, the obsolescence of the institution of marriage, and progressive models of education. After receiving the Nobel Prize for Literature in 1950, he became a vociferous member of the Campaign for Nuclear Disarmament. He is responsible for the creation of the Atlantic Peace Foundation, dedicated to research on peace, and the Bertrand Russell Peace Foundation, devoted to the study of disarmament and the defense of oppressed peoples. In 1966, Russell's efforts led to the creation of the first international court for war crimes. Named after him, the Russell Tribunal indicted the United States for genocide in the Vietnam War. Russell died at the age of ninety-two in 1970.

Russell's public profile was that of the political activist, because he understood public involvement as his personal contribution to specific pressing issues. The political activist, in the sense that I am trying to demarcate here, may freely choose whether to be politically involved, which causes to intervene in and fight for or against. Presupposing the availability of all these choices is to endorse the liberalist "live-and-let-live" conception of freedom in which the subject is accorded autonomous power of acting and deliberating beyond social constraint.

A condition for Russell's political activism is that philosophy be granted the same negative freedom by history that the individual citizen is granted by society. By binding knowledge to experience, empiricism seemed to him to be the only orientation that secures philosophy its independence from historical pressures. "The only philosophy that affords a theoretical justification of democracy in its temper of mind is empiricism."[5] "This is partly because democracy and empiricism (which are intimately interconnected) do not demand a distortion of facts in the interest of theory."[6] Take the controversy between Ptolemy's geocentric and Copernicus's heliocentric systems. Through observation, we simply know that Ptolemy was wrong and Copernicus was right. Philosophy's responsibility, Russell argued, "as pursued in the universities of the Western democratic world, is, at least in intention, part of the pursuit of knowledge, aiming at the same kind of detachment as is sought in science, and not required, by the authorities, to arrive at conclusions convenient to the government."[7]

For a political activist on the Russellean model, the specificity of a philosopher's contribution lies in sharing with the public her analytical tools, helping it think lucidly about confusing and multifaceted issues, sorting good from bad arguments, supporting the good ones and combating the bad ones. In more recent years, Noam Chomsky's public engagement, which includes a short book on 9/11,[8] continues in this Russellean tradition of political activism.

By contrast, the life and political commitment of Arendt provide a different definition of a philosopher's public profile. One of the foremost political thinkers of the twentieth century, Arendt experienced firsthand the upheaval of Nazism in Germany, from which she escaped to the United States, never to return as a resident. The only child of a secular Jewish family, at twenty-three she had her dissertation already in print. After the burning of the Reichstag in Berlin in 1933, she was arrested along with her mother, held, and questioned by the police for over a week. Released, she escaped via Czechoslovakia and Switzerland to finally land in Paris, where she spent seven years working for Jewish organizations that facilitated the channeling of children to Palestine. In 1940, she married her second husband, a German leftist Gentile who had just been released from a two-month detention in an internment camp. Yet, before the year was over Arendt herself was interned with her mother in an "enemy alien" camp for women, from which she eventually escaped. Reunited with her husband, she boarded a ship from Lisbon to New York. While in the United States she became critical of the Zionist movement's focus on Palestine rather than Europe: one of the causes she supported was the formation of a Jewish army to fight alongside the Allies. From 1933 until 1951, when she finally obtained U.S. citizenship, she spoke of herself as a "stateless person." She died at age sixty-nine, having taught at various U.S. universities and contributing to the press as a public intellectual.

If for Russell philosophy's first commitment is the pursuit of knowledge over and beyond the impact of time, for Arendt, philosophy's first commitment is to human laws and institutions, which by definition evolve over time. Such laws, for her, designate not only the boundaries between private and public interest but also the description of the relations between citizens. In her two major books, *The Human Condition* (1944) and *The Origins of Totalitarianism* (1958), Arendt underlines the need for philosophy to recognize the extreme fragility of human laws and institutions, which she sees dramatically increased by the onset of modernity, taken as a cultural and historical paradigm. In this sense, she understood her philosophical responsibility in terms of a critique of modernity—an evaluation of the peculiar challenges presented to thought by modern European history. In it, the concept of totalitarianism features as the ultimate challenge.

Unlike tyranny, which promotes lawlessness, the two totalitarian regimes of the mid-twentieth century, Stalinism and Nazism, were not lawless. Rather, they promoted inexorable laws that were presented as either laws of nature (the biological laws of racial superiority) or laws of history (the economic laws of class struggle). In Arendt's reading, totalitarianism is a distinctly *modern* political danger, which combines unprecedented serialized coercion with a totalizing secular ideology.[9] The "total terror" practiced in the extermination camps and the gulags is not the means but "the essence of totalitarian government."[10] In turn, the essence of terror is not the physical elimination of whomever is perceived to be different but the eradication of difference in people, namely, of their individuality and capacity for autonomous action. The monopoly of power sought by totalitarian regimes "can be achieved and safeguarded only in a world of conditioned reflexes, of marionettes

without the slightest trace of spontaneity. Precisely because man's resources are so great, he can be fully dominated only when he becomes
a specimen of the animal-species man."[11]

The objectification Arendt set as the defining core of totalitarianism was not restricted to the victims of the mass murders carried out in
the concentration camps and the gulags but was required of the perpetrators, too. In 1961, Arendt was asked by the *New Yorker* to cover the
trial of the fugitive Nazi criminal Adolf Eichmann, captured in Ar-
gentina by the Mossad, the Israeli secret service, and brought to stand
trial in Jerusalem, where he was eventually executed. Arendt's correspondence from Jerusalem broke her long self-imposed silence on the
"Jewish question" that dated to the establishment of the state of Israel
and the failure of Judah Magnes's efforts to establish a binational democratic federation in Palestine. Later revised and published as a book,[12]
Arendt's report focused on the description of Eichmann as an obtuse
individual who drifted with the times and refused to critically examine
any of his criminal actions. In his thoughtless ordinariness—his speaking in clichés, apparent lack of fanatical hatred for the Jews, and pride
in being a law-abiding citizen—Eichmann appeared to her as the incarnation of the "banality of evil."[13]

No doubt, her belief that philosophy revolves around the cultivation and protection of a healthy political space—forged out of popular
participation, human diversity, and equality—reflected the urgency of
her own personal response to total terror: a response that arose out
of trauma, displacement, loss, and exile. Yet, this is also the mark of
an ancient orientation that Arendt inherited from the Greeks. Since
Socrates, philosophy has involved the unresolvable but productive tension between action and speculation, timeliness and timelessness, *vita
activa* and *vita contemplativa*.

Philosophy and the Traumas of Twentieth-Century History

Despite their sharply distinct approaches to philosophy, Habermas
and Derrida seem to follow in the Arendtian model. Like Arendt and
unlike Russell, they do not look at political commitment as a supplement to their commitment to philosophy, an option that can be taken
up, postponed, or even rejected altogether. Both of them have encoun-

tered and embraced philosophy in the context of the traumas of twentieth-century European history: colonialism, totalitarianism, and the Holocaust. Their contributions to the subject of 9/11 and global terrorism follow in the same vein.

Habermas and Derrida were born only a year apart, in 1929 and 1930, respectively, and were adolescents during World War II. Habermas lived in Germany, under the ominous grip of the Third Reich, while Derrida lived in Algeria, a French colony at that time.

Habermas recalls the deep state of shock that he and his friends found themselves in as they learned about the Nazi atrocities at the Nuremberg trials and, subsequently, in a series of documentary films. "We believed that a spiritual and moral renewal was indispensable and inevitable."[14] The challenge of how to achieve a moral renewal in a country with an "unmasterable past"[15] has been Habermas's lifelong quest, which he has pursued with exceptional loyalty and passion both as a philosopher and as a public intellectual. The task was so monumental that one cannot avoid pondering how a man of his great talent, having been presented many times with academic offers from around the world, did not decide to leave Germany and remove the "German question" from the center stage of his life and thought. After all, it would have made perfect sense from the standpoint of his cosmopolitan beliefs. The fact that he never did leave is for me great cause for admiration. The crucial role he played during the Historians' Debate (*Historikerstreit*) represents compelling evidence for the depth of Habermas's public commitment.

In the mid-1980s several German historians began to question the "uniqueness" of Nazi crimes, thereby opening the way to a revisionist reading aimed at equating them with other twentieth-century political tragedies. Habermas was particularly outraged at the renowned Berlin historian Ernst Nolte, who suggested that "a conspicuous shortcoming of the literature on National Socialism is that it doesn't know, or doesn't want to admit, to what extent everything that was later done by the Nazis, with the sole exception of the technical procedure of gassing, had already been described in an extensive literature dating from the early 1920s."[16] Nolte claims that the Holocaust was fundamentally on a par with the Stalinist purges and even with the Bolshevik upheaval, except for the "technical procedure of gassing."

Habermas, on that occasion, represented the most eloquent voice against the normalization of the German past and in defense of Germany's absolute need to deal with the dark side of its past. He remarked that a "traumatic refusal" to face the reality of Nazism had been at work in the nation since the fall of the Third Reich. He also pointed to the danger of this denial. Describing the perspective of his own generation, he wrote, "The grandchildren of those who at the close of World War II were too young to be able to experience personal guilt are already growing up. Memory, however, has not become correspondently distantiated," for, regardless of one's subjective perspective, its point of departure is still the same—"the images of the unloading ramp at Auschwitz."17

Guilt is not simply individual, and responsibility does not only come with making personal choices. This is a point that both Habermas and Derrida share because, like Arendt, they are post-Holocaust philosophers.

Habermas articulates how guilt and responsibility are engrained in the context of our daily interaction with one another: quoting Ludwig Wittgenstein, he calls this context a "form of life."

> There is the simple fact that subsequent generations also grew up from within a form of life in which that was possible. Our own life is linked to the life context in which Auschwitz was possible not by contingent circumstances but intrinsically. Our form of life is connected to that of our parents and grandparents through a web of familial, local, political and intellectual traditions that is difficult to disentangle—that is, through a historical milieu that made us who we are. None of us can escape this milieu, because our identities, both as individuals and as Germans, are indissolubly interwoven with it.18

However, one should not presume that since Habermas foregrounds the constitutive role of history, he either downplays the importance of individual participation in the political arena or believes that political identity is automatically provided by a historically established tradition. On the contrary, particularly in the context of German national identity, he defends a notion of constitutional patriotism. Only such patriotism, which is based on the free allegiance to the constitution on the part of each individual citizen, can forge a progressive national alliance. For Habermas, it is essential that Germans understand themselves as a nation solely on their loyalty to the republican constitution, without hanging onto what he calls "the pre-political crutches of nationality and community of fate."[19]

Derrida experienced these crutches firsthand when, in October 1942, he was expelled from his school, the Lycée de Ben Aknoun, housed in a former monastery located near El-Biar in Algeria where he grew up and lived until he was nineteen years old. The reason for the expulsion was not rowdy behavior but the application of the racial laws in France and its colonial possessions, including Algeria. Identity emerged for Derrida as a cluster of unstable boundaries. As he painfully recollects, the boy who was expelled in 1942 was "a little black and very Arab Jew who understood nothing about it, to whom no one ever gave the slightest reason, neither his parents nor his friends."[20] Derrida's background highlights the challenge of existing at the boundaries of multiple territories: Judaism and Christianity, Judaism and Islam, Europe and Africa, mainland France and its colonies, the sea and the desert. This is the same challenge that Derrida presents to philosophy.

The language that Derrida recalls being used at the time of his expulsion from school highlights the polyphony of these voices:

> In my family and among the Algerian Jews, one scarcely ever said "circumcision" but "baptism," not Bar Mitzvah but "communion," with the consequences of softening, dulling through fearful acculturation, that I've always suffered from more or less consciously, of unavowable events, felt as such, not "Catholic," violent, barbarous, hard, "Arab," circumcised circumcision, interiorized, secretly assumed accusation of ritual murder.[21]

For Derrida, then and for the rest of his life, each word branches out into a network of historical and textual connections. His political interventions are often aimed at throwing light upon these hidden continents. As long as we use language unreflexively, we remain completely unaware of them; the problem with this blessed ignorance is that, just by relying on them, we iterate a number of normative assumptions of which we are not even aware.

Take the human being as an example. Most people would assume that it is a self-evident designation: a human being is a member of the human species. The problem is that both "human" and "species" are terms that branch out in historically constructed mazes that broaden and indefinitely complicate the semantic spectrum of this phrase. On the one hand, the human species, as is the case with all species, is inscribed in evolutionary history: the question of when we became human depends upon the principle of classification we adopt, which in theory could be different than what it is.[22] On the other hand, the adjective "human," which accompanies either the notion of an individual being or the whole species, puts us face to face with the issue of what 'human" means. Does it mean to act as a human? How do we demarcate human behavior? We cannot even begin to approach this question without referring to the notion of human nature, its humanity or inhumanity.

This question was crucial to Derrida's response to the events of 1968.[23] Derrida's contribution to that epoch of great ideological conflict and political turmoil was to interrogate which conception of the human being was in fact at stake. His considerations started via questioning the "anthropologism" that he saw dominating the French intellectual scene, which took for granted the humanistic heritage associated with the Greek ideal of *anthropos*. From the Italian Renaissance to the Enlightenment, humanism remained loyal to what Derrida has called the "unity of man." There would not be "human sciences" without a belief in the distinctly and uniquely "human" endeavor, which holds "man" together as a concept.

In the darkness of World War II, existentialist philosophers such as Jean-Paul Sartre hoped to launch a new version of classical humanism. Sartre proposed to redefine man in terms of "human reality," by which he meant that the human subject could not be understood separately from her world.[24] This interdependence between subject and world granted Sartre a way to firmly ground moral and political responsibility in the very constitution of the subject. Anchoring human reality in responsibility toward one's world seemed the necessary antidote for the inhumanity of totalitarianism.

Yet, Derrida contended, even if the existentialists were the first to ask the question of the meaning of man, they did not succeed in overcoming the classical ideal of the unity of man.[25] "Although the theme of history is quite present in the discourse of the period, there is still little practice of the history of concepts. For example, the history of the concept of man is never examined. Everything occurs as if the sign 'man' had no origin, no historical, cultural, or linguistic limit."[26] Derrida's position here is that once the concept of man is given historical, cultural, and linguistic boundaries it will be much harder to resort to any essentialist arguments. The very multiplicity of historical narratives will upset any attempt to construe the concept in terms of irreducible pairs—man versus woman, human versus inhuman, human versus animal, rationality versus instinct, culture versus nature—which, in Derrida's opinion, produces dangerous simplifications.

Particularly for a generation that had to make sense of the failure of the humanistic ideal to protect Europe from totalitarianism and genocide, Derrida's angle adds a whole new dimension to the concept of social critique. As for Habermas, for Derrida guilt and responsibility for the horrors of the twentieth century cannot be limited to those who were directly involved. In the same vein, for both of them the political commitment of philosophy is not a matter of personal choice. By engaging in philosophy, one automatically engages in the effort to reckon with its time: in this sense neither one of them is a political activist, whereas both of them, if in very different ways, are social critics. For Arendt, Habermas, and Derrida, philosophy's first commitment is to human laws and institutions as they evolve through time. This belief marks them as post-Holocaust philosophers. Their common challenge has been, necessarily, how to give a positive turn to the intellectual depression into which the generation of their teachers had fallen after the experience of personal exile and the horrors of the 1930s and 1940s.

On the one hand, Habermas takes the universal value of republican institutions and democratic participation as a given, passed on to us by the tradition of the Enlightenment. Speaking against the normalization of the German past he wrote, "After Auschwitz our national consciousness can be derived only from the better traditions in our history, a history that is not unexamined but instead appropriated critically."[27] The problem for him is not that the Enlightenment has failed as an intellectual project but that its original critical attitude toward history got lost, opening the way for political barbarism. On the other hand, Derrida believes that universalism is what republican institutions and democratic participation struggle toward in their infinite quest for justice. This quest is ensured only if we are open to considering the notions of republicanism and democracy, institution and participation, not as absolutes but as constructions whose validity evolves with time and are thus in need of constant revision.

The Legacy of the Enlightenment in a Globalized World

The explicit ideology of the terrorists who attacked the Twin Towers and the Pentagon on 9/11 is a rejection of the kind of modernity and secularization that in the philosophical tradition is associated with the concept of Enlightenment. In philosophy, the Enlightenment describes not only a specific period, which historically coincided with the eighteenth century, but also the affirmation of democracy and the separation of political power from religious belief that the French and American Revolutions made their focus.

Kant famously wrote that the "Enlightenment is man's emergence from his self-incurred immaturity. Immaturity is the inability to use one's own understanding without the guidance of another."[28] Rather than a coherent set of beliefs, the Enlightenment marks a break with the past, which becomes available only on the basis of the individual's independence in the face of authority. Precisely this independence is the mark of modernity. "If it is asked whether we at present live in an *enlightened* age, the answer is: No, but we do live in an age of *enlightenment*."[29]

On February 14, 1989, more than two-hundred years after the publication of Kant's words, the world was reminded that he was right: indeed, one can never trust that we live in an enlightened age but rather in an age where enlightenment is a process in constant need of cultivation. On that very day, the absolute leader of the Islamic Republic of Iran, the Ayatollah Khomeini, launched a *fatwa*, or death sentence, against the Indian-born writer Salman Rushdie with the following announcement on public radio: "I inform the proud Muslim people of the world that the author of *The Satanic Verses* book, which is against Islam, the Prophet and the Koran, and all involved in its publication who were aware of its content, are sentenced to death."[30] For nine years Rushdie had to live in hiding, a nightmare from which he was formally released in 1998, when representatives of the British and Iranian governments struck a deal at the United Nations to end the death threat against him.[31]

Where a philosopher stands vis-à-vis the heritage of the Enlightenment is thus not only a theoretical matter but also implies delicate political ramifications. Like many philosophers who came of age in the 1980s, I grew up convinced that Habermas and Derrida expressed sharply opposed views with regard to the Enlightenment: Habermas defended it, and Derrida rejected it. Later on, I came to realize that this was a skewed picture for which the intellectual obsession of that decade—the *querelle* between modernism and postmodernism—is the main culprit. If Habermas's identification with modernism and Enlightenment political values is indisputable, the predominant claim of those years that Derrida is a counter-Enlightenment thinker is simply mistaken.[32]

Habermas follows in the tradition of Critical Theory,[33] which attributes to philosophy a diagnostic function with regard to both the ills of modern society and the intellectual discourse that underlies their insurgence and justifies their scopes and motivations. As is the case with clinical medical practice, for Critical Theory diagnosis is not a speculative enterprise but an evaluation oriented toward the possibility of remedy. Such evaluation bestows on philosophy the burden and privilege of political responsibility. The interdependence of theory and practice is one of the axioms of Critical Theory. Its focus is emancipation, regarded as the demand for improvement of the present human situation. Habermas calls this demand the "unfinished project of modernity." Begun by Kant and other Enlightenment thinkers, this project requires belief in principles whose validity is universal because they hold across historical and cultural specificities.

By contrast, the intellectual grounding of Derrida's deconstruction owes much to the nineteenth- and twentieth-century lineage constituted by Nietzsche, Heidegger, and Freud. For Derrida, many of the principles to which the Western tradition has attributed universal validity do not capture what we all share or even hope for. Rather, they impose a set of standards that benefit some and bring disadvantage to others, depending on the context. For him, demarcating the historical and cultural boundaries of such principles is a precondition for embracing the Enlightenment demand of justice and freedom for all. Yet,

Derrida's approach to ethics and politics has an additional dimension: he calls it a responsibility before alterity and difference, that which is beyond the boundaries of description, excluded, and silent. For him, this sense of responsibility articulates the demand for universalism associated with the Enlightenment.

In light of the dialogues collected in this book, one cannot but be persuaded that Habermas and Derrida share an allegiance to the Enlightenment. The difference in their approaches is not only of historical interest (because it casts a new light on their relation) but an illustration of the richness and variety that philosophy is uniquely capable of offering to the interpretation of the present moment. The issue of tolerance, a key concept of both the Enlightenment and the self-representation of Western democracies, is a case in point.[34]

Derrida stresses the distinctly Christian matrix of the notion of tolerance, which makes it less neutral a political and ethical concept than it makes itself out to be. The religious origin and focus of the notion of tolerance makes it the remnant of a paternalistic gesture in which the other is not accepted as an equal partner but subordinated, perhaps assimilated, and certainly misinterpreted in its difference. "Indeed, tolerance is first of all a form of charity. A Christian charity, therefore, even if Jews and Muslims might seem to appropriate this language as well . . . In addition to the religious meaning of tolerance . . . we should also mention its biological, genetic or organicist connotations. In France the phrase 'threshold of tolerance' was used to describe the limit beyond which it was no longer decent to ask a national community to welcome any more foreigners, immigrant workers and the like." The notion of tolerance is for Derrida inadequate for use in secular politics. Its religious overtone, with deep roots in the Christian conception of charity, defeats any claim of universalism.[35] Attentive to all facts of language, Derrida points out that it is not a coincidence that tolerance has been appropriated by the biological discourse to indicate the fine line between integration and rejection. As is true with organ transplants and pain management, the threshold of tolerance designates tolerance as the extreme limit of the organism's struggle to maintain itself in balance before collapse.

Tolerance is thus the opposite of hospitality, which Derrida offers as its alternative. Clearly, the distinction between tolerance and hospitality is not a semantic subtlety but points to what is most important in

Derrida's approach to ethics and politics: the unique obligation that each of us has to the other.

But pure or unconditional hospitality does not consist in such an *invitation* ("I invite you, I welcome you into *my home,* on the condition that you adapt to the laws and norms of my territory, according to my language, tradition, memory, and so on"). Pure and unconditional hospitality, hospitality *itself,* opens or is in advance open to someone who is neither expected nor invited, to whomever arrives as an absolutely foreign *visitor,* as a new *arrival,* nonidentifiable and unforeseeable, in short, wholly other.

Derrida's endorsement of hospitality in place of tolerance is a sophisticated reworking of a key text by a key philosopher of the Enlightenment, Kant, who first posed the question of hospitality in the context of international relations.[36]

Those who interpret Derrida as a certain kind of postmodernist—a counter-Enlightenment thinker with a leaning toward relativism—would use his deconstruction of the universal reach of tolerance in support of their argument.[37] To the contrary, for Derrida, demarcating the historical and cultural limits of apparently neutral concepts of the Enlightenment tradition such as tolerance expands and updates rather than betrays its agenda.[38] To meet the specifically global challenges of our time, social critique and ethical responsibility require the deconstruction of falsely neutral and potentially hegemonic ideals. Far from curtailing the demand for universal justice and freedom, deconstruction renews it infinitely.

In contrast, Habermas stands by tolerance on both the ethical and legal front. His defense of tolerance emerges out of his conception of constitutional democracy as the only political situation that can accommodate free and uncoerced communication and the formation of a rational consensus. It is true, he says, that the term has a religious origin and that it was only subsequently appropriated by secular politics. Moreover, it is true that tolerance is intrinsically one-sided: "It is obvious that the threshold of tolerance, which separates what is still 'acceptable' from what is not, is arbitrarily established by the existing authority." However, in Habermas's view, the one-sidedness of tolerance is neutralized if tolerance is practiced in the context of a participatory political system such as that provided by parliamentary democracy. In a direct response to Derrida, during our dialogue he clarified this point:

However, from this example we can also learn that the straight deconstruction of the concept of tolerance falls into a trap, since the constitutional state contradicts precisely the premise from which the paternalistic sense of the traditional concept of "tolerance" derives. Within a democratic community whose citizens reciprocally grant one another equal rights, no room is left for an authority allowed to *one-sidedly* determine the boundaries of what is to be tolerated. On the basis of the citizens' equal rights and reciprocal respect for each other, nobody possesses the privilege of setting the boundaries of tolerance from the viewpoint of their own preferences and value-orientations.

The objection that Habermas addresses to Derrida and to his deconstruction of the notion of tolerance applies to a very specific political situation: a functional participatory democracy. In it, tolerance cannot possibly be practiced as the reason of the strongest.

Yet, I submit, globalization seems to have transformed the conditions and the meaning of participation both economically and politically. Who participates in what? If it is true that more avenues of global participation are opening up, why does the threshold of tolerance seem to recede, particularly on the part of those who supposedly have just entered the public forum as participants? Should we admit that globalization spreads more the illusion than the reality of universal participation? Is the affluent First World honest in presenting and promoting itself as tolerant? What are we to do with the concept of tolerance?

Habermas turns to modernity to rebuke these challenges. The paradigm of religious intolerance—and he considers fundamentalism to be its incarnation—appears to him as an exclusively modern phenomenon. Like Kant, Habermas understands modernity to be a change in belief attitude rather than a coherent body of beliefs. A belief attitude indicates the way in which we believe rather than what we believe in. Thus, fundamentalism has less to do with any specific text or religious dogma and more to do with the modality of belief. Whether we discuss Islamic, Christian, or Hindu fundamentalist beliefs, we are talking about violent reactions against the modern way of understanding and practicing religion. In this perspective, fundamentalism is not the simple return to a premodern way of relating to religion: it is a panicked response to modernity perceived as a threat rather than as an opportunity.

Sure enough, Habermas concedes, every religious doctrine is

based on a dogmatic kernel of belief; otherwise, it wouldn't entail faith. Yet, with the onset of modernity, religions had "to let go of the universally binding character and political acceptance of their doctrine" in order to coexist within a pluralistic society. The transition from the premodern belief attitude to the modern one has been a monumental challenge for world religions. These are religions whose exclusive claim to truth was supported and confirmed by political situations "whose peripheries seemed to blur beyond their boundaries." Modernity brings about a plurality of nations and such a growth in social and political complexity that the exclusivity of absolute claims becomes simply untenable. "In Europe, the confessional schism and the secularization of society have compelled religious belief to reflect on its nonexclusive place within a universal discourse shared with other religions and limited by a scientifically generated worldly knowledge."

Globalization has accelerated the defensive reaction that accompanies the fear of what Habermas defines as the "violent uprooting of traditional ways of life," of which modernization is generally accused. We cannot deny, Habermas says, that globalization has divided world society into winners, beneficiaries, and losers. In this sense, "[t]he West in its entirety serves as a scapegoat for the Arab world's own, very real experiences of loss." On a psychological level, such experience creates a situation favorable to a highly polarized worldview in which various spiritual sources are intended to resist the secularizing force of Western influence. To dispel this dangerous polarization between the a-morality of the West and the supposed spirituality of religious fundamentalism, Habermas calls for a rigorous self-examination on the part of Western culture. For if the normative message that Western liberal democracies export is one of consumerism, fundamentalism will go unchallenged.

The relation between fundamentalism and terrorism is mediated by violence that Habermas understands as a communicative pathology. "The spiral of violence begins as a spiral of distorted communication that leads through the spiral of uncontrolled reciprocal mistrust, to the breakdown of communication." However, the difference between the violence existing in Western societies—which are certainly haunted by social inequality, discrimination, and marginalization—and cross-cultural violence is that, in the latter "those who first become alienated from each other through systematically distorted communication" do not recognize each other as participating members of a community. The legal

framework of international relations does not do much in the way of
opening up new channels. For what is needed is a change in mentality,
which "happens rather through the improvement of living conditions,
through a sensible relief from oppression and fear. Trust must be able to
be developed in communicative everyday practices. Only then can a
broadly effective enlightenment extend into media, schools, and homes.
And it must do so by affecting the premises of its own political culture."
     The remedy against systematic distortions of communication lead-
ing to cross-cultural violence is to rebuild a fundamental link of trust
among people, which cannot take place while oppression and fear dominate. Such a link depends as much on the improvement of material
conditions as it does on the political culture in which individuals find
themselves interacting with each other, for in the absence of either one
mutual perspective-taking becomes impossible.
     While for Habermas reason, understood as the possibility of trans-
parent and nonmanipulative communication, can cure the ills of modernization, fundamentalism and terrorism among them, for Derrida
these destructive strains can be detected and named but not wholly
controlled or conquered. Whereas for Habermas the pathological
agents concern the speed at which modernization has imposed itself
and the defensive reaction that it has elicited on the part of traditional
ways of life, for Derrida the defensive reaction comes from modernity
itself. Terrorism is for him the symptom of an autoimmune disorder
that threatens the life of participatory democracy, the legal system that
underwrites it, and the possibility of a sharp separation between the religious and the secular dimensions. Autoimmune conditions imply the
spontaneous suicide of the defensive mechanism supposed to protect
the organism from external aggression. From the standpoint of this
somber analysis, Derrida's exhortation is to proceed slowly and patiently in the search for a cure.
     Derrida's thesis in the dialogue is that the kind of global terrorism
behind the attacks of 9/11 is not the first symptom of the autoimmune
crisis but only its most recent manifestation. Throughout the Cold War,
Western liberal democracies were arming and training their future enemies in a quasi-suicidal manner. The Cold War's symmetrical display of
power was undermined by the dissemination of the nuclear arsenal as
well as of bacteriological and chemical weapons. Now we are faced with

the reality of an a-symmetrical conflict, which as such represents a further stage of the autoimmune crisis. In the age of terror, there is no possibility of balance: since incalculable forces rather than sovereign states represent the real threat, the very concept of responsibility becomes potentially incalculable. Who is responsible for what, at what stage of planning, in the face of what juridical body?

Like the Cold War, the specter of global terrorism haunts our sense of the future because it kills the promise upon which a positive relation with our present depends. In all its horror, 9/11 has left us waiting for the worst. The violence of the attacks against the Twin Towers and the Pentagon has revealed an abyss of terror that is going to haunt our existence and thinking for years and perhaps decades to come. The choice of a date, 9/11, as a name for the attacks, has the aim of attributing to them historical monumentality, which is in the interest of both the Western media and the terrorists.

For Habermas as well as for Derrida, globalization plays a big role vis-à-vis terrorism. While for Habermas what is at issue is an increase of inequality due to accelerated modernization, Derrida has a differentiated reading of it depending on the context. Globalization, for him, rendered possible the rapid and relatively smooth process of democratization in most Eastern European nations, formerly part of the Soviet Union. There, Derrida believes that it was a good thing. "Recent movements toward democratization . . . owe a great deal, almost everything perhaps, to television, to the communication of models, norms, images, informational products, and so on." By contrast, Derrida is extremely worried about the effect of globalization on the dynamics of conflict and war. "Between the two supposed war leaders, the two metonymies, 'Bin Laden' and 'Bush,' the war of images and of discourses proceeds at an ever quickening pace over the airwaves, dissimulating and deflecting more and more quickly the truth that it reveals." In other cases yet globalization is nothing more than a rhetorical artifice, aimed at dissimulating injustice. This is, in Derrida's view, what is happening within Islamic cultures, where globalization is only *believed* to be taking place but in reality it isn't. Here Derrida comes close to Habermas not only by understanding globalization under the rubric of inequality but also by connecting it with the problem of modernity and of the Enlightenment.

In the course of the last few centuries, whose history would have to be carefully reexamined (the absence of an Enlightenment age, colonization, imperialism, and so on), several factors have contributed to the geopolitical situation whose effects we are feeling today, beginning with the paradox of a marginalization and an impoverishment whose rhythm is proportional to demographic growth. These populations are not only deprived of access to what we call democracy (because of the history I just briefly recalled) but are even dispossessed of the so-called natural riches of the land . . . These natural "riches" are in fact the only nonvirtualizable and non-deterritorializable goods left today.

The Islamic world's position is unique in two ways: on the one hand, it historically lacks exposure to the quintessentially modern experience of democracy that Derrida, with Habermas, regards as necessary for a culture to positively face modernization. On the other hand, many Islamic cultures flourished on soil rich in natural resources like oil, which Derrida defines as the last "nonvirtualizable and non-deterritorializable" resource. This situation makes the Islamic block more vulnerable to the savage modernization brought about by the globalized markets and dominated by a small number of states and international corporations.

While for Habermas terrorism is the effect of the trauma of modernization, which has spread around the world at a pathological speed, Derrida sees terrorism as a symptom of a traumatic element intrinsic to modern experience, whose focus is always on the future, somewhat pathologically understood as promise, hope, and self-affirmation. Both are somber reflections on the legacy of the Enlightenment: the relentless search for a critical perspective that must start with self-examination.

FUNDAMENTALISM
AND TERROR

‹‹

A Dialogue with Jürgen Habermas

‹‹

B O R R A D O R I :   Do you consider what we now tend to call "September 11" an unprecedented event, one that radically alters the way we see ourselves?

H A B E R M A S :   Allow me to say in advance that I shall be answering your questions at a distance of three months.[1] Therefore, it might be useful to mention my personal experience in relation to the event. At the start of October I was beginning a two-month stay in Manhattan. I must confess I somehow felt more of a stranger this time than I did on previous visits to the "capital of the twentieth century," a city that has fascinated me for more than three decades. It was not only the flag-waving and rather defiant "United We Stand" patriotism that had changed the climate, nor was it the peculiar demand for solidarity and the accompanying susceptibility to any presumed "anti-American-

Translated from the German by Luis Guzman. Revised by Jürgen Habermas in English.

ism." The impressive American liberality toward foreigners, the charm
of the eager, sometimes also self-consciously accepting embrace—this
noble openhearted mentality seemed to have given way to a slight mistrust. Would we, the ones who had not been present, now also stand by
them unconditionally? Even those who hold an unquestionable *record*,
as I do among my American friends, needed to be cautious with regard
to criticism. Since the intervention in Afghanistan, we suddenly began
to notice when, in political discussions, we found ourselves only
among Europeans (or among Israelis).

On the other hand, only there did I first feel the full magnitude of
the event. The terror of this disaster, which literally came bursting out
of the blue, the horrible convictions behind this treacherous assault, as
well as the stifling depression that set over the city, were a completely
different experience there than at home. Every friend and colleague
could remember exactly what they were doing that day shortly after
9:00 A.M. In short, only there did I begin to better comprehend the
foreboding atmosphere that already echoes in your question. Also
among the left there is a widespread awareness of living at a turning
point in history. I do not know whether the U.S. government itself was
slightly paranoid or merely shunning responsibility. At any rate, the repeated and utterly nonspecific announcements of possible new terror
attacks and the senseless calls to "be alert" further stirred a vague feeling of angst along with an uncertain readiness—precisely the intention
of the terrorists. In New York people seemed ready for the worst. As a
matter of course, the anthrax scares (even the plane crash in Queens)[2]
were attributed to Osama bin Laden's diabolical machinations.

Given this background, you can understand a certain tendency toward skepticism. But is what we contemporaries think at the moment
that important for a long-term diagnosis? If the September 11 terror attack is supposed to constitute a caesura in world history, as many
think, then it must be able to stand comparison to other events of
world historical impact. For that matter, the comparison is not to be
drawn with Pearl Harbor but rather with the aftermath of August 1914.
The outbreak of World War I signaled the end of a peaceful and, in retrospect, somewhat unsuspecting era, unleashing an age of warfare, totalitarian oppression, mechanistic barbarism and bureaucratic mass
murder. At the time, there was something like a widespread foreboding. Only in retrospect will we be able to understand if the symbolically

suffused collapse of the capitalistic citadels in lower Manhattan implies a break of that type or if this catastrophe merely confirms, in an inhuman and dramatic way, a long-known vulnerability of our complex civilization. If an event is not as unambiguously important as the French Revolution once was—not long after that event Kant had spoken about a "historical sign" that pointed toward a "moral tendency of humankind"—only "effective history" can adjudicate its magnitude in retrospect.

Perhaps at a later point important developments will be traced back to September 11. But for now we do not know which of the many scenarios depicted today will actually hold in the future. The clever, albeit fragile, coalition against terrorism brought together by the U.S. government might, in the most favorable case, be able to advance the transition from classical international law to a cosmopolitan order. At all events, a hopeful signal was the Afghanistan conference in Bonn, which, under the auspices of the UN, set the agenda in the right direction.[3] However, after September 11 the European governments have completely failed. They are obviously incapable of seeing beyond their own national scope of interests and lending at least their support to the U.S. Secretary of State Colin Powell against the hard-liners. The Bush administration seems to be continuing, more or less undisturbed, the self-centered course of a callous superpower. It is fighting now as it has in the past against the appointment of an international criminal court, relying instead on military tribunals of its own. These constitute, from the viewpoint of international law, a dubious innovation. It refuses to sign the Biological Weapons Convention. It one-sidedly terminated the ABM Treaty and absurdly sees its plan to deploy a missile defense system validated by the events of September 11. The world has grown too complex for this barely concealed unilateralism. Even if Europe does not rouse itself to play the civilizing role, as it should, the emerging power of China and the waning power of Russia do not fit into the *pax Americana* model so simply. Instead of the kind of international police action that we had hoped for during the war in Kosovo, there are wars again—conducted with state-of-the-art technology but still in the old style.

The misery in war-torn Afghanistan is reminiscent of images from the Thirty Years' War. Naturally there were good reasons, even normative ones, to forcibly remove the Taliban regime, which brutally oppressed not only women but the entire population. They also refused the legitimate demand to hand over bin Laden. However, the asymmetry between the concentrated destructive power of the electronically controlled clusters of elegant and versatile missiles in the air and the archaic ferocity of the swarms of bearded warriors outfitted with Kalashnikovs on the ground remains a morally obscene sight. This feeling is more properly understood when one recalls the bloodthirsty colonial history that Afghanistan suffered, its arbitrary geographic dismemberment, and its continued instrumentalization at the hands of the European power play. In any case, the Taliban regime already belongs to history.

BORRADORI: True, but our topic is terrorism, which seems to have taken up new meaning and definition after September 11.

HABERMAS: The monstrous act itself was new. And I do not just mean the action of the suicide hijackers who transformed the fully fueled airplanes together with their hostages into living weapons, or even the unbearable number of victims and the dramatic extent of the devastation. What was new was the symbolic force of the targets struck. The attackers did not just physically cause the highest buildings in Manhattan to collapse; they also destroyed an icon in the household imagery of the American nation. Only in the surge of patriotism that followed did one begin to recognize the central importance the towers held in the popular imagination, with their irreplaceable imprint on the Manhattan skyline and their powerful embodiment of economic strength and projection toward the future. The presence of cameras and of the media was also new, transforming the local event simultaneously into a global one and the whole world population into a benumbed witness. Perhaps September 11 could be called the first historic world event in the strictest sense: the impact, the explosion, the slow collapse—everything that was not Hollywood anymore but, rather, a gruesome reality, literally took place in front of the "universal eyewitness" of a global public. God only knows what my friend and colleague *experienced*, watching the second airplane explode into the top floors of the World Trade Center only a few blocks away from the roof of his house on Duane Street. No doubt it was something completely different from what I *experienced* in Germany in front of the television, though we *saw* the same thing.

Certainly, no observation of a unique event can provide an explanation per se for why terrorism itself should have assumed a new characteristic. In this respect, one factor above all seems to me to be relevant: one never really knows who one's enemy is. Osama bin Laden, the person, more likely serves the function of a stand-in. Compare the new terrorists with partisans or conventional terrorists, for example, in Israel. These people often fight in a decentralized manner in small, autonomous units, too. Also, in these cases there is no concentration of forces or central organization, a feature that makes them difficult targets. But partisans fight on familiar territory with professed political objectives in order to conquer power. This is what distinguishes them from terrorists who are scattered around the globe and networked in the fashion of secret services. They allow their religious motives of a fundamentalist kind to be known, though they do not pursue a program that goes beyond the engineering of destruction and insecurity. The terrorism we associate for the time being with the name "al-Qaeda" makes the identification of the opponent and any realistic assessment of the danger impossible. This intangibility is what lends terrorism a new quality.

Surely the uncertainty of the danger belongs to the essence of terrorism. But the scenarios of biological or chemical warfare painted in detail by the American media during the months after September 11, the speculations over the various kinds of nuclear terrorism, only betray the inability of the government to at least determine the magnitude of the danger. One never knows if there's anything to it. In Israel, people at least know *what* can happen to them if they take a bus, go into a department store, discotheque, or any open area—and *how frequently* it happens. In the U.S.A. or Europe, one cannot circumscribe the risk; there is no realistic way to estimate the type, magnitude, or probability of the risk, nor any way to narrow down the potentially affected regions.

This brings a threatened nation, which can react to such uncertain dangers solely through administrative channels, to the truly embarrassing situation of perhaps overreacting and, yet, because of the inadequate level of secret intelligence, remaining unable to know whether or not it is in fact overreacting. Because of this, the state is in danger of falling into disrepute due to the evidence of its inadequate resources: both domestically, through a militarizing of the security measures, which endanger the constitutional state, and internationally, through the mobilization of a simultaneously disproportionate and ineffective military and technological superiority. With transparent motives, U.S. Defense Secretary Donald Rumsfeld warned again of *unspecified* terror threats at the NATO conference in Brussels in mid-December [2001]: "When we look at the destruction they caused in the U.S.A., imagine what they could do in New York, or London, or Paris, or Berlin with nuclear, chemical or biological weapons."[4] Of a wholly different kind were the measures—necessary and prudent, but only effective in the long term—the U.S. government took after the attack: the creation of a worldwide coalition of countries against terrorism, the effective control over suspicious financial flows and international bank associations, the networking of relevant information flows among national intelligence agencies, as well as the worldwide coordination of corresponding police investigations.

B O R R A D O R I : You have claimed that the intellectual is a figure with historically specific characteristics, deeply intertwined with European history, the ninteenth century, and the onset of modernity. Does he or she play a particular role in our present context?

H A B E R M A S : I wouldn't say so. The usual suspects—writers, philosophers, artists, scholars working in the humanities as well as in the social sciences—who speak out on other occasions have done so this time, too. There have been the usual pros and cons, the same snarl of voices with the familiar national differences in style and public resonance—it has not been much different from the Gulf or Kosovo Wars. Perhaps the American voices were heard faster and louder than usual— in the end, also somewhat more devoutly gubernatorial and patriotic. On one side, even leftist liberals for the moment seem to be in agreement with Bush's politics. Richard Rorty's pronounced positions are, if I understand correctly, not completely atypical. On the other side, critics of the operation in Afghanistan started from a false prognosis in their pragmatic assessment of its chances for success. This time, what was required was not only anthropological-historical knowledge of a somewhat specialized kind but also military and geopolitical expertise. I am not subscribing to the anti-intellectual prejudice, according to which intellectuals regularly lack the required expertise. If one is not exactly an economist, one refrains from judging complex economic developments. With regard to military issues, however, intellectuals obviously do not act differently from other armchair strategists.

B O R R A D O R I : In your Paulskirche speech (Frankfurt, October 2001),[5] you defined fundamentalism as a specifically modern phenomenon. Why?

H A B E R M A S :   It depends, of course, on how one uses the term. "Fundamentalist" has a pejorative ring to it. We use this predicate to characterize a peculiar mindset, a stubborn attitude that insists on the political imposition of its own convictions and reasons, even when they are far from being rationally acceptable. This holds especially for religious beliefs. We should certainly not confuse fundamentalism with dogmatism and orthodoxy. Every religious doctrine is based on a dogmatic kernel of belief. Sometimes there is an authority such as the pope or the Roman congregation, which determines what interpretations deviate from this dogma and, therefore, from orthodoxy. Such orthodoxy first veers toward fundamentalism when the guardians and representatives of the true faith ignore the epistemic situation of a pluralistic society and insist—even to the point of violence—on the universally binding character and political acceptance of their doctrine.

Until the onset of modernity, the prophetic teachings were also *world* religions in the sense that they were able to expand within the cognitive horizons of ancient empires perceived from within as all-encompassing worlds. The "universalism" of those empires, whose peripheries seemed to blur beyond their boundaries, provided the appropriate background for the exclusive claim to truth by the world religions. However, in the modern conditions of an accelerated growth in complexity, such an exclusive claim to truth by one faith can no longer be naively maintained. In Europe, the confessional schism and the secularization of society have compelled religious belief to reflect on its nonexclusive place within a universal discourse shared with other religions and limited by scientifically generated secular knowledge. At the same time, the awareness of this double relativization of one's own position obviously should not imply relativizing one's own beliefs. This self-reflexive achievement of a religion that learned to see itself through the eyes of others has had important political implications. The believers could from then on realize why they had to renounce violence, in general, and refrain from state power, in particular, for the purpose of enforcing religious claims. This cognitive thrust made religious tolerance, as well as the separation between state and church, possible for the first time.

When a contemporary regime like Iran refuses to carry out this separation or when movements inspired by religion strive for the reestablishment of an Islamic form of theocracy, we consider that to be fundamentalism. I would explain the frozen features of such a mentality in terms of the repression of striking cognitive dissonances. This repression occurs when the innocence of the epistemological situation of an all-encompassing world perspective is lost and when, under the cognitive conditions of scientific knowledge and of religious pluralism, a return to the exclusivity of premodern belief attitudes is propagated. These attitudes cause such striking cognitive dissonances since the complex life circumstances in modern pluralistic societies are normatively compatible only with a *strict* universalism in which the same respect is demanded for everybody—be they Catholic, Protestant, Muslim, Jewish, Hindu, or Buddhist, believers or nonbelievers.

B O R R A D O R I :   How is the kind of Islamic fundamentalism we see today different from earlier fundamentalist trends and practices, such as the witch-hunts of the early modern age?

H A B E R M A S :   There is probably a motif that links the two phenomena you mention, namely, the defensive reaction against the fear of a violent uprooting of traditional ways of life. In that early modern age, the beginnings of political and economic modernization may have given rise to such fears in some regions of Europe. Of course, with the globalization of markets, particularly the financial markets, and with the expansion of foreign direct investments, we find ourselves today at a completely different stage. Things are different insofar as world society is meanwhile *split up* into winner, beneficiary, and loser countries. To the Arab world, the U.S.A. is the driving force of capitalistic modernization. With its unapproachable lead in development and with its overwhelming technological, economic, political, and military superiority, the U.S.A. appears as an insult to their self-confidence while simultaneously providing the secretly admired model. The West in its entirety serves as a scapegoat for the Arab world's own, very real experiences of loss, suffered by populations torn out of their cultural traditions during processes of accelerated modernization. What was experienced in Europe under more favorable circumstances as a process of *productive* destruction does not hold the promise of compensation for the pain of the disintegration of customary ways of life in other countries. They feel this compensation cannot even be achieved within the horizon of the next generations.

It is understandable on a psychological level for this defensive reaction to feed on spiritual sources, which set in motion, against the secularizing force of the West, a potential that already seems to have disappeared from it. The furious fundamentalist recourse to a set of beliefs, from which modernity has elicited neither any self-reflexive learning process nor any differentiation between religion, secular knowledge, and politics, gains certain plausibility from the fact that it feeds on a substance that apparently disappeared from the West. A materialist West encounters other cultures—which owe their profile to the imprint of one of the great world religions—only through the provocative and trivializing irresistibility of a leveling consumerist culture. Let's admit it—the West presents itself in a form deprived of any normative kernel as long as its concern for human rights only concerns the attempt at opening new free markets and as long as, at home, it allows free reign to the neoconservative division of labor between religious fundamentalism and a kind of evacuating depleting secularization.

B O R R A D O R I :   Philosophically speaking, do you consider terrorism to be a wholly political act?

H A B E R M A S :   Not in the subjective sense in which Mohammed Atta, the Egyptian citizen who came from Hamburg and piloted the first of the two catastrophic airplanes, would offer you a political answer. No doubt today's Islamic fundamentalism is also a cover for political motifs. Indeed, we should not overlook the political motifs we encounter in forms of religious fanaticism. This explains the fact that some of those drawn into the "holy war" had been secular nationalists only a few years before. If one looks at the biographies of these people, remarkable continuities are revealed. Disappointment over nationalistic authoritarian regimes may have contributed to the fact that today religion offers a new and subjectively more convincing language for old political orientations.

B O R R A D O R I :   How would you actually define terrorism? Can a meaningful distinction be drawn between national and international or even global terrorism?

H A B E R M A S :   In one respect, Palestinian terrorism still possesses a certain outmoded characteristic in that it revolves around murder, around the indiscriminate annihilation of enemies, women, and children—life against life. This is what distinguishes it from the terror that appears in the paramilitary form of guerilla warfare. This form of warfare has characterized many national liberation movements in the second half of the twentieth century—and has left its mark today on the

Chechnyan struggle for independence, for example. In contrast to this, the global terror that culminated in the September 11 attack bears the anarchistic traits of an impotent revolt directed against an enemy that cannot be defeated in any pragmatic sense. The only possible effect it can have is to shock and alarm the government and population. Technically speaking, since our complex societies are highly susceptible to interferences and accidents, they certainly offer ideal opportunities for a prompt disruption of normal activities. These disruptions can, with minimum expense, have considerably destructive consequences. Global terrorism is extreme both in its lack of realistic goals and in its cynical exploitation of the vulnerability of complex systems.

B O R R A D O R I : Should terrorism be distinguished from ordinary crime and other types of violence?

H A B E R M A S : Yes and no. From a moral point of view, there is no excuse for terrorist acts, regardless of the motive or the situation under which they are carried out. Nothing justifies our "making allowance for" the murder or suffering of others for one's own purposes. Each murder is one too many. Historically, however, terrorism falls in a category different from crimes that concern a criminal court judge. It differs from a private incident in that it deserves public interest and requires a different kind of analysis than murder out of jealousy, for example. Otherwise, we would not be having this interview. The difference between political terror and ordinary crime becomes clear during the change of regimes, in which former terrorists come to power and become well-regarded representatives of their country. Certainly, such a political transition can be hoped for only by terrorists who pursue political goals in a realistic manner; who are able to draw, at least retrospectively, a certain legitimation for their criminal actions, undertaken to overcome a manifestly unjust situation. However, today I cannot imagine a context that would some day, in some manner, make the monstrous crime of September 11 an understandable or comprehensible political act.

B O R R A D O R I : Do you think it was good to interpret 9/11 as a declaration of war?

H A B E R M A S : Even if the term "war" is less misleading and, morally, less controvertible than "crusade," I consider Bush' s decision to call for a "war against terrorism" a serious mistake, both normatively and pragmatically. Normatively, he is elevating these criminals to the status of war enemies; and pragmatically, one cannot lead a war against a "network" if the term "war" is to retain any definite meaning.

B O R R A D O R I :   If the West needs to develop greater sensitivity and adopt more self-criticism in its dealings with other cultures, how should it go about doing that? Philosophically, you have articulated the interrelation between "translation" and the "search for a common language." Can this be the key to a new political course?

H A B E R M A S :   Since September 11 I have often been asked whether or not, in light of this violent phenomenon, the whole conception of "communicative action" I developed in my theory has been brought into disrepute. We in the West do live in peaceful and well-to-do societies, and yet they contain a *structural* violence that, to a certain degree, we have gotten used to, that is, unconscionable social inequality, degrading discrimination, pauperization, and marginalization. Precisely because our social relations are permeated by violence, strategic action and manipulation, there are two other facts we should not overlook. On the one hand, the praxis of our daily living together rests on a solid base of common background convictions, self-evident cultural truths and reciprocal expectations. Here the coordination of action runs through the ordinary language games, through mutually raised and at least implicitly recognized validity claims *in the public space of more or less good reasons.* On the other hand, due to this, conflicts arise from *distortion in communication,* from misunderstanding and incomprehension, from insincerity and deception. When the consequences of these conflicts become painful enough, they land in court or at the therapist's office. The spiral of violence begins as a spiral of distorted communication that leads through the spiral of uncontrolled reciprocal mistrust, to the breakdown of communication. If violence thus begins with a distortion in communication, after it has erupted it is possible to know what has gone wrong and what needs to be repaired.

This trivial insight can be applied to the conflicts you speak of. The matter is more complicated here because cultures, ways of life, and nations are at a greater distance from and, thus, are more foreign to one another. They do not encounter each other like members of a society who might *become alienated* from each other only through systematically distorted communication. Furthermore, in *international relations,* the curbing power of the law plays a comparatively weak role. And in *intercultural* relations, the legal system achieves at best an institutional framework for formal meetings, such as the World Conference on Human Rights held in Vienna by the United Nations. As important as the multileveled intercultural discourse on the controversial interpretations of human rights may be, such formal encounters cannot by themselves interrupt the spiral of stereotyping. The desired transformation of a mentality happens, rather, through the improvement of living conditions, through a sensible relief from oppression and fear. Trust must be able to develop in communicative everyday practices. Only then can a broadly effective enlightenment extend into media, schools, and homes. And it must do so by affecting the premises of its own political culture.

In this context, the type of normative self-representation vis-à-vis other cultures becomes important for ourselves, too. In the process of such revision of its self-image, the West could learn, for example, how it would need to change its politics if it wants to be perceived as a shaping power with a civilizing impact. Without the political taming of an unbounded capitalism, the devastating stratification of world society will remain intractable. The disparities in the dynamic of world economic development would have to at least be balanced out regarding their most destructive consequences—the deprivation and misery of complete regions and continents comes to mind. This does not merely concern the discrimination toward, the humiliation of, or the offense to other cultures. The so-called "clash of civilizations" [Kampf der Kulturen] is often the veil masking the vital material interests of the West (accessible oilfields and a secured energy supply, for example).[6]

B O R R A D O R I :   In light of what you are suggesting, we should ask ourselves whether the dialogue model suits the intercultural exchange at all. Is it not always on our own terms that we swear to the solidarity between cultures?

H A B E R M A S :   The constant deconstructivist suspicion of our Eurocentric prejudices raises a counter-question: why should the hermeneutic model of understanding, which functions in everyday conversations and which since Humboldt has been methodologically developed from the practice of interpreting texts, suddenly break down beyond the boundaries of our own culture, of our own way of life and tradition? An interpretation must in each case bridge the gap between the hermeneutic preunderstanding of both sides—whether the cultural and spatiotemporal distances are shorter or longer, or the semantic differences smaller or larger. All interpretations are translations *in nuce.* It is not even necessary to reach back to Donald Davidson in order to understand that the *very idea of a conceptual scheme,* which constitutes one of several worlds, cannot be conceived of without contradiction. One can also show with Gadamerian arguments that the idea of a self-contained universe of meanings, which is incommensurable with other universes of this type, is an inconsistent concept.

From this, however, a methodical ethnocentrism does not necessarily follow. Rorty and Alasdair MacIntyre defend an assimilation model of understanding whereby radical interpretation means either the assimilation to one's own standards of rationality or a conversion and, thus, a kind of subjection to the rationality of a completely foreign conception of the world. We should only be able to understand what falls under the dictates of a world-disclosing language. That description fits at best the very beginning of an interpretation—a troubling situation that demands a hermeneutic effort since it makes participants painfully aware of the one-sided nature and limitations of their initial conjectures. Struggling with the difficulties of understanding, people must, step by step, widen their original perspectives and ultimately bring them together. And they can succeed in such a "fusion of horizons" by virtue of their peculiar capacity to take up the roles of "speaker" and "hearer." Taking up these roles in a dialogue, they engage in a fundamental symmetry, which, at bottom, all speech situations require. When a native speaker has learned how to use the system of personal pronouns, she has acquired competence in exchanging the perspectives between first and second person. And in the course of mutual perspective-taking there can develop a common horizon of background assumptions in which both sides accomplish an interpretation that is not ethnocentrically adopted or converted but, rather, *intersubjectively* shared.

This model explains why attempts at understanding have a chance only under symmetrical conditions of *mutual* perspective-taking. Good intentions and the absence of manifest violence are of course helpful, but not sufficient. Without the structures of a communicative situation free from distortion, the results are always under the suspicion of having been forced. Naturally, most of the time it is only the unavoidable fallibility of the human mind that is revealed by the election, and the need for revision and expansion of the interpretations obtained. However, such normal failures are often indistinguishable from that peculiar moment of blindness, which interpretations owe to the traces of forced assimilation to constraints imposed by a superior party. Due to this, communication is always ambiguous, suspect of latent violence. But when communication gets ontologized under this description, when "nothing but" violence is seen in it, one misses the essential point: that the critical power to put a stop to violence, without reproducing it in circles of new violence, can only dwell in the telos of mutual understanding and in our orientation toward this goal.

B O R R A D O R I : Globalization has brought us to reconsider the international-law concept of sovereignty. How do you see the role of international organizations in relation to it? Does cosmopolitanism, one of the central ideals of the Enlightenment, still play a useful role in today's circumstances?

H A B E R M A S : I believe that Carl Schmitt's existentialist idea, according to which "the political" consists merely in the self-assertion of a collective identity over against other collective identities, is false and dangerous in view of its practical consequences. The ontologization of the friend-foe relation suggests that attempts at a cosmopolitan juridification of the relations between the belligerent subjects of international law are fated to serve the masking of particular interests in universalistic disguise. But how can one, holding this opinion, ignore the fact that the totalitarian regimes of the twentieth century, with their political mass crimes, have repudiated in an unprecedented way the assumption of innocence found in classical international law? For this historical reason we have long found ourselves in the transition from classical international law to what Kant had anticipated as a state of world citizenry. This is a fact, and furthermore, normatively speaking, I do not see any meaningful alternative to such a development. This notwithstanding, there are drawbacks that cannot be ignored. Since the Nuremberg and Tokyo war crimes tribunals after the end of World War II, since the founding of the UN and the UN Declaration of Human Rights, since the more active human rights policy following the end of the Cold War, since the controversial NATO intervention in Kosovo, and finally, since the declaration of war against international terrorism, since all of these events, the ambivalence of this transition has emerged more clearly.

On the one hand, the idea of an international community that eliminates the state of nature between nations by effectively penalizing wars of aggression, genocide, and crimes against humanity and punishing violations of human rights has taken shape in the UN and its branches. The tribunal in The Hague is hearing the case against Slobodan Milosevic, a former head of state. The top British judges almost prevented the repatriation of Augusto Pinochet, a criminal ex-dictator. The establishment of an international criminal court is underway. The principle of nonintervention in the domestic affairs of a sovereign state has been undermined. Resolutions of the UN Security Council have revoked the Iraqi government's free use of its own airspace. UN soldiers are guaranteeing the safety of the post-Taliban government in Kabul. Macedonia, which stood at the brink of a civil war, has agreed under pressure from the EU to demands from the Albanian minority.

On the other hand, the world organization is often nothing more than a paper tiger. It is dependent on the willingness of the great powers to cooperate. The Security Council can provide only very selective observance for the avowed principles of the international community, even after the events of 1989. As the Srebrenica tragedy shows, UN troops are often not in a position to enforce given guarantees. If the Security Council is blocked in its decisions, as it was in the face of the Kosovo conflict, and if in its place a regional alliance like NATO acts without a mandate, it reveals the fatal power differential that exists between the legitimate but weak authority of the international community and the actual strength of nation-states capable of military action but pursuing their own interests.

The discrepancy between what should and what can be done, between justice and power, sheds a negative light both on the credibility of the UN and on the practice of intervention of unauthorized states that merely usurp a mandate—even for good reasons—and turn what would be justified as a police action into an act of war. The supposed police action often becomes indistinguishable from an all too ordinary war. This unclear jumble of classical power politics, consideration for regional alliances, and attempts at a cosmopolitan regime not only strengthens the opposing interests existing between North and South, East and West within the UN. It also fosters the superpower's apprehension toward all normative restrictions of its scope of discretion.

This, in turn, fosters growing dissent within the Western camp between the Anglo-Saxon and the continental countries. The former draw their inspiration from the "realistic school" of international relations while the latter favor a normative legitimation and a gradual transformation of international law into a cosmopolitan order.

During the war in Kosovo, or even in the policy toward Afghanistan, one could clearly see corresponding differences in the setting of an agenda. This tension between rather power-pragmatic and more normative goals will only be resolved if one day the large continentwide alliances, like the EU, NAFTA, and ASEAN,[7] develop into empowered actors capable of reaching transnational agreements and taking over responsibility for an ever more closely tied transnational network of organizations, conferences, and practices. Only with this type of global players able to form a political counterbalance to the global expansion of markets running ahead of any political frame would the UN find a base for the implementation of high-minded programs and policies.

B O R R A D O R I : Many have admired the universalism you defend in your writings on moral and political philosophy; many have criticized it. What does this universalism have to do with tolerance? Is tolerance not a paternalistic term that would be better off being replaced by the concept of "hospitality" or "friendship?"

H A B E R M A S : The concept of tolerance has certainly had this connotation throughout history. Remember, for example, the Edict of Nantes, under which the French king permitted the Huguenots, a religious minority, to profess their beliefs and observe their rituals on the condition that they not question the authority of the king's throne or the supremacy of Catholicism. Tolerance has been practiced for centuries in this paternalistic spirit. The one-sided nature of the declaration that a sovereign ruler or the culture of the majority is willing at its own discretion to "tolerate" the deviant practices of the minority is paternalistic. In this context, the act of toleration retains an element of an act of mercy or of "doing a favor." One party allows the other a certain amount of deviation from "normality" under one condition: that the tolerated minority does not overstep the "threshold of tolerance." Criticism has been aimed, and rightly so, against this authoritarian "conception of allowance," for it is obvious that the threshold of tolerance, which separates what is still "acceptable" from what is not, is arbitrarily established by the existing authority. And the impression then arises that tolerance, since it can only be practiced within a boundary beyond which it would cease, possesses itself a kernel of intolerance. This consideration is reflected in your question.

Today, for example, we encounter this paradox in the concept of "militant democracy": no freedom for the enemies of freedom. However, from this example we can also learn that the straight deconstruction of the concept of tolerance falls into a trap, since the constitutional state contradicts precisely the premise from which the paternalistic sense of the traditional concept of "tolerance" derives. Within a democratic community whose citizens reciprocally grant one another equal rights, no room is left for an authority allowed to *one-sidedly* determine the boundaries of what is to be tolerated. On the basis of the citizens' equal rights and reciprocal respect for each other, nobody possesses the privilege of setting the boundaries of tolerance from the viewpoint of their own preferences and value-orientations. Certainly, to tolerate other people's beliefs without accepting their truth, and to tolerate other ways of life without appreciating their intrinsic value as we do with regard to our own, requires a common standard. In the case of a democratic community, this common value base is found in the principles of the constitution. Of course, there arise disputes over the true understanding of these principles, too. What is important, however, is the peculiar character of reflexivity that constitutional principles enjoy. The explanation of this intricate issue brings us back to the question of universalism.

For conflicts of constitutional interpretation, the constitution itself has made the necessary provisions. There are institutions and procedures for settling the question of the limits for what might still, or no longer, be taken as "being loyal to the constitution." The question applies in particular to a kind of public agitation that renounces the "foundations of the constitution" (as is the case today with Islamic extremism). Interestingly, in a community that tolerates "civil disobedience" constitutional protection extends even beyond the established order, beyond all practices and institutions in the shape of which its own normative content has been spelled out and has assumed binding force. In its tolerance of civil disobedience, the constitution self-reflexively stretches to cover even the conditions for overstepping its own boundaries. A democratic constitution can thus tolerate resistance from dissidents who, after exhausting all legal avenues, nonetheless oppose legitimately reached decisions. It only imposes the condition that this rule-breaking resistance be plausibly justified in the spirit and wording of the constitution and conducted by symbolic means that lend the fight the character of a nonviolent appeal to the majority to once again reflect on their decisions. In this way, the democratic project of the realization of equal civil rights actually feeds off the resistance of minorities, which, although appearing as enemies of democracy to the majority today, *could* actually turn out to be their authentic friends tomorrow.

To return to your question, this reflexive overstepping of the boundaries of tolerance within a "militant democracy" is due to the universalistic nature of the legal and moral foundation of a liberal order. In the strict sense, "universalism" amounts to the egalitarian individualism of a morality that demands mutual recognition, in the sense of equal respect and reciprocal consideration for everybody. Membership in this inclusive moral community, which is therefore open to all, promises not only solidarity and a nondiscriminating inclusion, but at the same time equal rights for the protection of everybody's individuality and otherness.

Discourses inspired by this idea are distinguished from all other discourses by two essential features. On the one hand, the universalistic discourses of law and morality can be abused as a particularly insidious form of legitimation since particular interests can hide behind the glimmering façade of reasonable universality. This ideological function, which had already been denounced by the young Marx, forms the basis of Carl Schmitt's resentment when he throws "humanity"—the insistence on standards of egalitarian individualism—together with "bestiality" in one pot. What fascists like Schmitt seem to overlook, and what Marx clearly saw, is the other characteristic of this discourse: the peculiar self-reference that makes it the vehicle for self-correcting learning processes. Just as every objection raised against the selective or one-eyed application of universalistic standards must already presuppose these same standards, in the same manner, any deconstructive unmasking of the ideologically concealing use of universalistic discourses actually presupposes the critical viewpoints advanced by these same discourses. Moral and legal universalism is, thus, self-reflexively closed in the sense that its imperfect practices can only be criticized on the basis of its own standards.

B O R R A D O R I :   One last question: What are your ideas on heroism?

H A B E R M A S :   The courage, discipline, and selflessness demonstrated by the New York firemen who on September 11 spontaneously put their lives on the line to save others is admirable. But why do they need to be called "heroes"? Perhaps this word has different connotations in American English than it does in German. It seems to me that whenever "heroes" are honored the question arises as to who needs them and why. Even in this looser sense of the term one can understand Bertolt Brecht's warning: "Pity the land that needs heroes."

RECONSTRUCTING
TERRORISM

Habermas

For over four decades Habermas's thought has been centered on the
idea that democracy, and the public struggle for its best form, is the key
to solving apparently insurmountable problems. Democracy, in its
structural perfectibility, is both the means and the end of individual
and social emancipation. In the eighteenth century, Kant defined
emancipation as the process of civic maturation that provides individuals with the self-confidence to use their own reason and understanding. Such maturity is a prerequisite for participating, equally and freely,
in a community politically structured as a constitutional democracy.
Habermas grew up in post–World War II Germany, where democracy
was not only a reality but a passionately embraced one. This position
makes him stress emancipation as "a very special kind of self-experi-
ence, because in it processes of self-understanding link up with an increase of autonomy."[1] In other words, the kind of emancipation that
democracy stimulates in individuals brings them to live firsthand the

interdependence between self-knowledge and freedom. The more one discursively examines oneself, through conversation and dialogue, the more freely one can think and act.

The cultivation of self-knowledge is among the oldest pursuits of philosophy. "Know thyself" was the inscription above the entrance of the sanctuary at Delphi, dedicated to Apollo, the most devotedly rational god of all. Yet, for Habermas, self-knowledge must be oriented to the very specific scope of developing autonomy of judgment and freedom of action—the two pillars of the political project of modernity canonized by Kant. This understanding of self-knowledge is an ongoing theme in Habermas's philosophy, reaching back to *Knowledge and Human Interests* (1962). In it, Habermas compares social theory to psychoanalysis. This move underlines that Habermas does not take individual autonomy for granted, as if it were given to human subjects by nature. Rather, he sees it as a function of interpersonal exchange. The dialogue a patient has with a therapist is not manipulative or exploitative but aimed at stimulating the human potential for self-reflection and self-knowledge. However, the comparison between psychoanalysis and social theory holds true only at the level of methodological structures and basic concepts. For Habermas never conceived of society as a unitary subject that entertains with the social theorist the same asymmetrical relation that a patient has with her therapist. Autonomy, for him, has always been a function of the fundamental symmetry, or equality, between interlocutors, a symmetry embedded in the concept of democratic participation.

Starting in the late 1970s, Habermas began to frame the issues of autonomy and participation within the practice of everyday communication. Since the publication of his monumental *Theory of Communicative Action* (1981), his assumption has been that we learn who we are as autonomous agents from our basic relations with others. The most basic among these relations is the act of communicating through language. Habermas's standpoint is thus that the substance of communication is mutual understanding; and yet, understanding cannot occur in a completely unregulated context, namely, one in which lies, mystification, and manipulation predominate. For communication to succeed there needs to be, on the part of both speaker and listener, some commitment to telling the truth and meaning exactly what one is saying. This establishes communication as a rational practice, which allows for the formation of a freely achieved consensus among interlocutors. Such consensus is structurally analogous to the open-ended nature of the debate that founds democratic deliberation.

It's really quite simple: whenever we mean what we say, we raise the claim that what we said is true, or right, or truthful. With this claim, a small bit of ideality breaks into our everyday lives, because such validity claims can in the end be resolved only with arguments. At the same time, we know that arguments that appear valid to us today can prove to be false tomorrow, in light of new experiences and new information.[2]

The claim that what I am saying is valid—whether by valid I mean true, right, or truthful—is the "bit of ideality" that Habermas sees breaking "into our everyday lives." While it is possible for individuals to decide not to tell the truth, for information to circulate in a distorted form whether for political, commercial, or personal reasons, not everyone can behave manipulatively all the time. If that were to happen, the category of lying, defined in opposition to that of telling the truth, would be lost; the appropriation of tradition would become impossible; and ultimately, communication would not occur.

For Habermas, more bits of ideality trickle down into our everyday life, the more we communicate effectively with others, and the more we grow in the understanding of ourselves and of others. This allows us to become more autonomous individuals, more mature and emancipated agents, and ultimately, more rational citizens. As emancipation is relocated in everyday communicative practice, it loses the character of an extraordinary experience: the unique historical event of Kant's imagination. Fundamentally, Habermas reframes it as the claim of validity that is attached to every act of speech directed from a speaker to a listener in a nonmanipulative and nonmystifying situation.

Philosophy's aim is to offer a *reconstruction* of the conditions that make communication not only possible but also effective and productive, both at the individual and social levels. The reconstruction of these conditions gives philosophy a sharp critical tool with which to evaluate the present and its distortions in communication. Unlike classical political philosophy, whose task is to draft the requirements for a well-ordered and just society, Habermas's approach provides philosophy with the possibility of diagnosing the ills of society in terms of defects in communication.

Is terrorism a defect in communication? If so, does it occur at the level of local communication—within the bounds of a single culture, nation, or religion—or at the level of global communication? Whether it is local or global or both, who is accountable for it?

My dialogue with Habermas revolved around these crucial questions. In it, Habermas exposed his entire philosophical framework to interpret the attacks of 9/11, the most heinous and gigantic terrorist mission ever perpetrated. As a whole, the dialogue has the structure of a case study: the analysis of this specific occurrence allows for an interpretation of global terrorism that helps expose its dangerous conceptual elusiveness. The purpose of my essay is to review the main arguments Habermas puts forth and place them in the larger context of his philosophy. Understanding how they fit into his philosophical project will help the reader walk along the same path that Habermas took to arrive at his judgments on terrorism. It will also highlight a number of implications that, particularly for those new to Habermas's theory, may easily be overlooked.

9/11: The First Historic World Event

It is a great privilege to have a mind of the caliber of Habermas's apply itself to the reading and interpretation of an event that so powerfully defused a certain sense of safety afforded by the end of the Cold War. By coincidence, he was in New York in the weeks after the terrorist attacks that destroyed the Twin Towers, a portion of the Pentagon in Washington, D.C., and took down a commercial plane full of passengers in western Pennsylvania. The direct experience of that aftermath gave him a completely different perspective on the degree of emotional devastation that New Yorkers suffered on 9/11.

Our dialogue began from Habermas's acknowledgment of the irreducible chasm between fact and representation, first-person and third-person perspectives. Plainly, he concedes that only after arriving in New York did the full emotional intensity of this chasm become palpable for him. Even Habermas, a stern defender of the endless benefits of what can be articulated through speech, admitted the strength of the unspeakable as he recounted the tale of a friend who watched the tragedy unfold from the roof of his house. As graphic and shocking as they were, the images he saw on his TV screen in Germany were delivered in the "breaking news" format, leaving the possibility of a third-person perspective. By contrast, New Yorkers like me were left in existential and sensory chaos: not only did a pervasive smell hang over Manhattan for weeks, but the acute scream of the sirens, usually lost in acoustic pollution, kept puncturing the silence left by the empty airspace—the great dome of contrails and roars crisscrossing above the city.

And yet, as Habermas points out, never before did anyone get as much reality from a TV screen as people worldwide got on 9/11. The footage of 9/11 wasn't edited or even produced for its own media coverage, and this renders it, in his words, the "first historic world event."[3]

> "Perhaps September 11 could be called the first historic world event in the strictest sense: the impact, the explosion, the slow collapse—everything that was not Hollywood anymore but, rather, a gruesome reality, literally took place in front of the "universal eyewitness" of a global public.

A comparison with Habermas's reaction to the Gulf War further clarifies his take on the uniqueness of 9/11. In that case, too, he was an active public voice. In January 1991, when the Gulf War broke out, the world was struck at how "staged" the war seemed: it invited, he later wrote, "comparisons with video games, with the maddeningly irresistible playback of an electronic program."[4] Nonetheless, "we outside observers were all too aware that a good portion of the reality—in fact, the warlike dimension of the war—was being withheld, and this awareness may have stimulated our own powers of imagination. The censor's black patch on the TV screen sets one's own imagination in motion."[5] The Gulf War exposed the public to a minimal amount of footage of what happened on the ground. While in 1991, proving the old saying that "Truth is the first casualty of war," the global public was given a media construction; in 2001 that same global public became a "universal eyewitness." This very fact, for Habermas, makes 9/11 the "first historic world event."

While Habermas underlines the absolute uniqueness of 9/11 from the standpoint of its communicative modality, he prefers to let history judge its relative importance. Whether or not 9/11 will "stand comparison to other events of world historical impact," he said, is for history itself to decide. But how is history going to judge? The answer to this question lies, for Habermas, in the notion of "effective history" (*Wirkungsgeschichte*), first theorized by another German philosopher: Hans Georg Gadamer. With effective history Gadamer indicates that the interpreter of a past event is conditioned, in her evaluation, by the effects of her own present. This denies historical knowledge any degree of objectivity, for the simple reason that we are always already immersed in history. By contrast, historical judgments are based on a peculiar interplay between past and present, which Gadamer calls "fusion of horizons."[6]

Contrary to most political commentators, Habermas's bet is that 9/11 is closer to August 1914, the onset of World War I, than to the surprise attack against the U. S. naval fleet by the Japanese army at Pearl Harbor, in 1943. In his reading, precisely like 1914, 9/11 marks the beginning of an era of pronounced instability not only with regard to the relations between East and West but also, and perhaps even more unsettling, between the United States and Europe. The U.S. response to terrorism has produced a fundamental mistrust toward foreigners and, at the same time, the expectation of unconditional support on the part of their political partners, the European Community first and foremost. These two stances, mistrust toward foreigners and the expectation of unconditional support, run against the very grain of Habermas's approach to the political and ethical realms, which he sees ruled by dialogue and rational argumentation.

The emphasis on rational argumentation as the ultimate condition for justice is the central theme of Habermas's philosophical approach. It grows out of the enormous challenge presented by being a post–World War II German intellectual. Coming to age in a country physically and culturally devastated by an "unmasterable past" made Habermas embrace the responsibility of being a German and a European citizen to the fullest. Europe "must use one of its strengths, namely its potential for self-criticism, its power of self-transformation, in order to relativize itself far more radically vis-à-vis the others, the strangers, the misunderstood. That's the opposite of Eurocentrism. But *we* can overcome Eurocentrism only out of the better spirit of Europe."[7] For Habermas, the better spirit of Europe is the rationalist tradition in which support is never granted without rational argumentation. Within this tradition Kant towers as the unsurpassed master.

Indeed, Kant's conception of the Enlightenment is set against the notion of unconditional support, which Habermas feels the United States solicited from its allies after 9/11. For Kant, the Enlightenment marks the liberation of humanity from blind obedience to authority, gained through rational self-affirmation. Enlightenment is the "freedom to make *public use* of one's reason in all matters."[8] To declare that the exercise of reason is dependent on its "public use" means to assert that there is an exponential enlightening effect if public freedom is established. Public freedom stimulates "private" freedom because, according to Kant, any individual "naturally" embraces her autonomy of judgment if external conditions allow it. Autonomous judgment or private freedom is the formulation of a rational argument: since arguments, for Kant, consist in the exchange among interlocutors who consider each other equal, the very form of rational argumentation is modeled after the public use of reason even when arguments are being formulated in the privacy of one's own mind.

If private freedom is dependent on its public use, as it is for Kant, it also depends on the availability of an interlocutor open to listen and respond truthfully. To take up the Kantian perspective, as Habermas does, means to reject de facto any requests for unconditional support.[9]

From Classical International Law to a New Cosmopolitan Order

The request for unconditional support advanced by the U.S. administration not only to its political allies but to the "civilized world," is for Habermas only one feature of the post-9/11 era. Another is that the threat of global terrorism has accelerated the need for the conversion from classical international law to a new cosmopolitan order on the world scale.

For at least three decades, financial and political globalization has put pressure on the organizational form of the nation-state conceived as territorial state. This aging poses the question of how long the form of the nation-state will last, and eventually, what will replace it. Habermas's political intervention on the occasion of the unification of the two German republics in 1989 speaks directly to his position concerning the destiny of the nation-state. Kant's long shadow can be found in Habermas's declaration that it would be a mistake for German citizens to found their identity in tradition. For him, the only legitimate political articulation of the identity of a nation, with or without an unmasterable past, is "constitutional patriotism" in which loyalty to the constitution attests for the consensual participation of all citizens. Such loyalty also expresses loyalty to the idea of universal rights that he takes as the condition for the coexistence of human beings, particularly in a complex and multicultural society. A few months after the fall of the Berlin Wall, which led to the unification of the two German republics, Habermas wrote the following:

> If we do not free ourselves from the diffuse notions about the nation-state, if we do not rid ourselves of the pre-political crutches of nationality and community of fate, we will be unable to continue unburdened on the very path that we have long since chosen: the path to a multicultural society, the path to a federal state with wide regional differences and strong federal power, and above all the path to a unified European state of many nationalities. A national identity which is not based predominantly on republican self-understanding and constitutional patriotism necessarily collides with the universalist rules of mutual coexistence for human beings.[10]

The notion of constitutional patriotism is a useful point of departure to address Habermas's view concerning the possibility of a new cosmopolitan order, which he recognizes as the most urgent challenge facing the geopolitical scene after the terrorist attacks of 9/11.

To get rid of all atavisms, political thought has to abandon the idea that politics is anything other than a communicative exchange whose key requirement is reaching rational agreement on what we mean when we talk to each other. Speakers and listeners implicitly sign this agreement every time they communicate on any subject and in whatever arena, private or public, ethical or political. Politics is thus indistinguishable from the communicative modality proper to everyday exchanges. In politics as well as in ordinary speech, lying and manipulation, deception and misunderstanding, cannot dominate, because communication would be precluded. As is the case with everyday speech, our objective should be to make the communicative core of politics more effective, for this would automatically strengthen each citizen's identification with her community solely on the basis of its constitutional rules.

Habermas considers the German philosopher of law Carl Schmitt to be the emblem of the wrong way of thinking about politics. His opposition to this very controversial figure,[11] is indicative of how implacable Habermas is toward the aspects of German and European culture that he associates with nationalist policies and prepolitical values such as ethnicity or "community of fate." Habermas feels that his first civic duty as a German citizen is to recover only what is rationally justified and agreed upon.

A member of the Nazi Party since 1933, Schmitt was perhaps the most prominent constitutionalist of the Third Reich; arrested in 1945, Schmitt was banned from teaching and retreated into a largely self-imposed exile. Schmitt believed that the dynamic of modern European history is driven by a search for a neutral sphere free from violent conflict and intellectual contestation. This history grows out of a reaction against the religious wars that crippled Europe in the sixteenth century. According to Schmitt, a number of expansionist threats menace Europe, making its desire for peace unattainable. Since his early writings from the 1920s during the Weimer Republic, Schmitt was obsessed by the expansion of Soviet Russia, where civil war had followed the abdication of the tsar in 1917. In his eyes, Russia was dedicated to absorbing all the technological opportunities in order to develop an ever stronger army. In his writings after World War II, Schmitt extended his obsession to the other giant on the international scene: the United States. In the face of these threats, Europe remained for Schmitt the homeland of the concept and the practice of sovereign states, balancing each other through international law.[12]

In our dialogue, Habermas affirms that for Schmitt the bounds of the political realm are set by the self-assertion of one collective identity against another: a sovereign nation is not based on the self-determination of civic liberties but on the uniqueness of one ethnic nationality against all others. To define the political in this way means, for Habermas, to "ontologize" the friend-foe relation and turn it into the substance or the essence of politics. It is precisely in relation to this premise that Schmitt develops the suspicion that international law may be at the service of expansionist interests of stronger actors. Habermas rejects this line of reasoning not only because it grounds politics in values and assumptions that are prepolitical but also because it plays down the internal legitimacy of international law, reducing it to the contingent mediation between national political actors.

> But how can one, holding this opinion, ignore the fact that the totalitarian regimes of the twentieth century, with their atrocities of political mass crimes, have repudiated in an unprecedented way the assumption of innocence found in classical international law?

Schmitt's position disavows what Habermas deems to be an obvious fact: namely, that international law is a freely achieved agreement between equal partners—and needs to be unmasked in all its danger.

Habermas commends Europe's overcoming of nationalism as evidence of civic maturity and prudence. However, even within the European Community, the possibility of conceiving international law from a new cosmopolitan angle will arise only after nation-states have exited center stage. As that will happen, other "continentwide alliances" could become the major political actors on the international scene. ASEAN (Association of Southeast Asian Nations) and NAFTA (North American Free Trade Agreement) are just two examples already in place.

More than two hundred years ago, Kant anticipated the possibility of transforming classical international law into a new cosmopolitan order. With remarkable political acumen, Kant specified that only constitutional republican states could be part of this order, for "each nation, for the sake of its own security, can and ought to demand of the others that they should enter along with it into a constitution, similar to the civil one, within which the rights of each could be secured. This would mean establishing a *federation of peoples*."[13] Kant's idea requires that civil society coincide with the international community; this coincidence would automatically eliminate the state of nature between nations, which Schmitt describes within the friend-foe scheme.

In the Kantian cosmopolitan picture, a sense of hospitality replaces enmity among nations. "Hospitality means the right of a stranger not to be treated with hostility when he arrives on someone else's territory."[14] Prefaced by the remark that the concept of hospitality is not about philanthropy but about right, Kant goes on to specify its meaning. The stranger cannot claim the *right of a guest*, for that would entail friendliness with the host. But the guest can claim a *right of resort*, "for all men are entitled to present themselves in the society of others by virtue of their right of communal possession of the earth's surface. Since the earth is a globe, they cannot disperse over an infinite area, but must necessarily tolerate one another's company."[15] Just by virtue of sharing possession of the earth's surface, people will thus become members of a universal and cosmopolitan community conceived according to the principle that "a violation of rights in one part of the world is felt everywhere."[16] This would give all human beings the status of "world citizens."

Both Habermas and Derrida are heavily indebted to Kant in their construal of cosmopolitanism. Yet, while Derrida expands on Kant's notion of hospitality as the alternative to the friend-foe relation, Habermas insists on the elimination of the state of nature on the basis of mutual respect between constitutional republican states. In Habermas's view, the institution of an international criminal court is the first station on the cosmopolitan line. Another is the overcoming of the principle of nonintervention in domestic affairs of foreign states. Two examples of this overcoming have been the UN ban against Iraq's use of its own airspace after the Gulf War and the controversy surrounding the extradition of the Chilean dictator, Augusto Pinochet, from Great Britain, where he was detained under house arrest.[17]

However, Habermas is convinced that what separates the present moment from a full transition to cosmopolitanism is not only a theoretical matter but a practical one, too, for the decisions of the international community need to be respected. The example of the 1995 massacre in the Bosnian city of Srebrenica, while under the protection of Dutch United Nations peacekeepers, is an example of Habermas's worry concerning "the fatal power differential that exists between the legitimate but weak authority of the international community and the actual strength of nation-states, capable of military action but pursuing their own interests." Unfortunately, the power differential between national and international authorities threatens to weaken the legitimacy of any military intervention and to retool police action as war.

Terrorism and the Public Sphere

The question of nationalism lies at the center of Habermas's discussion of terrorism. Today's holy warriors, he claimed, were yesterday's secular nationalists: disappointment toward nationalistic authoritarian regimes like Iran, Iraq, Saudi Arabia, and possibly even Pakistan makes religion "more subjectively convincing" than any secular political motivation. Objectively, however, terrorism can be granted political content only if it has politically realistic goals. Otherwise, it is on a par with ordinary criminal activity. Since only the future can judge whether the goals of terrorism have been accomplished, terrorism is a retrospective designation.

For Habermas, linking the political scope of terrorism to the accomplishment of its goals offers the possibility of distinguishing between at least three different kinds of terrorism: indiscriminant guerilla warfare, paramilitary guerilla warfare, and global terrorism.[18] The first is epitomized by Palestinian terrorism, in which murder is often carried out by a suicide militant. The model of paramilitary guerilla warfare is proper to the national liberation movements and is retrospectively legitimized by the formation of the state. The third, global terrorism, does not seem to have politically realistic goals other than exploiting the vulnerability of complex systems. In this sense, global terrorism has the smallest chance of being retrospectively recognized as advancing political claims.

Unlike the global terrorists' multinational networks, both the indiscriminant model and the paramilitary model of terrorist activities share what Habermas calls a "partisan" profile, which anchors them to specific locations. By contrast, elusiveness and intangibility represent the novelty of global terrorism as well as its greatest destructive potential that, for Habermas, has to do with the delegitimation of democratic governments. The risk of overreaction on the part of the United States after 9/11, and of any nation under the threat of global terrorism, has for him a paradoxical and tragic implication: in spite of not expressing realistic political objectives, global terrorism succeeds in the supremely political goal of delegitimizing the authority of the state.

Since the beginning of his career, Habermas has devoted a great deal of attention to the question of legitimacy, which he sees inextricably related to the workings of the public sphere. In *The Structural*

Transformation of the Public Sphere (1962), Habermas analyzes the key role of the public sphere in the formation of political decisions within a democracy.

Kant is again Habermas's point of departure. Habermas gets from Kant a view of the public sphere as the definitive institution of democracy, that without which no theory of constitutional republicanism can exist. Only an actively involved public sphere opens the way for a truly democratic exchange. While Habermas admires Kant for having presented the public sphere as constituted around rational argument rather than the identities of the arguers, he is critical of Kant for his elitist and somewhat bourgeois understanding of its dynamics. For Habermas, Kant's description of the public sphere is the expression of a bourgeois ideology that conceives participation as a prerogative of the upper class, predominantly educated, affluent, and male.[19]

Thus Habermas embarks on a critical and historical reconstruction of the development of the public sphere in modern Western democracies. Since Kant, the advent of mass communication clearly represents the fundamental change. On the one hand, it has had the positive effect of progressively expanding the public sphere, enlarging participation to a much wider spectrum of citizens. On the other hand, the quantitative expansion of participation has meant a decrease in its quality. A number of factors have contributed to it: the pace at which information is processed by and circulates within the public sphere makes it hard to keep up with the model of communication that Kant has in mind when he discusses the public sphere, namely, the academic exchange.

While in the academic exchange the participants in a discussion are given enough time to think and formulate their arguments, the speed involved in mass communication works in the interest of those who select and distribute the information rather than those who receive it. Habermas suggests that the pressure of thinking and evaluating data quickly has a political import, because it facilitates an experience of politics based on the persona of the actors rather than the ideas that each of them defends.[20] The difficulty in bracketing the dramatic packaging of personal attributes is due to the power of the public relations industry, whose objective is to engineer consent among consumers of mass culture. For Habermas, mass consumption and its ideology, consumerism, not only silences rational-critical consensus but imposes itself onto the most vulnerable participants in the public sphere: those whose level of wealth is greater than their level of education.

This type of analysis is in line with the original theoretical orientation of Critical Theory,[21] both in the sense of its strong historical and sociological background and because of its preoccupation with the negative effects of mass culture. With the early phase of Critical Theory, Habermas shares a certain description of the political and social workings of late capitalism: more people are being informed, which creates additional opportunities for them to participate in the public sphere. But he also shares the belief that this expansion is often induced forcefully and manipulatively upon, rather than freely achieved by, the entire strata of the general population. In a paradoxical turn, more information becomes the cause for the atrophy of the various democratic functions. Maneuvered by multinational corporations and the unbridled free market, mass culture thus imposes its own rules of democratic participation: namely, utilitarian rules serving private interests rather than universal rules serving the public interest.

Critical Theorists of the early 1930s were still hoping that this problem had a material solution, consisting of a combination of Enlightenment ideals and Marxism: not a radical overthrowing of capitalism but rather a conversion to a socialist democracy with vast state participation. Yet, after these same Critical Theorists came back from a long and painful exile from Germany, they became radically pessimistic about both theoretical and concrete possibilities for change. Adorno in particular suggested that the only escape from the suffocating grip of cultural homogenization and consumerism was to be found in the experience of art and music.[22] By contrast, for Habermas, a committed citizen and public intellectual of the new Federal Republic of Germany, this pessimism has never been a solution: posing the question of the legitimacy of the public sphere was the beginning of his own answer, his own very original demarcation of a new agenda for Critical Theory.

Habermas's starting point was that our late-capitalist or postindustrial mass democracies "can claim to continue the principles of the liberal constitutional state only as long as they seriously try to live up to the mandate of a public sphere that fulfills political functions."[23] But how can the public set in motion a critical process through the very means of mass communication that manipulate and control it? To avoid Adorno's retreat from the social and political aspects of his theory into the utopian dimension of art, only two solutions seemed available: either hoping for a reversal of the capitalist trend in a Marxist sense, which was rendered less and less appealing by the failed promise of communist states,[24] or formulating the concept of the public sphere on a new foundation. The latter was Habermas's strategy, which reached full maturity with the publication of *The Theory of Communicative Action* (1981).

Following Habermas's retracing of the concept of the public sphere in relation to his theory of communicative action is a necessary prelude to understanding both his interpretation of violence and global terrorism as defects of communication as well as the solution that he envisages for these problems.

The Democracy of Everyday Speech

The model of the public sphere defended by Kant is firmly anchored in the material conditions of late eighteenth-century society, a society nonmediatized, nonglobalized, and characterized by a relatively well-demarcated distinction between political and economic levels. In Habermas's reading these conditions limit Kant's conception of the public sphere within "monological" boundaries. Monologism refers to the idea that the individual's participation in the public sphere is limited to the simple *sharing* of her already constituted opinions and moral decisions. In the monological perspective, moral reasoning is defined as a hypothetical conversation with oneself (or with an imaginary listener).

With the notion of monologism, Habermas wants to underline two concurrent elements in Kantian ethics and politics. First is the solitary nature of the categorical imperative: the mental experiment in which one asks oneself whether one's actions are based on a principle according to which the rest of humanity would choose to act, in any culture, at any time in history.[25] Second is the priority of subjectivity over intersubjectivity in the Kantian conception of individual autonomy: this priority posits autonomy as a natural given for human beings as opposed to the product of their rational communicative exchange, which is Habermas's own belief.

Habermas's attempts to capture communication at a deeper level than Kant, one at which opinions and moral decisions are being shaped *through* intersubjective dialogue. Capturing communication at this deeper level implies a radical shift from the subject-centered paradigm of monologism. While in the monological model the individual speaker preexists intersubjective communication, for Habermas intersubjective communication is the condition of possibility for the individual speaker. In this light, the speaker is not a freestanding agent but a functioning unit of a community of speakers. Habermas calls this new approach "universal pragmatics."[26] The argument that allows Habermas to establish the interdependence between the individual speaker and her community is that an isolated individual cannot establish rules for her own private use, or at least rules that she could meaningfully follow.[27] Since both the act of speech and the various modalities of communication depend on rules, they also depend on a plurality of users. It follows that individual language use presupposes a community of users.

The linguistic "competence" required by the process of communication covers both the grammatical rules of natural languages and an orientation toward consensus that Habermas sees intrinsically present in every speech act.[28] When I say something, so the argument goes, I make myself implicitly available to defend it: this is what he calls a speech act's "universal validity claim." Every speech act, if challenged, requires the speaker to justify it or "redeem it." In Habermas's mind, some form of validity claim is implicit in the very structure of speech, a premise that leads him to conclude that rationality provides the structure as well as the scope of communication. His crucial argument is that every time we communicate with one another, we automatically commit to the possibility of a freely achieved dialogic agreement in which the better argument will win.[29] This is why whenever we are faced with disagreements or at least with the pluralism of different convictions we are always seeking a future resolution. Communicative action is Habermas's name for the residue of rationality built into our everyday exchange.

In communicative action individuals arrive at judgments by conversing with other participants who in turn will be affected by those judgments. This dynamic between participants renders communicative action fundamentally emancipatory because it affirms the need to resolve disagreements through argument. In addition, communicative action is emancipatory because it expresses reason's systematic interest in pursuing the material conditions that facilitate its fullest development. Communicative action, Habermas writes eloquently, "is renewed with each act of unconstrained understanding, with each moment of living together in solidarity, of successful individuation, and of saving emancipation . . . Communicative reason operates in history as an avenging force."[30]

While the monological voice of Kantian ethics operates in the first person and the second-person singular ("I" and "thou"), the dialogical voice of communicative action speaks in the first-person plural ("we"). This "we" makes it possible for moral maxims not to linger in abstraction but rather to spring from individual concrete needs and socially situated commitments. Insofar as communicative action "intends to bring into the open the rational potential intrinsic in everyday communicative practices,"[31] it functions from the bottom up rather than from the top down.

For Habermas, it is important that the emphasis on the concrete and the particular does not slide into giving relative value to each position: for him, rationality is not a matter of personal preference. Unlike Richard Rorty and other defenders of the neopragmatist approach, Habermas is totally opposed to the notion that there is no criterion to establish the universal validity of a belief, so that my belief, in principle, is as valid as any other. To hold a position, for him, means that this *is* a valid position in light of the rational arguments that make it appear as the best available until a better one is offered to me. If a position is valid in this sense, it is not just valid to me but to anyone honestly involved in the discussion. Habermas's defense of "universalism" in ethical and political theory stems from the possibility of rationally justifying individual belief as well as public consensus.

Universalism relies on the classical Socratic distinction between knowledge and opinion, where the former is founded on truth while the latter is the result of provisional subjective assessment. Affirming the difference between knowledge and opinion, between objective understanding and subjective evaluation, serves the purpose of highlighting what separates temporary utilitarian agreements from proper consensus. If all we allowed were utilitarian agreements, it would be hard, in Habermas's view, to establish the boundaries between truthful communication and mendacious communication. Basically, it would be impossible to tell who is manipulating whom, who is telling the truth, and who is lying.

The possibility of rationally justified consensus is absolutely crucial from a political perspective: for without it, not only would philosophy lose its critical edge but the door would be left open for a definition of solidarity either in terms of prepolitical values or in terms of the volatility of subjective feelings of compassion. For Habermas, solidarity and the social bond are a structural function of communication that can be strengthened once we become aware of the validity claims embedded in any of our statements. As soon as we enter into meaningful discussions with one another our commitment to redeem such claims will systematically propel us to seek rational solutions that will be evident to everyone who is not under the spell of manipulation or distortion. These kinds of solutions will allow for the formation of lasting and rationally validated consensus rather than shifting alliances of convenience or utilitarian agreements.[32]

Any discussion of the public sphere is about the nature of our interest in others and the reach of political involvement. Without an interest in others and a sense of involvement with the well-being of the collectivity there is no public sphere. The theory of communicative action claims to have found a way to weave together the abstract level, pertaining to the validity of moral norms (the demand that beliefs are not a matter of preference or inclination but of validity, based on rational argumentation), with the concrete, flesh-and-bones dimension of existence. If Habermas is right, the classic difficulty of reconciling individual autonomy and social bond would be fundamentally solved. Also, stating that interest and motivation toward others is constitutive of who one is rather than the result of an intention that may at any time be revoked, reinforces both engagement in the democratic process and commitment to social justice, as it imbues these political experiences with self-reflection and the promise of self-transformation.

This conception of communication modifies the notion of public sphere in a substantial way. Being the arena in which participants debate their already formulated positions, the public sphere becomes the dialogical framework within which the individual and her moral principles and beliefs emerge in response to a community of fellow speakers. While Kant's categorical imperative is well illustrated by a scene of solitary conversation with oneself (or with an imaginary listener) in which one seeks to identify the principle such that the rest of humanity would choose to act accordingly, the principle of communicative action corresponds to a forum in which a plurality of speakers either agree or disagree based on the strength of their arguments. Habermas identifies the freedom of either agreeing ·or disagreeing on the basis of the strongest argument as both the formal feature of rationality and the founding principle of democracy.

Habermas is aware that this freedom describes a theoretical model not found in the real world, where communication gets distorted by a variety of factors: from the engineering of consensus by the public relations industry to all sorts of power games inflicted by the speaker on the listener. However, it is the very abstractness of what he calls "ideal speech situation" that makes it a regulative principle and a guide to our conduct.[33]

Violence as Distorted Communication

According to Habermas's argument, if global terrorism does not have a realistic political goal it can be categorized as regular criminal activity— unlawful violence. So the questions arise: What is violence? Why does violence occur? Is there a way to stop it? Habermas admits that violence exists in any society.

> We in the West do live in peaceful and well-to-do societies, and yet they contain a *structural* violence that, to a certain degree, we have gotten used to, i.e., unconscionable social inequality, degrading discrimination, pauperization, and marginalization.

The reason why Habermas thinks violence does not explode in democratic societies stems from his theory of communicative action.

> The praxis of our daily living together rests on a solid base of common background convictions, self-evident cultural truths and reciprocal expectations. Here the coordination of action runs through the ordinary language games, through mutually raised and at least implicitly recognized validity claims *in the public space of more or less good reasons.*

Our everyday life, says Habermas, is structured by the communicative practices that allow us to understand each other. Just by the act of speaking, we implicitly agree on a set of grammatical rules that we all use truthfully, for the sake of communication and not manipulation. Habermas's point is that in this same way we implicitly agree on the rules of the culture, society, and community within which we function. These rules are what he defines as "a solid base of common background convictions, self-evident cultural truths, and reciprocal expectations." The common background grants us the possibility of putting ourselves in the other's shoes, which Habermas articulates as "symmetrical conditions of *mutual* perspective-taking." But if the mutual perspective-taking for some reason cannot occur, speaker and listener become estranged from each other and indifferent to the redemption of their claims. This is the beginning of a distortion in communication, a misunderstanding or a deception, of which terrorism is the most extreme version.

One of the central arguments that emerged from our dialogue is precisely that terrorism is a communicative pathology that feeds its own destructive input. He says: "The spiral of violence begins as a spiral of distorted communication that leads through the spiral of uncontrolled reciprocal mistrust to the breakdown of communication." In Western liberal democracies there are established channels to ease communicative breakdowns. At the individual level, psychotherapy helps recover one's internal moments of silence. In the intersubjective public arena, legal suits settle conflicts between individuals who have exhausted all avenues of discussion. Globalization seems to inject fuel into the spiraling movement of communicative violence. By intensifying communication, globalization puts on stage distributive injustice, starkly dividing the world into winners, beneficiaries, and losers. Mutual perspective-taking becomes harder and harder in the face of such challenges. The burden of responsibility clearly falls on the shoulders of the stronger nations. This is why Habermas calls on liberal Western democracies to rebuild channels of communication, for unbounded capitalism and the rigid stratification of world society are at the root of the collapse of dialogue.

The idea that globalization may be interpreted as a communicative pathology intersects the debate on the clash of civilizations.[34] Initiated by political scientist Samuel Huntington in 1993, the year of the first terrorist attack on the World Trade Center by an Islamic fundamentalist group, this debate revolves around the hypothesis that world politics is undergoing an important shift. The shift is determined by a radical change in the nature of conflicts, which for Huntington will be progressively anchored in cultural and religious motives rather than in ideological differences or economic inequality. In his reading, despite individual desires for power or money, the driving and mobilizing force in today's conflicts is culture. Huntington identifies Islamic civilization as most likely to be the primary challenger in the twenty-first century.

Habermas rejects Huntington's hypothesis. The cause of the communicative ailment brought about by globalization is not cultural but economic. To cure it, the Western coalition needs to work on two fronts. On the one hand, on its self-representation: it is important for developing countries to stop perceiving the foreign policy of Western nations as an imperialist front seeking financial expansion. On the other hand, what these democracies have to do is not reducible to a marketing strategy, for it is a sad fact that Western consumerism explodes like a land mine in the midst of the most disadvantaged layers of the world population. This consumerist blast, Habermas suggests, elicits the spiritual reaction, which too many people see as the only alternative to silence and resignation.

Starting in the late 1970s, as he achieves a systematic articulation of the theory of communicative action, Habermas begins to refer to the public sphere in terms of "life-world." Coined by the phenomenological tradition initiated by Edmund Husserl, the notion of life-world refers to the preinterpreted and prereflective background against which our everyday life unfolds. It encompasses the whole range of taken-for-granted daily social activities, but it also, and conjointly, indicates the role of tradition as well as any established modes of thinking and acting on communication.

The transition from the public sphere to the notion of life-world marks an important conceptual shift in Habermas's theoretical development. The reference to "life" certainly underlines his commitment to the concreteness and utter specificity of the subject's place within her community of fellow speakers. The concept of "world" frees the public realm from the model of eighteenth-century European society in relation to which the notion of a public sphere was first conceived. Such a notion understands society as a totality, neatly divided into private and public domains: in it, individuals participate in the process of democratic deliberation as if they were members of an encompassing organization. This premise, says Habermas, is simply unfit to describe the complexity of contemporary society where the flow of argumentative dialogue is systematically menaced by nonpolitical forces: from religious fundamentalism to all brands of fanaticism, from the market to state administration. The hope to radically change these forces by politicizing them is the guiding illusion of Marx's critique of ideology, which Habermas considers too totalizing a model to deal with the complexity of global postindustrial society.

The publication of *The Theory of Communicative Action* (1981) marks Habermas's turn toward a new framework of inquiry that weaves together a wide array of sources both from analytic philosophy, with a particular focus on the ordinary language school of J. L. Austin and John Searle, and from the social sciences. Strong influences on this new framework are Noam Chomsky's generative approach to linguistics, the psychological and moral development theories of Jean Piaget and Lawrence Kohlberg, and the social model of analysis elaborated by Talcott Parsons and George Herbert Mead.

The encounter with the new web of sources contributes in different ways to Habermas's belief that postindustrial societies are arranged in a two-tiered body, each governed by different rules and modes of development.

> From that time on I have considered state apparatus and economy to be systemically integrated action fields that can no longer be transformed democratically from within, that is, be switched over to a political mode of integration, without damage to their proper systematic logic and therewith their ability to function. The abysmal collapse of state socialism has only confirmed this. Instead, radical democratization now aims for a shifting of forces within a "separation of powers" that itself is to be maintained in principle. The new equilibrium to be attained is not one between state powers but between different resources for societal integration. The goal is no longer to supersede an economic system having a capitalist life of its own and a system of domination having a bureaucratic life of its own but to erect a democratic dam against the colonializing *encroachment* of system imperatives on areas of the life-world.[35]

In this passage, Habermas underlines the irreducibility of two economic, social, and cognitive domains. The first is the system, a nonintegrated, nonparticipatory model of development; both state apparatus and the economy function as self-subsisting systems of this kind. The concept of a self-subsisting or boundary-maintaining system is the product of Habermas's intense debate with Niklas Luhmann on the meaning and worth of the systems theory approach to sociology.[36] Parallel but irreducible to the system is the life-world, which denotes "all those conditions of communication under which there can come into being a discursive formation of opinion and will on the part of a public composed of the citizens of the state."[37] These two domains designate the contrast between two types of actions: the system corresponds to strategic action; and the life-world, to the realm of communicative action.[38]

Habermas uses the contrast between strategic and communicative action and the associated distinction between system and life-world as the analytical framework to interpret a new range of social movements whose focus is the well-being of the life world in the face of what he calls the encroachment of system-imperatives. Examples are social movements such as environmentalism, civil rights, and pacifism, to which we could add, from more recent years, the antiglobalization movement. In Habermas's view, all these movements are new historical occurrences because they do not coalesce around individual grievances, which would fall under a strategic practical horizon, but rather form around principles of free discourse and communicative action. This is proved by their lack of interest in gaining any shares of state power as well as by persistent debates concerning their self-identity.[39]

If the domains of the system and the life-world are indeed heterogeneous, the challenge is to protect the life-world from shrinking under the pressure of particular interests. The real threat is, for Habermas, that the system tends to colonize the life-world. If this assault were to succeed, the dogmatic, economic, and bureaucratic machines would supersede the emancipatory potential of rationality embodied in democratic institutions. Only by appropriating through reflection and affirming in practice the conditions of communication in the life-world can we resist the sprawling influence of nonpolitical imperatives.

The emphasis on the communicative model is relevant to Habermas's new articulation of the concept of critique. While in classical

Critical Theory and in Marxism, the aim of critique was to make explicit the contradictions produced in the world by the social injustice inherent in capitalism, for Habermas the function of critique is to affirm communicative rationality and its potential for self-reflection and self-examination. Provided that rationality is not an abstract function but the conceptual underpinning of every-day communicative practice, critique becomes the effort to enhance the production of consensus based on free and undistorted discussion among speakers. Critique thus becomes the examination of the conceptual and practical procedures allowing the formation of rational consensus.

The turn toward communicative action causes Habermas's focus to shift from historically and sociologically founded analyses to a more formal approach in which the investigation of institutional processes and argumentative structures is given more prominence than material conditions.

The arguments through which we redeem validity claims are units of what Habermas calls "discourse." The notion of discourse was elaborated by ethnolinguistists such as Emile Benveniste,[40] who analyzed language with reference to the speaker and her spatio-temporal location, including all variables that specify the context of utterance. Habermas makes the term "discourse" the cornerstone of his communicative approach to ethics and political philosophy. Since one of his most recent books, *Between Facts and Norms* (2000), he has been stretching it to cover legal theory, too. Discourse entails a certain suspension of belief in a given norm and indicates the procedure through which one can test its validity. Once its validity is reassessed through rational (discursive) argumentation, the norm is presumed to be valid not only for the individual who happens to accept it or the rational speakers involved in the discussion, but for all possible rational speakers involved in any feasible discussion. The ideal of a discourse-based approach to ethics is a moral community whose norms and practices are fully accepted by those who are subject to them. This community forms a society based on the agreement of all free and equal partners from which imposition and manipulation have been expunged.

The discursive approach to ethics and political philosophy is less focused on the discussion of the normative content of specific norms or principles and more focused on identifying which norms can be redeemed discursively and the kind of rational procedures their redemption requires. Habermas's interpretation of the *locus classicus* of Critical Theory, the concept and fate of modernity, occurs against the background of his newly forged discursive orientation. For Habermas, modernity is the name for a way of thinking and acting in line with communicative rationality. Discussing in more detail his treatment of modernity underscores the premises of his understanding of religious fundamentalism as a uniquely modern disruption, which is at the core of his reading of global terrorism. Also, the debate on what to do with the intellectual heritage of modernity is the axis of Habermas's response to Derrida, which I will articulate by addressing Habermas's and Derrida's readings of a third philosopher, Walter Benjamin. Benjamin stands between Habermas and Derrida in a Janus-like pose, casting an intense gaze upon both Critical Theory and deconstruction.

The Iron Cage of Fundamentalism

Habermas's interest in the concept of modernity, posited as the heritage of the Enlightenment political legacy, comes to him from his mentors, Adorno and Horkheimer. Since the foundation of the Frankfurt School, Critical Theorists agreed that the Enlightenment was the just and necessary cry against the oppression of unilateral authorities, such as religion. However, in the post–WWII period, this noble agenda seemed hardly reconcilable with what many German intellectuals, including Adorno and Horkheimer, interpreted as the Enlightenment's self-destructive strains: How did it happen that the shared sense of civic responsibility, cultivated for two centuries by post-Kantian Enlightenment thinking and society, did not prevent two world wars and the upsurge of totalitarian regimes? The threat of global terrorism that has inaugurated the start of the third millennium could easily be used as further evidence to support this dark suspicion.

In the midst of the ruins of bombed German cities and shattered German culture, Adorno and Horkheimer looked back at the work of sociologist Max Weber, who explicitly laid out the hypothesis that Enlightenment culture held self-destructive seeds.[41] Weber's argument revolves around the possibility that the secularization of knowledge mandated by the Enlightenment ignites a "disenchantment of the world," which erodes the foundations of traditional ways of life. Such disenchantment leaves the human subject alone: as all ideals of cosmic harmony are dispelled, the world comes to be perceived as an external object to be used for utilitarian ends. Disenchantment is thus the breeding ground for an instrumental conception of rationality, which Weber refers to as *Zweckrationalität,* whose agenda is the reductive causal terms of means and ends. Reason, understood in this way, represents the pure and simple promotion of control—the control of human beings over the world and of the individual human being over others.

After living firsthand the unspeakable atrocities of totalitarianism, many German intellectuals and Critical Theorists were convinced that history had provided the ultimate corroboration for the worst of Weber's fears. *Dialectic of Enlightenment,* published in 1947 by Adorno and Horkheimer on their return to Germany from a decade of exile in the United States, is the quintessential expression of the belief that Weber was right.

Adorno exerted the greatest influence on the young Habermas. However, theirs is a complicated relation: as Habermas struggled to overcome the pessimism and nihilism of his teacher, he did it using Adorno's own means.

> Rereading Adorno had given me the courage to take up systematically . . . the theory of reification as a theory of rationalization, in Max Weber's sense. Already at that time, my problem was a theory of modernity, a theory of the pathology of modernity from the viewpoint of the realization— the deformed realization—of reason in history.[42]

Since his earliest days, Habermas has been seeking a positive and constructive theory of modernity. "The pathology of modernity" mentioned in the passage can be read to mean either that there are pathological strains within modernity or that modernity itself is the illness. Habermas takes the latter stance, that the pathological strains existing *within* modernity can be separated out of the healthier whole.

Reading Weber's theory of rationalization in connection with the theory of reification is the first step Habermas takes in this direction. Reification indicates the way in which social relations have been deformed, and even disfigured, by the capitalist mode of production. Capitalism, according to the Marxist diagnosis, imposes on the working class the unbearable weight of alienation, which reduces the labor force to just another kind of commodity. In capitalist modernity, so the argument goes, the life of the working class is understood as a means to implement profit. This mechanism impedes the worker from appropriating the meaning of her own labor. Eventually, if alienation is the result of her activity, she is also denied an autonomous relationship with her surroundings. In post–World War II Germany, Habermas combined Weber's theory that modernity carried out a destructive kind of rationalization with the Marxist theory of reification. Precisely this combination of rationalization and reification is the pathological strain of modernity.

At the center of Weber's dark scenario is the figure of the iron cage, a prison of efficient bureaucratic blindness created by the indiscriminate growth of utilitarian or instrumental rationality. Habermas's conception of the two-tiered modes of development of complex societies, in which the economy and administrative apparatus are described as self-feeding "systems," is clearly inherited from Weber. Very much in line with Weber, Habermas sees the danger of the expanding power of impersonal economic forces and bureaucratically organized administration processes. However, very much unlike Weber, Habermas does not think that societal rationalization amounts to the growing power of technology and calculation, organization and administration, and that the triumph of reason is a hindrance to freedom rather than its ultimate chance. On the contrary, Habermas endorses unconditionally the political agenda of the Enlightenment, which he renames the "discourse of modernity." It is this discourse, which the Enlightenment left unfinished, that today complex postindustrial societies should devote themselves to completing.

Habermas's critique of Weber's pessimism toward modernity provides a unique key to interpret religious fundamentalism. Weber's negative description of the effects of instrumental rationality and secularization eerily fits the religious fundamentalist perception that Western culture is uprooting traditional forms of life. Fundamentalism echoes Weber's contention that such uprooting, in homogenizing cultures and estranging individual members from their communities, tends to destroy the possibility of spiritual and moral identity. Fundamentalism, precisely because of its opposition to modernity and modernization, is for Habermas a distinctively and uniquely modern phenomenon.

Every religion entails a dogmatic kernel of belief, observed Habermas, which is the reason why every religion needs an authority entitled to discriminate between orthodox, or valid, and unorthodox, or invalid, interpretations of dogma. Yet, as he stated in our dialogue, "such orthodoxy first veers toward fundamentalism when the guardians and representatives of the true faith ignore the epistemic situation of a pluralistic society and insist—even to the point of violence—on the universally binding character and political acceptance of their doctrine." Modernity does not simply confine religion within the spiritual dimension of life, pushing it away from the political management of the public sphere; it demands that it embraces, at the cognitive level, its location in a pluralistic society. In other words, religion has to face the complex challenge of relativizing its position vis-à-vis other religions without relativizing its own dogmatic core. This is what Habermas called "the epistemic situation" of religion in modernity.

Starting with the Reformation, which caused the internal schism of Western Christianity into Roman Catholicism and Protestantism, for four hundred years religion in Europe has withstood a situation of this kind. Seeing oneself through the eyes of others is what modernity has asked of religion. The other in this case is a competing plurality of others, including different religious faiths, scientific knowledge, and political institutions. Fundamentalism is the rejection of this cluster of challenges, which Habermas described as "the repression of striking cognitive dissonances" and the return to "the exclusivity of pre-modern belief attitudes." A belief attitude indicates the way in which we believe rather than what we believe in. Fundamentalism has less to do with any specific text or religious dogma and more to do with the modality of belief. For this reason, he added, "modern pluralistic societies are normatively compatible only with a *strict* universalism in which the same respect is demanded for everybody—be they Catholic, Protestant, Muslim, Jewish, Hindu, or Buddhist, believers or nonbelievers." This universalism is "strict" because it applies to the way in which any religion relates itself to others and to its own faith. A pure universalism is the ground on which Habermas strongly defends the notion of tolerance.

Tolerance describes the constraint of strict universalism demanded by modern pluralist societies. In our dialogue, Habermas recalled the Edict of Nantes (1598), in which Henry IV, king of France, "permitted the Huguenots, a religious minority, to profess their beliefs and observe their rituals under the condition that they do not question the authority of the king's throne or the supremacy of Catholicism." The Protestant minority was thus "tolerated" provided that it renounced any claim to political power or antagonism toward the Catholic majority. Habermas easily recognized that these are paternalistic conditions for which acceptance of the other has the character of an "act of mercy."

While this is the reason why Derrida rejects the concept of tolerance, the paternalistic character of tolerance does not impede Habermas from defending it on the basis of an argument that he also uses against the notion that democracy may be a culturally specific, and thus not universally preferable, form of government. In our dialogue, he tersely expressed it with the following words:

> Within a democratic community whose citizens reciprocally grant one another equal rights, no room is left for an authority allowed to *one-sidedly* determine the boundaries of what is to be tolerated. On the basis of the citizens' equal rights and reciprocal respect for each other, nobody possesses the privilege of setting the boundaries of tolerance from the viewpoint of their own preferences and value orientations.

For Habermas, tolerance is defensible if practiced in the context of a democratic community. In such a context, given that citizens grant each other equal rights, no one has the privilege to set the boundaries of what has to be tolerated. While Henry IV one-sidedly proclaimed tolerance toward Protestants, in modern Western democracies tolerance acquires a dialogical profile. What is being tolerated is not one-sidedly or *monologically* established but *dialogically* achieved through the rational exchange among citizens.

In a liberal democracy, the only common standard required by tolerance—the condition under which a religious person tolerates an atheist—is loyalty to the constitution. The constitution, for Habermas, is the political incarnation of the ideal of a moral community whose norms and practices are fully accepted by its members. Allegiance to the constitution thus means allegiance to a society in which the agreement of all free and equal partners is achieved independently from imposition and manipulation. In Habermas's account, the constitution of a republican democratic state is the quintessential model of discursive validation. The case of conflicts regarding the interpretation of the constitution illustrates this discursive element in it, for "the constitution itself has made the necessary provisions. There are institutions and procedures for settling the question of the limits for what might still, or no longer, be taken as 'being loyal to the constitution.'" As long as commonly agreed upon procedures are in place, the possibility of rationally articulating conflicts is also in place. This possibility entails two concurrent commitments: one is the speaker's commitment to telling the truth and defending it through the redemption of its validity claims; the other is the listener's commitment to either accept it or oppose it with a better argument. If these two commitments have been made, even being loyal to the constitution is subject to constant revision on the part of all involved agents.

The case of civil disobedience is interesting from the standpoint of Habermas's appreciation of the constitution's discursive structure and self-reflective potential. In the dialogue he underlined that "in its tolerance of civil disobedience, the constitution self-reflexively stretches to cover even the conditions for overstepping its own boundaries." This is to say that the constitution has provisions for the most radical situation in which a dissident decides not to abide by it anymore. Such provisions mandate that the dissident's resistance be carried out according to certain procedures. It is the constitutional procedures that allow the majority to remain critically engaged with their own decisions. Formulated in these terms, the democratic project feeds off the resistance of minorities, whose hostility to the will of the majority at the present moment may renew the majority's own self-understanding in the future.

According to Habermas, rights are not features that individuals naturally possess but relations that have their basis in mutual recognition.

> *At the conceptual level*, rights do not immediately refer to atomistic and estranged individuals who are possessively set against one another. On the contrary, as elements of the legal order they presuppose collaboration among subjects who recognize one another, in their reciprocally related rights and duties, as free and equal consociates under law. This mutual recognition is constitutive for the legal order from which actionable

rights are derived. In this sense "subjective" rights emerge equiprimordially with "objective" law.[43]

Individuals confer upon each other rights as soon as they agree to regulate their common life through law. In liberal democracies, law is not and should not be interpreted as an internally coherent system of abstract norms; rather the legal body is, and should be taken to correspond to, subjective liberty. Underlying this belief, which is central to Habermas's more recent contributions to political and legal theory, is the Kantian principle that guarantees to the individual the greatest amount of liberty that can be granted to all.

The Unfinished Project of Modernity

Modernity is for Habermas the very emblem of the political promise of rationality. The problem, as Habermas sees it, is that this promise has not been fulfilled. The articulation of this unfulfilled promise has sharply distinguished him from the tradition of German thinkers—which includes Weber, Adorno, and Horkheimer—that made Enlightenment rationality responsible for infecting modernity with the virus of self-destruction.

In Habermas's eyes, the French thinkers associated with the critique of Enlightenment rationality and very loosely affiliated with the label of postmodernism radicalize this position and buy into a fundamentally irrationalist claim, which makes us more and not less vulnerable to the threat of fascism. In complex postindustrial societies, fascism corresponds to the colonization of the life-world by the systemic pressures of unbridled global markets, wild technological sprawl, and I might add, religious fundamentalism. Habermas simply does not see how to counter such colonization if rationality is not recognized, in line with Enlightenment tenets, as the universally valid political tool.

Against the negative interpretations of modernity, Habermas advances the thesis that modernity has produced moral progress. Such progress rests on the awareness that the process of socialization has to be structured by a system of norms requiring argumentative justification without any appeal to tradition. As the life-world is structurally threatened, this awareness arises as the positive and constructive effort that frees society to build its identity independently from any sense of debt toward the past. As he declared publicly in 1990 following German reunification, national identity cannot be built on past traditions or on the notion of a common fate. The moral progress of modernity consists in having showed that, if a nation wants to avoid totalitarian risks, it needs to rely only and exclusively on the freely and rationally reached commitment to its own rules and norms. The gift of Western modernity is to have showed the benefits of excluding from the range of acceptable political norms any mythical or religious parameters. What Habermas calls postconventional morality rests on the rational procedure of testing validity claims in an intersubjective setting.

As Habermas developed his reflection of modernity in opposition to tradition, and in relation to the form in which rationality affirms itself in a democratic setting, the question arose as to whether modernity has the character of a historical experience or is simply a set of formal requirements applying to all ages and places. This is a crucial question if one wants, as Habermas does, to strictly universalize the agenda of modernity as the unique carrier of moral progress. Sorting out the details of the distinction between modernity, assumed as the political agenda emerged at a particular historical moment, and modernization, understood as a process that can occur at any time or place, helps understand Habermas's view of religious fundamentalism as a modern phenomenon. But what exactly does Habermas mean by "modern?" Is fundamentalism the panicked reaction to modernity or modernization? In this last section, I would like to reconstruct the historical foundations of this distinction and show how Habermas, following Hegel, locates a middle way between them.

In *The Philosophical Discourse of Modernity* Habermas discusses Weber as a powerful supporter of the interpretation of modernity as a historical epoch. For Weber, modernity is strongly rooted in the European historical and cultural context because Europe is the region in which religious worldviews were first translated into a secular culture. This premise led him to ask the question of why, outside of Europe, "the scientific, the artistic, the political, or the economic development . . . did not enter upon that path of rationalization which is peculiar to the Occident."[44] Weber's answer was that there is a necessary connection between the notion of modernity and the intellectual orientation of Western rationalism.

Other sociologists, Habermas points out,[45] offered related views, according to which the secularization of modern societies is brought about by some kind of internal "aging" of traditions, which, having lost their spontaneity and vitality, have become self-reflective and self-examining. In these models, rationality is not conceived as specifically Western or attributed with the uplifting role of emancipating people from constraining conditions.

Instead of interpreting modernity as a historically specific experience, a third group of social scientists see it as a general scheme of social development consisting in a number of conditions: mobilization of resources, implementation of productivity, formation of centralized political powers, rise of national identity, demand for a universal educational system, secularization of values and norms, affirmation of urban forms of life. The descriptive term for this general scheme is modernization, which emerges as an evolutionary social dynamics.

Habermas's understanding of modernity combines elements from all these interpretations but also revives the perspective offered by the thinker who inaugurated the philosophical discussion of this notion: Georg Wilhelm Friedrich Hegel.

> As modernity awakens to consciousness of itself, a need for self-reassurance arises, which Hegel understands as a need for philosophy. He sees philosophy confronted with the task of grasping *its own* time—and for him that means the modern age—in thought. Hegel is convinced that he cannot possibly obtain philosophy's concept of itself independently of the philosophical concept of modernity.[46]

For Hegel, modernity has a historical function but is not unique to a historical epoch. The modern time is the epoch in which an individual and a community develop a historical consciousness of themselves and their actions: an awareness of their own place in history and their potential for changing it. Any modern subject is confronted with "the task of grasping *its own* time" independently from what is mandated by a sacred Scripture or tradition. Philosophy is the name for the emergence of this historical consciousness, which is uniquely emancipatory, for Hegel as well as for Habermas, because it discloses the possibility of critically appropriating the present. Modernity is renewed every time the present is taken as a door opened onto the future. As Habermas claims, the modern age "*has to create its normativity out of itself.*" Modernity sees itself cast back upon itself without any possibility of escape."[47]

Like Hegel, Habermas thinks that a truly democratic society has to be committed to its norms independent of any external authority, whether it is the past, tradition, or religious orthodoxy. This implies that modernity is not a historically bound phenomenon, irreducibly determined by the course of European history and culture, but rather a project endorsed deliberately at a certain point *in* history by whatever community of citizens.[48] Fundamentalism is the violent reaction against this very project. Modernity is thus the name for the possibility of critically appropriating any tradition so that individuals and communities may pursue, freely and consensually, their own deliberations.

Giving up modernity for Habermas means to give up the commitment to freedom and social justice, which is the very core of his philosophical system. This explains why he took so much to heart the debate over the fate of modernity and strongly opposed any suggestion that our epoch may be projected onto a postmodern one. Since the 1980s, his commitment to modernity led him to take up the task of unmasking the political irresponsibility of postmodern philosophers operating under the influence of Nietzsche and Heidegger. In the preface to *The Philosophical Discourse of Modernity*, he declares how this topic occupied him almost obsessively since 1980, the year of his reception of the prestigious Adorno Prize.[49] Since that day, he writes,

> This theme, disputed and multifaceted as it is, never lost its hold on me. Its philosophical aspects have moved even more starkly into public consciousness in the wake of the reception of French neostructuralism . . . The challenge from the neostructuralist critique of reason defines the perspective from which I seek to reconstruct here, step by step, the philosophical discourse of modernity. Since the late eighteenth century, modernity has been elevated to a *philosophical* theme in this discourse.[50]

Habermas's intense involvement with the issue of modernity stems from his anxiety that the postmodern orientation encourages political responsibility and the potential to develop into a dangerous reactionary revival.[51] Habermas accuses this breed of thinkers, including Derrida, of not giving due respect to the political underpinning of modernity: a universalist call for freedom and equality that cannot be relativized in any form.

I will address Habermas's critique of Derrida indirectly by discussing Habermas's response to Walter Benjamin.[52] In Habermas's view, Benjamin is Derrida's direct antecedent for the messianic sense that he attributes to the modern moment. Habermas's opinion of Benjamin is significant not only because he extends his judgment of Benjamin to Derrida but also because Derrida, perhaps in response to Habermas, uses Benjamin as a main source of one of his crucial text on political philosophy, "The Force of Law."[53] Habermas introduces his discussion of Benjamin's theory of modernity by contrasting it with the French poet Charles Baudelaire.

> Whereas Baudelaire had contented himself with the idea that the constellation of time and eternity comes to pass in the authentic work of art, Benjamin wanted to translate this basic aesthetic experience back into a historical relationship. He fashioned for this purpose the concept of a "now-time" (*Jetztzeit*), which is shot through with fragments of messianic or completed time ... On the one hand, the idea of a homogeneous and empty time that is filled in by "the stubborn belief in progress" of evolutionism and the philosophy of history; on the other hand, the neutralization of all standards fostered by historicism when it imprisons history in the museum and "tell[s] the sequence of events like the beads of a rosary.[54]

Baudelaire is an unrestrained defender of aesthetic modernity: for him, the unprecedented freedom enjoyed by the modern work of art gives it the opportunity to express the clash between the impermanence of the present and the weight of eternity. In Habermas's reading, Benjamin is even more exacting in his demands. For him, the work of art achieves authentic modernity not just because of its subjective freedom and defiance of convention but as a result of its productive connection with the present, understood in a messianic vein.

In Benjamin's mind, modern philosophy of history has suffocated messianism in two ways: either by looking at history as a predetermined course of events or by accepting everything historical indiscriminately and placing it, with the same degree of respect, in a museum. By contrast, Benjamin's own call for a new messianism is the call for a present that is neither predictable—as those who view history as a predetermined course of events would like it to be—nor indifferent to its past—as those who revere all that is past to the same degree would view it. The present needs to be a response to the complete unpredictability of the future and a critical assessment of the past, construed as the horizon of unfulfilled expectations.

> This need for redemption on the part of past epochs who have directed their expectations to us is reminiscent of the figure familiar in both Jewish and Protestant mysticism of man's responsibility for the fate of a God who, in the act of creation, relinquished his omnipotence in favor of human freedom, putting us on an equal footing with himself.[55]

The two conditions that Benjamin considers essential to a meaningful connection with the present—that it be oriented toward an unpredictable future and that it be selective with respect to the value of the past based on its unfulfilled expectations—conjointly reveal the absolute uniqueness of our location in history. Benjamin calls it messianism.

An attentive look at Benjamin's position reveals that it is fundamentally connected with Hegel's articulation of modernity, which I have showed as being close to that of Habermas's. If this holds true, there is an overlap between Habermas and Benjamin on Hegelian grounds. Although this is certainly the case, the ground of overlap is limited. Hegel did conceive the meaning of modernity along the lines of the absolute uniqueness of the present with respect to its location in history. It is only in the modern epoch, for Hegel as well as for Benjamin, that this uniqueness has come to the fore as an empowering weapon in the hands of individuals and communities. However, Hegel was suspicious of the past's limited vision of the overall trajectory of history, which in his mind became visible only from the modern standpoint. By contrast, Benjamin thought of the past as a range of unfulfilled expectations for which the modern subject should still feel responsible, because it is only on the basis of this very call from the past that the future can be faced as the wholly new. Benjamin, and later on Derrida, develop a strain of Hegel's reflection on the significance of modernity that is precisely what Habermas, who also looks back to Hegel for inspiration, suppresses. This strain concerns a past that cannot be articulated discursively. There is nothing more dangerous, in Habermas's view, than the idea of building the future as response to a quasi-messianic call from the past.[56]

AUTOIMMUNITY:
REAL AND SYMBOLIC
SUICIDES

~~~~~~

A Dialogue with Jacques Derrida

~~~~~~

B O R R A D O R I : September 11 (*Le 11 septembre*) gave us the impression of being a *major event*,[1] one of the most important historical events we will witness in our lifetime, especially for those of us who never lived through a world war. Do you agree?

D E R R I D A : *Le 11 septembre,* as you say, or, since we have agreed to speak two languages, "September 11."[2] We will have to return later to this question of language. As well as to this act of naming: a date and nothing more. When you say "September 11" you are already citing, are you not? You are inviting me to speak here by recalling, as if in quotation marks, a date or a dating that has taken over our public space and our private lives for five weeks now. Something *fait date,* I would say in

Translated from the French by Pascale-Anne Brault and Michael Naas. Revised by Jacques Derrida in French.

a French idiom, something marks a date, a date in history; that is always what's most striking, the very impact of what is at least *felt*, in an apparently immediate way, to be an event that truly marks, that truly makes its mark, a singular and, as they say here, "unprecedented"[3] event. I say "apparently immediate" because this "feeling" is actually less spontaneous than it appears: it is to a large extent conditioned, constituted, if not actually constructed, circulated at any rate through the media by means of a prodigious techno-socio-political machine. "To mark a date in history" presupposes, in any case, that "something" comes or happens for the first and last time, "something" that we do not yet really know how to identify, determine, recognize, or analyze but that should remain from here on in unforgettable: an ineffaceable event in the shared archive of a universal calendar, that is, a *supposedly* universal calendar, for these are—and I want to insist on this at the outset—only suppositions and presuppositions. Unrefined and dogmatic, or else carefully considered, organized, calculated, strategic—or all of these at once. For the index pointing toward this date, the bare act, the minimal deictic, the minimalist aim of this dating, also marks something else. Namely, the fact that we perhaps have no concept and no meaning available to us to name in any other way this "thing" that has just happened, this supposed "event." An act of "international terrorism," for example, and we will return to this, is anything but a rigorous concept that would help us grasp the singularity of what we will be trying to discuss. "Something" took place, we have the feeling of not having seen it coming, and certain consequences undeniably follow upon the "thing." But this very thing, the place and meaning of this "event," remains ineffable, like an intuition without concept, like a unicity with no generality on the horizon or with no horizon at all, out of range for a language that admits its powerlessness and so is reduced to pronouncing mechanically a date, repeating it endlessly, as a kind of ritual incantation, a conjuring poem, a journalistic litany or rhetorical refrain that admits to not knowing what it's talking about. We do not in fact know what we are saying or naming in this way: September 11, *le 11 septembre,* September 11. The brevity of the appellation (September 11, 9/11) stems not only from an economic or rhetorical necessity. The telegram of this metonymy—a name, a number—points out the unqualifiable by recognizing that we do not recognize or even cognize, that we do not yet know how to qualify, that we do not know what we are talking about.

This is the first, indisputable effect of what occurred (whether it was calculated, well calculated, or not), precisely on September 11, not far from here: we repeat this, *we must* repeat it, and it is all the more necessary to repeat it insofar as we do not really know what is being named in this way, as if to exorcise two times at one go: on the one hand, to conjure away, as if by magic, the "thing" itself, the fear or the terror it inspires (for repetition always protects by neutralizing, deadening, distancing a traumatism, and this is true for the repetition of the televised images we will speak of later), and, on the other hand, to deny, as close as possible to this act of language and this enunciation, our powerlessness to name in an appropriate fashion, to characterize, to think the thing in question, to get beyond the mere deictic of the date: something terrible took place on September 11, and in the end we don't know what. For however outraged we might be at the violence, however much we might genuinely deplore—as I do, along with everyone else—the number of dead, no one will really be convinced that this is, in the end, what it's all about. I will come back to this later; for the moment we are simply preparing ourselves to say something about it.

I've been in New York for three weeks now. Not only is it impossible not to speak on this subject, but you feel or are made to feel that it is actually *forbidden,* that you do not have the right, to begin speaking of anything, especially in public, without ceding to this obligation, without making an always somewhat blind reference to this date (and this was already the case in China, where I was on September 11, and then in Frankfurt on September 22).[4] I gave in regularly to this injunction, I admit; and in a certain sense I am doing so again by taking part in this friendly interview with you, though trying always, beyond the commotion and the most sincere compassion, to appeal to questions and to a "thought" (among other things, a real political thought) of what, it seems, has just taken place on September 11, just a few steps from here, in Manhattan or, not too far away, in Washington, D.C.

I believe always in the necessity of being attentive first of all to this phenomenon of language, naming, and dating, to this repetition compulsion (at once rhetorical, magical, and poetic). To what this compulsion signifies, translates, or betrays. Not in order to isolate ourselves in language, as people in too much of a rush would like us to believe, but on the contrary, in order to try to understand what is going on precisely *beyond* language and what is pushing us to repeat endlessly and without knowing what we are talking about, precisely there where language and the concept come up against their limits: "September 11, September 11, *le 11 septembre, 9/11.*"

We must try to know more, to take our time and hold onto our freedom so as to begin to think this first effect of the so-called event: From where does this menacing injunction itself come to us? How is it being forced upon us? *Who* or *what* gives us this threatening order (others would already say this terrorizing if not terrorist imperative): name, repeat, rename "September 11," "le 11 septembre," even when you do not yet know what you are saying and are not yet thinking what you refer to in this way. I agree with you: without any doubt, this "thing," "September 11," "gave us the impression of being a *major event.*" But what is an impression in this case? And an event? And especially a "*major* event"? Taking your word—or words—for it, I will underscore more than one precaution. I will do so in a seemingly "empiricist" style, though aiming beyond empiricism. It cannot be denied, as an empiricist of the eighteenth century would quite literally say, that there was an "impression" there, and the impression of what you call in English—and this is not fortuitous—a "*major event.*" I insist here on the English because it is the language we speak here in New York, even though it is neither your language nor mine; but I also insist because the injunction comes first of all from a place where English predominates. I am not saying this only because the United States was targeted, hit, or violated on its own soil for the first time in almost two centuries—since 1812 to be exact[5]—but because the world order that felt itself targeted through this violence is dominated largely by the Anglo-American idiom, an idiom that is indissociably linked to the political discourse that dominates the world stage, to international law, diplomatic institutions, the media, and the greatest technoscientific, capitalist, and military power. And it is very much a question of the still enigmatic but also *critical* essence of this hegemony. By *critical,* I mean at once decisive, potentially decisionary, decision-making, and *in crisis:* today more vulnerable and threatened than ever.

Whether this "impression" is justified or not, it is in itself an event, let us never forget it, especially when it is, though in quite different ways, a properly global effect. The "impression" cannot be dissociated from all the affects, interpretations, and rhetoric that have at once reflected, communicated, and "globalized" it, from everything that also and first of all formed, produced, and made it possible. The "impression" thus resembles "the very thing" that produced it. Even if the so-called "thing" cannot be reduced to it. Even if, therefore, the *event* itself cannot be reduced to it. The event is made up of the "thing" itself (that which happens or comes) and the impression (itself at once "spontaneous" and "controlled") that is given, left, or made by the so-called "thing." We could say that the impression is "informed," in both senses of the word: a predominant system gave it form, and this form then gets run through an organized information machine (language, communication, rhetoric, image, media, and so on). This informational apparatus is from the very outset political, technical, economic. But we can and, I believe, must (and this duty is at once philosophical and political) distinguish between the supposedly brute fact, the "impression," and the interpretation. It is of course just about impossible, I realize, to distinguish the "brute" fact from the system that produces the "information" about it. But it is necessary to push the analysis as far as possible. To produce a "major event," it is, sad to say, not enough, and this has been true for some time now, to cause the deaths of some four thousand people, and especially "civilians," in just a few seconds by means of so-called advanced technology. Many examples could be given from the world wars (for you specified that this event appears even more important to those who "have never lived through a world war") but also from after these wars, examples of quasi-instantaneous mass murders that were not recorded, interpreted, felt, and presented as "major events." They did not give the "impression," at least not to everyone, of being unforgettable catastrophes.

We must thus ask why this is the case and distinguish between two "impressions." On the one hand, compassion for the victims and indignation over the killings; our sadness and condemnation should be without limits, unconditional, unimpeachable; they are responding to an undeniable "event," beyond all simulacra and all possible virtualization; they respond with what might be called the heart and they go straight to the heart of the event. On the other hand, the interpreted, interpretative, informed impression, the conditional evaluation that makes us *believe* that this is a "major event." *Belief,* the phenomenon of *credit* and of *accreditation,* constitutes an essential dimension of the evaluation, of the dating, indeed, of the compulsive inflation of which we've been speaking. By distinguishing impression from belief, I continue to make as if I were privileging this language of English empiricism, which we would be wrong to resist here. All the philosophical questions remain open, unless they are opening up again in a perhaps new and original way: What is an impression? What is a belief? But especially: what is an event worthy of this name? And a "major" event, that is, one that is actually more of an "event," more actually an "event," than ever? An event that would bear witness, in an exemplary or hyperbolic fashion, to the very essence of an event or even to an event beyond essence? For could an event that still conforms to an essence, to a law or to a truth, indeed to a concept of the event, ever be a major event? A major event should be so unforeseeable and irruptive that it disturbs even the horizon of the concept or essence on the basis of which we believe we recognize an event *as such*. That is why all the "philosophical" questions remain open, perhaps even beyond philosophy itself, as soon as it is a matter of thinking the event.

B O R R A D O R I :   You mean "event" in the Heideggerian sense?

D E R R I D A :   No doubt, but, curiously, to the extent that the thought of *Ereignis* in Heidegger would be turned not only toward the *appropriation* of the proper (*eigen*) but toward a certain *expropriation* that Heidegger himself names (*Enteignis*). The undergoing of the event, that which in the undergoing or in the ordeal *at once opens itself up to and resists experience,* is, it seems to me, a certain *unappropriability* of what comes or happens. The event is what comes and, in coming, comes to surprise me, to surprise and to suspend comprehension: the event is first of all *that which* I do not first of all comprehend. Better, the event is first of all *that* I do not comprehend. It consists in *that, that* I do not comprehend: *that which* I do not comprehend and first of all *that* I do not comprehend, the fact that I do not comprehend: my incomprehension. That is the limit, at once internal and external, on which I would like to insist here: although the experience of an event, the mode according to which it affects us, calls for a movement of appropriation (comprehension, recognition, identification, description, determination, interpretation on the basis of a horizon of anticipation, knowledge, naming, and so on), although this movement of appropriation is irreducible and ineluctable, there is no event worthy of its name except insofar as this appropriation *falters* at some border or frontier. A frontier, however, with neither front nor confrontation, one that incomprehension does not run into head on since it does not take the form of a solid front: it escapes, remains evasive, open, undecided, indeterminable. Whence the unappropriability, the unforesee-ability, absolute surprise, incomprehension, the risk of misunderstand-ing, unanticipatable novelty, pure singularity, the absence of horizon. Were we to accept this minimal definition of the event, minimal but double and paradoxical, could we affirm that "September 11" consti-tuted an event without precedent? An unforeseeable event? A singular event through and through?

Nothing is less certain. It was not impossible to foresee an attack on American soil by those called "terrorists" (we will have to return to this word, which is so equivocal and so politically charged), against a highly sensitive, spectacular, extremely symbolic building or institu-tion. Leaving aside Oklahoma City (where, it will be said, the attacker came from the United States, even though this was the case of "Sep-tember 11" as well), there had already been a bombing attack against the Twin Towers a few years back, and the fallout from this attack re-mains very much a current affair since the presumed authors of this act of "terrorism" are still being held and tried.[6] And there have been so many other attacks of the same kind, outside American national terri-tory but against American "interests." And then there are the notable failures of the CIA and FBI, these two antennae of the American or-ganism that were supposed to see these attacks coming, to avert just such a surprise. (Let me say in passing, since I've just spoken of the "American national territory" and of American "interests," that "Sep-tember 11" reveals, or actually recalls, that for countless reasons we would have real difficulty defining rigorous *limits* for these "things," "national territory" and "American interests." Where do they end today? Who is authorized to answer this question? Only American cit-izens? Only their allies? It is perhaps here that we might get to the very bottom of the problem—and to one of the reasons why we would have difficulty knowing if there is here, *stricto sensu,* where and when, an "event.")

Let us accept nonetheless such a hypothesis and proceed slowly and patiently in speaking of this as an "event." After all, every time something happens, even in the most banal, everyday experience, there is *something* of an event and of singular unforeseeability about it: each instant marks an event, everything that is "other" as well, and each birth, and each death, even the most gentle and most "natural." But should we then say, to cite you, that September 11 was a "major event"?

Even though the word "major" suggests height and size, the evaluation here cannot be merely *quantitative,* a question of the size of the towers, the territory attacked, or the number of victims. You know, of course, that one does not count the dead in the same way from one corner of the globe to the other. It is our duty to recall this, without it attenuating in the least our sadness for the victims of the Twin Towers, our horror or our outrage in the face of this crime. It is our duty to recall that the shock waves produced by such murders are never purely natural and spontaneous. They depend on a complex machinery involving history, politics, the media, and so on. Whether we are talking about a psychological, political, police, or military response or reaction, we must acknowledge the obvious—at once qualitative and quantitative: for Europe, for the United States, for their media and their public opinion, quantitatively comparable killings, or even those greater in number, whether immediate or indirect, never produce such an intense upheaval when they occur outside European or American space (Cambodia, Rwanda, Palestine, Iraq, and so on). What *appears* new and "major" is not the weapon used, either: planes to destroy buildings full of civilians. There is no need, alas, to go back to the bombings during World War II, to Hiroshima and Nagasaki, to find countless examples of this. The least we can say about such aggressions is that, whether by quantitative or other measures, they were not inferior in scope to "September 11." And the United States was not always, let it be said by way of a litotes, on the side of the victims.

We must thus look for other explanations—meaningful and *qualitative* explanations. First of all, whether one is or is not an ally of the United States, whether one approves or not of what has remained more or less constant and continuous in U.S. policy from one administration to the next, no one, I think, will contest an obvious fact that determines the horizon of the "world" since what is called *the end of the Cold War* (and we will have to reinterpret this thing, the so-called *end of the Cold War,* from several different perspectives, and I will do so later, but for the moment allow me to recall only that "September 11" is also, still, and in many respects, a distant effect of the Cold War itself, before its "end," from the time when the United States provided training and weapons, and not only in Afghanistan, to the enemies of the Soviet Union, who have now become the enemies of the U.S.). The obvious fact is that since the "end of the Cold War" what can be called the

world order, in its relative and precarious stability, depends largely on
the solidity and reliability, on the *credit,* of American power. On every
level: economic, technical, military, in the media, even on the level of
discursive logic, of the axiomatic that supports juridical and diplomatic
rhetoric worldwide, and thus international law, even when the United
States violates this law without ceasing to champion its cause. Hence,
to destabilize this superpower, which plays at least the "role" of the
guardian of the prevailing world order, is to risk destabilizing the entire
world, including the declared enemies of the United States. What is
therefore threatened? Not only a great number of forces, powers, or
"things" that depend, even for the most determined adversaries of the
United States, on the order that is more or less assured by this superpower; it is also, *more radically still* (and I would underscore this
point), the system of interpretation, the axiomatic, logic, rhetoric, concepts, and evaluations that are supposed to allow one to *comprehend*
and to explain precisely something like "September 11." I am speaking
here of the *discourse* that comes to be, in a pervasive and overwhelming, hegemonic fashion, *accredited* in the world's public space. What is
legitimated by the prevailing system (a combination of public opinion,
the media, the rhetoric of politicians and the presumed authority of all
those who, through various mechanisms, speak or are allowed to speak
in the public space) are thus the norms inscribed in every apparently
meaningful phrase that can be constructed with the lexicon of violence,
aggression, crime, war, and terrorism, with the supposed differences
between war and terrorism, national and international terrorism, state
and nonstate terrorism, with the respect for sovereignty, national territory, and so on. Is, then, what was touched, wounded, or traumatized
by this double *crash* only some particular thing or other, a "what" or a
"who," buildings, strategic urban structures, symbols of political, military, or capitalist power, or a considerable number of people of many
different origins living on the body of a national territory that had remained untouched for so long? No, it was not *only* all that but perhaps
especially, through all that, the conceptual, semantic, and one could
even say hermeneutic apparatus that might have allowed one to see
coming, to comprehend, interpret, describe, speak of, and name "September 11"—and in so doing to neutralize the traumatism and come to
terms with it through a "work of mourning." What I am suggesting
here might appear abstract and overly reliant on what seems like a sim-

ple conceptual or discursive activity, a question of knowledge; it is as if I were in fact content to say that what is terrible about "September 11," what remains "infinite" in this wound, is that we do not *know* what it is and so do not know how to describe, identify, or even name it. And that is, in fact, what I'm saying. But in order to show that this horizon of nonknowledge, this nonhorizon of knowledge (the powerlessness to comprehend, recognize, cognize, identify, name, describe, foresee), is anything but abstract and idealist, I will need to say more. And, precisely, in a more concrete way.

I shall do this in *three moments*, twice by reference to what has been called the "Cold War," the "end of the Cold War," or "the balance of terror." These three moments or series of arguments all appeal to the same logic. The same logic that elsewhere I proposed we extend without limit in the form of an implacable law: the one that regulates every *autoimmunitary process*.[7] As we know, an autoimmunitary process is that strange behavior where a living being, in quasi-*suicidal* fashion, "itself" works to destroy its own protection, to immunize itself *against* its "own" immunity.

1. *First moment, first autoimmunity. Reflex and reflection. The Cold War in the head.*

Well beyond the United States, the whole world feels obscurely affected by a transgression that is not only presented as a transgression without precedent in history (the first violation of U.S. national territory in almost two centuries, or at least that's the phantasm that has prevailed for so long) but as a transgression of a new *type*. But what *type?* Before answering this question, let me recall once more the obvious: this transgression violates the territory of a country that, even in the eyes of its enemies and especially since the so-called "end of the Cold War," plays a virtually sovereign role among sovereign states. And thus the role of guarantor or guardian of the entire world order, the one that, in principle and in the last resort, is supposed to assure credit in general, credit in the sense of financial transactions but also the credit granted to languages, laws, political or diplomatic transactions. The United States holds this credit, for which everyone—including those who are trying to ruin it—feel the need, and it shows it not only through its wealth and its technoscientific and military power but also, at the same time, through its role as arbitrator in all conflicts, through its dominant presence on the Security Council and in so many other international institutions. Even when—and with impunity—it respects neither the spirit nor the letter of these institutions and their resolutions. The United States still retains the power of accrediting before the world a certain self-presentation: it represents the ultimate presumed unity of force and law, of the greatest force and the discourse of law.

But here is the first symptom of suicidal autoimmunity: not only is the ground, that is, the literal figure of the founding or foundation of this "force of law," *seen* to be *exposed* to aggression, but the aggression of which it is the *object* (the *object exposed,* precisely, to violence, but also, "in a loop,"[8] to its own cameras in its own interests) comes, *as from the inside,* from forces that are apparently without any force of their own but that are able to find the means, through ruse and the implementation of *high-tech* knowledge, to get hold of an American weapon in an American city on the ground of an American airport. Immigrated, trained, prepared for their act in the United States by the United States, these *hijackers* incorporate, so to speak, two suicides in one: their own (and one will remain forever defenseless in the face of a suicidal, autoimmunitary aggression—and that is what terrorizes most) but also the suicide of those who welcomed, armed, and trained them. For let us not forget that the United States had in effect paved the way for and consolidated the forces of the "adversary" by training people like "bin Laden," who would here be the most striking example, and by first of all creating the politico-military circumstances that would favor their emergence and their shifts in allegiance (for example, the alliance with Saudi Arabia and other Arab Muslim countries in its war against the Soviet Union or Russia in Afghanistan—though one could endlessly multiply examples of these suicidal paradoxes).

Doubly suicidal, this force will have been *adjusted* with an extraordinary *economy* (the maximum amount of security, of preparation, of technical proficiency, of destructive capability, with a minimum of borrowed means!). It will have targeted and hit the heart or, rather, the symbolic head of the prevailing world order. Right at the level of the head (*cap, caput, capital, Capitol*), this double suicide will have touched two places at once symbolically and operationally essential to the American corpus: the economic place or capital "head" of world capital (the World Trade Center, the very archetype of the genre, for there are now—and under this very name—WTCs in many places of the world, for example, in China) and the strategic, military, and administrative place of the American capital, the head of American political representation, the Pentagon, not far from the Capitol, the seat of Congress.

In speaking here of the Capitol, I'm already moving on to a *second* aspect of the same "event," of what might make it a "major event." At issue again is an autoimmunitary terror, and again, of the "Cold War," of what one calls a bit too quickly its "end" and of what, when seen from the Capitol, might be worse than the Cold War.

2. *Second moment, second autoimmunity.*
Reflex and reflection. Worse than the Cold War.

What is a traumatic event? First of all, any event worthy of this name, even if it is a "happy" event, has within it something that is traumatizing. An event always inflicts a wound in the everyday course of history, in the ordinary repetition and anticipation of all experience. A traumatic event is not only marked as an event by the memory, even if unconscious, of what took place. In saying this, I seem to be going against the obvious, namely, that the event is linked to presence or to the past, to the taking place of what has happened, once and for all, in an undeniable fashion, so that the repetition compulsion that might follow would but reproduce what has already happened or been produced. Yet I believe we must complicate this schema (even if it is not completely false); we must question its "chrono-logy," that is, the thought and order of temporalization it seems to imply. We must rethink the temporalization of a traumatism if we want to comprehend in what way "September 11" *looks like* a "major event." For the wound remains open by our terror before the *future* and not only the past. (You yourself, in fact, defined the event in relation to the future in your question; you were already anticipating by speaking of "one of the most important historical events we *will* witness in our lifetime.") The ordeal of the event has as its tragic correlate not what is presently happening or what has happened in the past but the precursory signs of what threatens to happen. It is the future that determines the unappropriability of the event, not the present or the past. Or at least, if it is the present or the past, it is only insofar as it bears on its body the terrible sign of what might or perhaps will take place, which will be *worse than anything that has ever taken place.*

Let me clarify. We are talking about a trauma, and thus an event, whose temporality proceeds neither from the now that is present nor from the present that is past but from an im-presentable to come (*à venir*). A weapon wounds and leaves forever open an unconscious scar; but this weapon is terrifying because it comes from the to-come, from the future, a future so radically to come that it resists even the grammar of the future anterior. Imagine that the Americans and, through them, the entire world, had been told: what has just happened, the spectacular destruction of two towers, the theatrical but invisible deaths of thousands of people in just a few second, is an awful thing, a terrible crime, a pain without measure, but it's all over, it won't happen again, there will never again be anything as awful as or more awful than that. I assume that mourning would have been possible in a relatively short period of time. Whether to our chagrin or our delight, things would have quite quickly returned to their normal course in ordinary history. One would have spoken of the work of mourning and turned the page, as is so often done, and done so much more easily when it comes to things that happen elsewhere, far from Europe and the Americas. But this is not at all what happened. There is traumatism with no possible work of mourning when the evil comes from the possibility to come of the worst, from the repetition to come—though worse. Traumatism is produced by the *future,* by the *to come,* by the threat of the worst *to come,* rather than by an aggression that is "over and done with."[9] What happened, even though this has not been said with the requisite clarity—and for good reason—is that, for the future and for always, the threat that was indicated through these signs might be worse than any other, worse even, and we shall explain this, than the threat that organized the so-called "Cold War." The threat of a *chemical* attack, no doubt, or *bacteriological* attack (recall that in the weeks immediately following September 11 it was thought that this was actually taking place), but especially the threat of a *nuclear* attack. Though rather little has been said about this, those responsible in the administration and in Congress quickly took the necessary measures to ensure that a constitutional state might survive a *nuclear* attack against Washington, the head of state, and the Congress (the Pentagon, White House, and the Capitol building). Certain representatives of Congress made this known during a televised public debate I happened to see here: from now on the *heads* of state (president, vice-president, members of the cabinet and of congress) will no longer all come together in the same place at the same time, as used to be the case, for example, with the State of the Union address. This suggests that the "major event" of "September 11" will not have consisted in a past aggression, one that is still present and effective. X will have been traumatized (X? Who or what is X? Nothing less than the "world," well beyond the United States, or in any case, the possibility of the "world"), but traumatized not in the present or from the memory of what will have been a past present. No, traumatized from the unpresentable future, from the open threat of an aggression capable one day of striking—for you never know—the *head* of the sovereign nation-state par excellence.

Why is this threat signaled by the "end of the Cold War"? Why is it worse than the "Cold War" itself? Like the formation of Arab Muslim terrorist networks equipped and trained during the Cold War, this threat represents the residual consequence of *both* the Cold War *and* the passage beyond the Cold War. On the one hand, because of the now uncontrollable proliferation of nuclear capability, it is difficult to measure the degrees and forms of this force, just as it is difficult to delimit the responsibility for this proliferation, a point we cannot pursue here. On the other hand, and here we touch upon what is worse than the Cold War, there can now no longer be a balance of terror, for there is no longer a duel or standoff between two powerful states (U.S.A., USSR) involved in a game theory in which both states are capable of neutralizing the other's nuclear power through a reciprocal and organized evaluation of the respective risks. From now on, the nuclear threat, the "total" threat, no longer comes from a state but from anonymous forces that are absolutely unforeseeable and incalculable. And since this absolute threat will have been secreted by the end of the Cold War and the "victory" of the U.S. camp, since it threatens what is supposed to sustain world order, the very possibility of a world and of any world-wide effort [*mondialisation*] (international law, a world market, a universal language, and so on), what is thus put at risk by this *terrifying* autoimmunity logic is nothing less than the existence of the world, of the worldwide itself. There is no longer any limit to this threat that at once looks for its antecedents or its resources in the long history of the Cold War and yet appears infinitely more dangerous, frightening, terrifying than the Cold War. And there are, in fact, countless signs that this threat is accelerating and confirming the end of this Cold War, hastening the at least apparent reconciliation of two equally frightened enemies. When Bush and his associates blame "the axis of evil," we ought both to smile at and denounce the religious connotations, the childish stratagems, the obscurantist mystifications of this inflated rhetoric. And yet there is, in fact, and from every quarter, an absolute "evil" whose threat, whose shadow, is spreading. Absolute evil, absolute threat, because what is at stake is nothing less than the *mondialisation* or the worldwide movement of the world, life on earth and elsewhere, without remainder.

But, and here's another paradox, even if this is in fact the origin of the "terror" that "terrorisms" are playing off, even if this terror is the very worst, even if it touches the geopolitical unconscious of every living being and leaves there indelible traces, even if this is what we are trying to get at when we speak, as you just did, and as is done so often, of "September 11" as a "major event" because it is the first (conscious-unconscious) sign of this absolute terror, well, at the same time, because of the anonymous invisibility of the enemy, because of the undetermined origin of the terror, because we cannot put a face on such terror (individual or state), because we do not know what an event *of* the unconscious or *for* the unconscious is (though we must nonetheless take it into account), the worst can simultaneously appear insubstantial, fleeting, light, and so seem to be denied, repressed, indeed forgotten, relegated to being just one event among others, *one* of the "major events," if you will, in a long chain of past and future events. Yet all these efforts to attenuate or neutralize the effect of the traumatism (to deny, repress, or forget it, to get over it) are but so many desperate attempts. And so many autoimmunitary movements. Which produce, invent, and feed the very monstrosity they claim to overcome.

What will never let itself be forgotten is thus the perverse effect of the autoimmunitary itself. For we now know that repression in both its psychoanalytical sense and its political sense—whether it be through the police, the military, or the economy—ends up producing, reproducing, and regenerating the very thing it seeks to disarm.

3. *Third moment, third autoimmunity.*
Reflex and reflection. The vicious circle of repression.

It cannot be said that humanity is defenseless against the threat of this evil. But we must recognize that defenses and all the forms of what is called, with two equally problematic words, the "war on terrorism"[10] work to regenerate, in the short or long term, the causes of the evil they claim to eradicate. Whether we are talking about Iraq, Afghanistan, or even Palestine, the "bombs" will never be "smart" enough to prevent the victims (military and/or civilian, another distinction that has become less and less reliable) from responding, either in person or by proxy, with what it will then be easy for them to present as legitimate reprisals or as counterterrorism. And so on ad infinitum . . .

For the sake of clarity and because the analysis required it, I have distinguished three autoimmunitary terrors. But in reality these three resources of terror cannot be distinguished; they feed into and overdetermine one another. They are, at bottom, the same, in perceptual "reality" and especially in the unconscious—which is not the least real of realities.

BORRADORI : Whether or not September 11 is an event of major importance, what role do you see for philosophy? Can philosophy help us to understand what has happened?

DERRIDA : Such an "event" surely calls for a philosophical response. Better, a response that calls into question, at their most fundamental level, the most deep-seated conceptual presuppositions in philosophical discourse. The concepts with which this "event" has most often been described, named, categorized, are the products of a "dogmatic slumber" from which only a new philosophical reflection can awaken us, a reflection *on* philosophy, most notably on political philosophy and its heritage. The prevailing discourse, that of the media and of the official rhetoric, relies too readily on received concepts like "war" or "terrorism" (national or international).

A *critical* reading of Schmitt, for example, would thus prove very useful. On the one hand, so as to follow Schmitt as far as possible in distinguishing classical war (a direct and declared confrontation between two enemy states, according to the long tradition of European law) from "civil war" and "partisan war" (in its modern forms, even though it appears, Schmitt acknowledges, as early as the beginning of the nineteenth century). But, on the other hand, we would also have to recognize, *against* Schmitt, that the violence that has now been unleashed is not the result of "war" (the expression "war on terrorism" thus being one of the most confused, and we must analyze this confusion and the interests such an abuse of rhetoric actually serve). Bush speaks of "war," but he is in fact incapable of identifying the enemy against whom he declares that he has declared war. It is said over and over that neither the civilian population of Afghanistan nor its armies are the enemies of the United States. Assuming that "bin Laden" is here the sovereign decision-maker, everyone knows that he is not Afghan, that he has been disavowed by his own country (by every "country" and state, in fact, almost without exception), that his training owes much to the United States and that, of course, he is not alone. The states that help him indirectly do not do so as states. No state as such supports him publicly. As for states that "harbor" terrorist networks, it is difficult to identify them as such. The United States and Europe, London and Berlin, are also sanctuaries, places of training or formation and information for all the "terrorists" of the world. No geography, no "territorial" determination, is thus pertinent any longer for locating the seat of these new technologies of transmission or aggression. To say it all too quickly and in passing, to amplify and clarify just a bit what I said earlier about an absolute threat whose origin is anonymous and not related to any state, such "terrorist" attacks already no longer need planes, bombs, or kamikazes: it is enough to infiltrate a strategically important computer system and introduce a virus or some other disruptive element to paralyze the economic, military, and political resources of an entire country or continent. And this can be attempted from just about anywhere on earth, at very little expense and with minimal means. The relationship between earth, *terra,* territory, and terror has changed, and it is necessary to know that this is because of knowledge, that is, because of technoscience. It is technoscience that blurs the distinction between war and terrorism. In this regard, when compared to the possibilities for destruction and chaotic disorder that are *in reserve,* for the future, in the computerized networks of the world, "September 11" is still part of the archaic theater of violence aimed at striking the imagination. One will be able to do even worse tomorrow, invisibly, in silence, more quickly and without any bloodshed, by attacking the computer and informational networks on which the entire life (social, economic, military, and so on) of a "great nation," of the greatest power on earth, depends. One day it might be said: "September 11"—those were the ("good") old days of the last war. Things were still of the order of the gigantic: visible and enormous! What size, what height! There has been worse since. Nanotechnologies of all sorts are so much more powerful and invisible, uncontrollable, capable of creeping in everywhere. They are the micrological rivals of microbes and bacteria. Yet our unconscious is already aware of this; it already knows it, and that's what's scary.

If this violence is not a "war" between states, it is not a "civil war" either, or a "partisan war," in Schmitt's sense, insofar as it does not involve, like most such wars, a national insurrection or liberation movement aimed at taking power on the ground of a nation-state (even if one of the aims, whether secondary or primary, of the "bin Laden" network is to destabilize Saudi Arabia, an ambiguous ally of the United States, and put a new state power in place). Even if one were to insist on speaking here of "terrorism," this appellation now covers a new concept and new distinctions.

B O R R A D O R I : Do you think that these distinctions can be safely drawn?

D E R R I D A : It's more difficult than ever. If one is not to trust blindly in the prevailing language, which remains most often subservient to the rhetoric of the media and to the banter of the political powers, we must be very careful using the term "terrorism" and especially "international terrorism." In the first place, what is terror? What distinguishes it from fear, anxiety, and panic? When I suggested earlier that the event of September 11 was "major" only to the extent that the traumatism it inflicted upon consciousness and upon the unconscious had to do not with what happened but with the undetermined threat of a future more dangerous than the Cold War, was I speaking of terror, fear, panic, or anxiety? How does a terror that is organized, provoked, and instrumentalized differ from that *fear* that an entire tradition, from Hobbes to Schmitt and even to Benjamin, holds to be the very condition of the authority of law and of the sovereign exercise of power, the very condition of the political and of the state? In *Leviathan* Hobbes speaks not only of "fear" but of "terror."[11] Benjamin speaks of how the state tends to appropriate for itself, and precisely through threat, a monopoly on violence ("Critique of Violence").[12] It will no doubt be said that not every experience of terror is necessarily the effect of some terrorism. To be sure, but the political history of the word "terrorism" is derived in large part from a reference to the Reign of Terror during the French Revolution, a terror that was carried out in the name of the state and that in fact presupposed a legal monopoly on violence. And what do we find in current definitions or explicitly legal definitions of terrorism? In each case, a reference to a crime against human life in violation of national or international laws entails at once the distinction between civilian and military (the victims of terrorism are assumed to be civilians) and a political end (to influence or change the politics of a country by terrorizing its civilian population). These definitions do not therefore exclude "state terrorism." Every terrorist in the world claims to be responding in self-defense to a prior terrorism on the part of the state, one that simply went by other names and covered itself with all sorts of more or less credible justifications. You know about the accusations leveled against, for example, and especially, the United States, suspected of practicing or encouraging state terrorism.[13] In addition, even during declared wars between states, in accordance with the long tradition of European law, there were frequently terrorist excesses. Well before the massive bombing campaigns of the last two world wars, the intimidation of civilian populations was commonly resorted to. For centuries.

A word must also be said about the expression "international terrorism," which has become a staple of official political discourse the world over. It is also being used in numerous official condemnations on the part of the United Nations. After September 11, an overwhelming majority of states represented in the UN (it may have actually been unanimous, I would have to check) condemned, as has happened more than once in the past few decades, what it calls "international terrorism." During a televised session of the UN, Secretary-General Kofi Annan had to recall in passing some of their previous debates. For just as they were preparing to condemn "international terrorism," certain states expressed reservations about the clarity of the concept and the criteria used to identify it. As with so many other crucial juridical notions, what remains obscure, dogmatic, or precritical does not prevent the powers that be, the so-called legitimate powers, from making use of these notions when it seems opportune. On the contrary, the more confused the concept the more it lends itself to an opportunistic appropri-

ation. It was, thus, after a few very hasty decisions, without any philosophical debate on the subject of "international terrorism" and its condemnation, that the UN authorized the United States to use *any* means
deemed necessary and appropriate by the American administration to
protect itself against this so-called "international terrorism."

Without going back too far in time, without even recalling, as is
often done these days, and rightly so, that terrorists might be praised as
freedom fighters in one context (for example, in the struggle against the
Soviet occupation of Afghanistan) and denounced as terrorists in another (and, these days, it's often the very same fighters, using the very
same weapons), let's not forget the trouble we would have deciding between "national" and "international" terrorism in the cases of Algeria,
Northern Ireland, Corsica, Israel, or Palestine. No one can deny that
there was state terrorism during the French repression in Algeria from
1954 to 1962. The terrorism carried out by the Algerian rebellion was
long considered a domestic phenomenon insofar as Algeria was supposed to be an integral part of French national territory, and the French
terrorism of the time (carried out by the state) was presented as a police
operation for internal security. It was only in the 1990s, decades later,
that the French Parliament retrospectively conferred the status of
"war" (and thus the status of an *international* confrontation) upon this
conflict so as to be able to pay the pensions of the "veterans" who
claimed them. What did this law reveal? That it was necessary, and that
we were able, to change all the names previously used to qualify what
had earlier been so modestly called, in Algeria, precisely the "events"
(the inability, once again, of popular public opinion to name the
"thing" adequately). Armed repression, an internal police operation,
and state terrorism thus all of a sudden became a "war." On the other
side, the terrorists were considered and from now on are considered in
much of the world as freedom fighters and heroes of national independence. As for the terrorism of the armed groups that helped force
the foundation and recognition of the state of Israel, was that national
or international? And what about the different groups of Palestinian
terrorists today? And the Irish? And the Afghans who fought against
the Soviet Union? And the Chechnyans? At what point does one terrorism stop being denounced as such to be hailed as the only recourse
left in a legitimate fight? And what about the inverse? Where does one
draw the line between the national and the international, the police and

the army, a "peacekeeping" intervention and war, terrorism and war, civilian and military, in a territory and within the structures that assure the defensive or offensive capacity of a "society"? I say simply "society" here because there are cases where a more or less organic and organized political entity is neither a state nor a completely nonstate entity but virtually a state: just look at what is today called Palestine or the Palestinian Authority.

Semantic instability, irreducible trouble spots on the borders between concepts, indecision in the very concept of the border: all this must not only be analyzed as a speculative disorder, a conceptual chaos or zone of passing turbulence in public or political language. We must also recognize here strategies and relations of force. The dominant power is the one that manages to impose and, thus, to legitimate, indeed to legalize (for it is always a question of law) on a national or world stage, the terminology and thus the interpretation that best suits it in a given situation. It was thus in the course of a long and complicated history that the United States succeeded in gaining an intergovernmental consensus in South America to officially call "terrorism" any organized political resistance to the powers in place—those put in place, in truth—so that an armed coalition could then be called upon to combat the so-called "terrorism." So that the U.S. could, without compunction, delegate responsibility to South American governments and so avoid the very legitimate accusation of violent interventionism.

But rather than continue in this direction by multiplying examples, I will settle for underscoring once more the novelty that makes so urgent both a refoundation, if we can still say this, of the juridico-political and a conceptual mutation, at once semantic, lexical, and rhetorical. Let's look again at many of the phenomena that some are trying to identify and interpret as (national or international) "terrorist" acts, acts of war, or peacekeeping interventions. They no longer aim at conquering or liberating a territory and at founding a nation-state. No one any longer aspires to this, not the United States or the (wealthy) so-called "northern" states, which no longer exercise their hegemony through the colonial or imperial model of occupying a territory, and not the countries formerly subject to this colonialism or imperialism. The "terrorist/freedom fighter" opposition also belongs to the categories of the past. Even when there is "state terrorism" it is no longer a question of occupying a territory but of securing some technoeconomic power or political control that has but a minimal need for territory. If oil reserves remain among the rare territories left, among the last nonvirtualizable terrestrial places, one can simply secure the rights to lay down a pipeline. Though it is also true that, for the moment, the whole technoindustrial structure of hegemonic countries depends on these resources, so that, however complex and overdetermined it may be, the possibility of everything we have just spoken about remains anchored, so to speak, in these nonreplaceable places, these nondeterritorializable territories. These territories continue to belong, by law, in the still solid tradition of international law, to sovereign nation-states.

BORRADORI : What you are suggesting calls for profound changes at the level of international institutions and international law.

DERRIDA : Such a mutation *will have* to take place. But it is impossible to predict at what pace. In all the transformations we have been discussing, what remains incalculable is first of all the pace or rhythm, the time of acceleration and the acceleration of time. And this is for essential reasons that have to do with the very speed of technoscientific advances or shifts in speed. Just like the shifts in size or scale that nanotechnologies have introduced into our evaluations and our measures. Such radical changes in international law are necessary, but they might take place in one generation or in twenty. Who can say? Though I am incapable of knowing who today deserves the name philosopher (I would not simply accept certain professional or organizational criteria), I would be tempted to call philosophers those who, in the future, reflect in a responsible fashion on these questions and demand accountability from those in charge of public discourse, those responsible for the language and institutions of international law. A "philosopher" (actually I would prefer to say "philosopher-deconstructor") would be someone who analyzes and then draws the practical and effective consequences of the relationship between our philosophical heritage and the structure of the still dominant juridico-political system that is so clearly undergoing mutation. A "philosopher" would be one who seeks a new criteriology to distinguish between "comprehending" and "justifying." For one can describe, comprehend, and explain a certain chain of events or series of associations that lead to "war" or to "terrorism" without justifying them in the least, while in fact condemning them and attempting to invent other associations. One can condemn unconditionally certain acts of terrorism (whether of the state or not) without having to ignore the situation that might have brought them about or even legitimated them. To provide examples it would be necessary to conduct long analyses, in principle interminably long. One can thus condemn *unconditionally,* as I do here, the attack of September 11 without having to ignore the real or alleged conditions that made it possible. Anyone in the world who either organized or tried to justify this attack saw it as a response to the state terrorism of the United States and its allies. This was the case, for example—and I cite this only as an example—in the Middle East, even though Yasir Arafat also condemned "September 11" and refused bin Laden the right to speak in the name of the Palestinian people.

B O R R A D O R I :   If the distinction between war and terrorism is problematic and we accept the notion of state terrorism, then the question still remains: who is the most terrorist?

D E R R I D A :   The *most* terrorist? This question is at once necessary and destined to remain without any answer. Necessary because it takes into account an essential fact: all terrorism *presents itself* as a response in a situation that continues to escalate. It amounts to saying, "I am resorting to terrorism as a last resort, because the other is more terrorist than I am; I am defending myself, counterattacking; the real terrorist, the worst, is the one who will have deprived me of every other means of responding before presenting himself, the first aggressor, as a victim." It is in this way that the United States, Israel, wealthy nations, and colonial or imperialist powers are accused of practicing state terrorism and thus of being "more terrorist" than the terrorists of whom they say they are the victims. The pattern is well known, so I won't belabor it. But it is difficult to write it off purely and simply, even if it is sometimes applied in a simplistic and abusive fashion. Yet the question you are asking, that of a "more or less" in terrorism, should also not be settled through a purely and objectively *quantitative* logic. For this question can give rise to no such formal evaluation. "Terrorist" acts try to produce psychic effects (conscious or unconscious) and symbolic or symptomatic reactions that might take numerous detours, an incalculable number of them, in truth. The *quality* or *intensity* of the emotions provoked (whether conscious or unconscious) is not always proportionate to the number of victims or the amount of damage. In situations and cultures where the media do not spectacularize the event, the killing of thousands of people in a very short period of time might provoke fewer psychic and political effects than the assassination of a single individual in another country, culture, or nation-state with highly developed media resources. And does terrorism have to work only through death? Can't one terrorize without killing? And does killing necessarily mean putting to death? Isn't it also "letting die"? Can't "letting die," "not wanting to know that one is letting others die"—hundreds of millions of human beings, from hunger, AIDS, lack of medical treatment, and so on—also be part of a "more or less" conscious and deliberate terrorist strategy? We are perhaps wrong to assume so quickly that all terrorism is voluntary, conscious, organized, deliberate, intentionally calculated: there are historical and political "situations" where terror operates, so to speak, as if by itself, as the simple result of some apparatus, because of the relations of force in place, without anyone, any conscious subject, any person, any "I," being really conscious of it or feeling itself responsible for it. All situations of social or national structural oppression produce a terror that is not natural (insofar as it is organized, institutional), and all these situations depend on this terror without those who benefit from them ever organizing terrorist acts or ever being treated as terrorists. The narrow, too narrow meaning commonly given today to the word "terrorism" gets circulated in various ways in the discourse that dominates the public space, and first of all through the technoeconomic power of the media. What would "September 11" have been without television? This question has already been asked and explored, so I will not insist on it here. But we must recall that maximum media coverage was in the *common* interest of the perpetrators of "September 11," the terrorists, and those who, in the name of the victims, wanted to declare "war on terrorism." Between these two parties, such media coverage was, like the good sense of which Descartes speaks, the most widely shared thing in the world. More than the destruction of the Twin Towers or the attack on the Pentagon, more than the killing of thousands of people, the real "terror" consisted of and, in fact, began by exposing and exploiting, having exposed and exploited, the image of this terror by the target itself. This target (the United States, let's say, and anyone who supports or is allied with them in the world, and this knows almost no limits today) had it in its own *interest* (the *same* interest it shares with its sworn enemies) to expose its vulnerability, to give the greatest possible coverage to the aggression against which it wishes to protect itself. This is again the same autoimmunitary perversion. Or perhaps it would be better to say "pervertibility," so as to name a possibility, a risk, or a threat whose virtuality does not take the form of an evil intention, an evil spirit, or a will to do harm. But this virtuality alone is enough to frighten, even terrify. It is the ineradicable root of terror and thus of a terrorism that announces itself even before organizing itself into terrorism. Implacably. Endlessly.

Let me add here a reminder: there is nothing purely "modern" in this relation between media and terror, in a terrorism that operates by propagating within the public space images or rumors aimed at terrifying the so-called civilian population. It is true, of course, that with radio and television what is called organized "propaganda" (something that is in fact relatively modern) has, in the last century, and already during World War I, played an essential role in "declared" war. It will have gone hand in hand with bombing campaigns (whether conventional or atomic) that could not differentiate between "civilian" and "military" any more than the "resistance" movements and the repressions of those movements could. It was thus *already* impossible during the two "world wars" to distinguish rigorously between war and terrorism. Look, for example, at the heroes of the French Resistance who pursued the "war" even after the armistice and often in the name of De Gaulle's "free France." These members of the Resistance were regularly treated as "terrorists" by the Nazis and the Vichy collaborators. The accusation ceased with the liberation of France, since it had been an instrument of Nazi propaganda, but who could deny that it was entirely untrue?

BORRADORI: Where were you on September 11?

DERRIDA: I was in Shanghai, at the end of a long trip to China. It was nighttime there, and the owner of the cafe I was in with a couple of friends came to tell us that an airplane had "crashed" into the Twin Towers. I hurried back to my hotel, and from the very first televised images, those of CNN, I note, it was easy to foresee that this was going to become, *in the eyes* of the world, what you called a "major event." Even if what was to follow remained, to a certain extent, invisible and unforeseeable. But to feel the gravity of the event and its "worldwide" implications it was enough simply to mobilize a few already tested political hypotheses. As far as I could tell, China tried during the first few days to circumscribe the importance of the event, as if it were a more or less local incident. But this organized interpretation, informed by the current state of U.S.-China relations (diplomatic tensions and incidents of various sorts), ended up having to yield to other exigencies: CNN and other international media outlets have penetrated Chinese space, and China too, after all, has its own "Muslim" problem. It thus became necessary to join in some way the "antiterrorist" "coalition." It would be necessary to analyze, in the same vein, the motivations and interests behind all the different geopolitical or strategico-diplomatic shifts that have "invested," so to speak, "September 11." (For example, the warming in relations between Bush and Putin, who has been given a freer hand in Chechnya, and the very useful but very hasty identification of Palestinian terrorism with international terrorism, which now calls for a universal response. In both cases, certain parties have an interest in presenting their adversaries not only as terrorists—which they in fact are to a certain extent—but *only* as terrorists, indeed as "*international* terrorists" who share the same logic or are part of the same network and who must thus be opposed, it is claimed, not through counterterrorism but through a "war," meaning, of course, a "nice clean" war. The "facts" clearly show that these distinctions are lacking in rigor, impossible to maintain, and easily manipulated for certain ends.

B O R R A D O R I : A radical deconstruction of the distinction between war and terrorism, as well as between different types of terrorism (such as national and international), makes it very difficult to conceive of politics in a strategic sense. Who are the actors on the world stage? How many of them are there? Isn't there here the risk of total anarchy?

D E R R I D A : The word "anarchy" risks making us abandon too quickly the analysis and interpretation of what indeed *looks like* pure chaos. We must do all that we can to account for this appearance. We must do everything possible to make this new "disorder" as intelligible as possible. The analysis we sketched out earlier tried to move in that direction: an end of the "Cold War" that leaves just one camp, a coalition, actually, of states claiming sovereignty, faced with anonymous and nonstate organizations, armed and virtually nuclear powers. And these powers can also, without arms and without explosions, without any attacks in person, avail themselves of incredibly destructive computer technologies, technologies capable of operations that in fact have no name (neither war nor terrorism) and that are no longer carried out in the name of a nation-state, and whose "cause," in all senses of this word, is difficult to define (there's the theological cause, the ethnic cause, the socioeconomic cause, and so on). On no side is the logic of sovereignty ever put into question (political sovereignty or that of the nation-state—itself of ontotheological origin, though more or less secularized in one place and purely theological and nonsecularized in another): not on the side of the nation-states and the great powers that sit on the Security Council, and not on the other side, or other sides, since there is precisely an indeterminate number of them. Everyone will no doubt point to existing international law (the foundations of which remain, I believe, perfectible, revisable, in need of recasting, both conceptually and institutionally). But this international law is nowhere respected. And as soon as one party does not respect it the others no longer consider it respectable and begin to betray it in their turn. The United States and Israel are not the only ones who have become accustomed to taking all the liberties they deem necessary with UN resolutions.

To answer your question more specifically, I would say that the United States is perhaps not the sole target, perhaps not even the central or ultimate target, of the operation with which the name "bin Laden" is associated, at least by metonymy. The point may be to provoke a military and diplomatic situation that destabilizes certain Arab countries torn between a powerful public opinion (which is anti-American if not anti-Western, for countless reasons stemming from a complex, centuries old history, but then also, in the aftermath of an era of colonialism or imperialism, from poverty, oppression, and ideologico-religious indoctrination) and the necessity of basing their nondemocratic authority on diplomatic, economic, and military ties with the United States. First on the list here would be Saudi Arabia, which remains the privileged enemy of everything that might be represented by a "bin Laden" (a name I use always as a synecdoche) or a Saddam Hussein. Yet Saudi Arabia (an important family and an important oil-producing power), while maintaining its ties with its American "protector," "client," and "boss," fuels all the hotbeds of Arab Islamic fanaticism if not "terrorism" in the world. This is one of the paradoxical situations, once again autoimmunitary, of what you called "total anarchy": the movements and shifts in the strategic oil alliances between the United States (self-styled champion of the democratic ideal, of human rights, and so on) and regimes about which the least that can be said is that they do not correspond to this model. Such regimes (I used the example of Saudi Arabia, though it would be necessary to speak of the equally serious case of Pakistan) are also the enemies or targets of those who organize so-called "international terrorism" against the U.S. and, at least virtually, their allies. That makes for more than one triangle. And with all the angling going on between these triangles, it is difficult to disentangle the real from the alleged motivation, oil from religion, politics from economics or military strategy. The "bin Laden" type of diatribe against the American devil thus combines such themes as the perversion of faith and nonbelief, the violation of the sacred places of Islam, the military presence near Mecca, the support of Israel, and the oppression of Arab Muslim populations. But if this rhetoric clearly resonates with the populations and even the media of the Arab and Muslim world, the governments of Arab Muslim states (the majority of which care about as much for human rights and democracy as bin Laden does) are almost all hostile in principle, as "governments," to the "bin Laden" network and its discourse. One thus has to conclude that "bin Laden" is also working to destabilize them . . .

B O R R A D O R I : Which would be the standard objective of terrorists, to overturn but not take over, to destabilize the current situation.

D E R R I D A : The most common strategy consists always in destabilizing not only the principal, declared enemy but also, at the same time, in a kind of quasi-domestic confrontation, those much closer. Sometimes even one's own allies. This is another necessary consequence of the same autoimmunitary process. In all wars, all civil wars, all partisan wars or wars for liberation, the inevitable escalation leads one to go after one's rival partners no less than one's so-called principal adversary. During the Algerian War, between 1954 and 1962, what sometimes looked like "fratricidal" acts of violence between different insurrectional forces proved sometimes just as extreme as those between these groups and the French colonial forces.

This is yet one more reason not to consider everything that has to do with Islam or with the Arab Muslim "world" as a "world," or at least as one homogeneous whole. And wanting to take all these divisions, differences, and differends into account does not necessarily constitute an act of war; nor does trying to do everything possible to ensure that

in this Arab Muslim "world," which is not a *world* and not a world that
is *one*, certain currents do not take over, namely, those that lead to fanaticism, to an obscurantism armed to the teeth with modern technoscience, to the violation of every juridico-political principle, to the
cruel disregard for human rights and democracy, to a nonrespect for
life. We must help what is called Islam and what is called "Arab" to free
themselves from such violent dogmatism. We must help those who are
fighting heroically in this direction *on the inside,* whether we are talking
about politics in the narrow sense of the term or else about an interpretation of the Koran. When I say that we must do this for what is called
Islam and what is called "Arab," I obviously mean that we must not do
any less when it comes to Europe, the Americas, Africa, and Asia!

B O R R A D O R I : Earlier you emphasized the essential role of international organizations and the need to cultivate a respect for international law. Do you think that the kind of terrorism linked to the al-
Qaeda organization and to bin Laden harbors international political
ambitions?

D E R R I D A : What appears to me unacceptable in the "strategy"
(in terms of weapons, practices, ideology, rhetoric, discourse, and so
on) of the "bin Laden effect" is not only the cruelty, the disregard for
human life, the disrespect for law, for women, the use of what is worst
in technocapitalist modernity for the purposes of religious fanaticism.
No, it is, above all, the fact that such actions and such discourse *open
onto no future and, in my view, have no future.* If we are to put any faith
in the perfectibility of public space and of the world juridico-political
scene, of the "world" itself, then there is, it seems to me, *nothing good*
to be hoped for from that quarter. What is being proposed, at least implicitly, is that all capitalist and modern technoscientific forces be put
in the service of an interpretation, itself dogmatic, of the Islamic revelation of the One. Nothing of what has been so laboriously secularized in
the forms of the "political," of "democracy," of "international law," and
even in the nontheological form of sovereignty (assuming, again, that
the value of sovereignty can be completely secularized or detheolo-
gized, a hypothesis about which I have my doubts), none of this seems
to have any place whatsoever in the discourse "bin Laden." That is
why, in this unleashing of violence without name, if I had to take one of
the two sides and choose in a binary situation, well, I would. Despite
my very strong reservations about the American, indeed European, po-

litical posture, about the "international antiterrorist" coalition, despite all the de facto betrayals, all the failures to live up to democracy, international law, and the very international institutions that the states of this "coalition" themselves founded and supported up to a certain point, I would take the side of the camp that, in principle, by right of law, leaves a perspective open to perfectibility in the name of the "political," democracy, international law, international institutions, and so on. Even if this "in the name of" is still merely an assertion and a purely verbal commitment. Even in its most cynical mode, such an assertion still lets resonate within it an invincible promise. I don't hear any such promise coming from "bin Laden," at least not one for *this world.*

BORRADORI : It seems that you place your hopes in the authority of international law.

DERRIDA : Yes. In the first place, as imperfect as they may be, these international institutions should be respected in their deliberations and their resolutions by the sovereign states who are members of them and who have thus subscribed to their charters. I mentioned just a moment ago the serious failings of certain "Western" states with regard to these commitments. Such failings would stem from at least two series of causes.

First, they would have to do with the very structure of the axioms and principles of these systems of law and thus of the charters and conventions that institutionalize them. Reflection (of what I would call a "deconstructive" type) should thus, it seems to me, without diminishing or destroying these axioms and principles, question and refound them, endlessly refine and universalize them, without becoming discouraged by the aporias such work must necessarily encounter.

But second, such failings, in the case of states as powerful as the United States and Israel (which is supported by the U.S.), are not subject to any dissuasive sanctions. The United Nations has neither the force nor the means for such sanctions. It is thus necessary to do everything possible (a formidable and imposing task for the very long term) to ensure that these current failings in the present state of these institutions are effectively sanctioned and, in truth, discouraged in advance by a new organization. This would mean that an institution such as the UN (once modified in its structure and charter—and I'm thinking here particularly of the Security Council) would have to have at its disposal an effective intervening force and thus no longer have to depend in order to carry out its decisions on rich and powerful, actually or virtually hegemonic, nation-states, which bend the law in accordance with their force and according to their interests. Sometimes quite cynically.

I'm not unaware of the apparently utopic character of the horizon I'm sketching out here, that of an international institution of law and an international court of justice with their own autonomous force. Though I do not hold law to be the last word in ethics, politics, or anything else, though this unity of force and law (which is required by the very concept of law, as Kant explains so well) is not only *utopic* but *aporetic* (since it implies that beyond the sovereignty of the nation-state, indeed beyond democratic sovereignty—whose ontotheological foundations must be deconstructed—we would nonetheless be reconstituting a new figure, though not necessarily state-related, of universal sovereignty, of absolute law with an effective autonomous force at its disposal), I continue to believe that it is faith in the possibility of this impossible and, in truth, undecidable thing from the point of view of knowledge, science, and conscience that must govern all our decisions.[14]

BORRADORI: It might be said that this terrorist attack was, in one sense, an attack against the principle of sovereignty that the United States has over its own land, yet also an attack on the sovereign role the United States plays vis-à-vis the Western world, at once politically, economically, and culturally. Have these two attacks destabilized the concept of sovereignty as it has been developed by Western modernity?

DERRIDA: Those called "terrorists" are not, in this context, "others," absolute others whom we, as "Westerners," can no longer understand. We must not forget that they were often recruited, trained, and even armed, and for a long time, in various Western ways by a Western world that itself, in the course of its ancient as well as very recent history, invented the word, the techniques, and the "politics" of "terrorism." Next, one has to divide, or at least differentiate, all the "wholes" or "groups" to which we might be tempted to attribute responsibility for this terrorism. It's not "the Arabs" in general, nor Islam, nor the Arab Islamic Middle East. Each of these groups is heterogeneous, filled with tensions, conflicts, and essential contradictions, with, in truth, what we have been calling self-destructive, quasi-suicidal, autoimmunitary processes. The same goes for the "West." What is, to my eyes, very important for the future, and I will return to this later, is also a difference, indeed up to a certain point and within certain limits, an opposition, between the United States (or let's say, more honestly, so as not to be too unfair to American society, what *dominates* and even *governs* in the United States) and a certain Europe. And precisely in relationship to the problems we are discussing. For the "coalition" that has just formed around the United States remains fragile and heterogeneous. It is not only Western, and the "front" without front of this "war" without war does not pit the West against the East or against the Far East (indeed China ended up joining, in its own way, the coalition), or the Middle East, where every country condemned, more or less sincerely, the terrorism and agreed to fight it. Some are doing so with rhetoric alone, others by providing military and logistical support. As for the European nations and NATO, their commitment to the so-called "coalition" remains very complex; it varies from one country to the next and public opinion is far from being won over to the American initiatives. The shifts in these alliances, the warming in relations between Putin's Russia and Bush's United States, the at least partial solidarity of China in the same struggle, are changing the geopolitical landscape and strengthening, though also complicating, the American position, which needs all these agreements in order to act.

What would give me the most hope in the wake of all these upheavals is a potential difference between a new figure of Europe and the United States. I say this without any Eurocentrism. Which is why I am speaking of a *new* figure of Europe. Without forsaking its own memory, by drawing upon it, in fact, as an indispensable resource, Europe could make an essential contribution to the future of the international law we have been discussing.[15] I hope that there will be, "in Europe," "philosophers" able to measure up to the task (I use quotation marks here because these "philosophers" of European tradition will not necessarily be professional philosophers but jurists, politicians, citizens, even European noncitizens; and I use them because they might be "European," "in Europe," without living in the territory of a nation-state in Europe, finding themselves in fact very far away, distance and territory no longer having the significance they once did). But I persist in using this name "Europe," even if in quotation marks, because, in the long and patient deconstruction required for the transformation to-come, the experience Europe inaugurated at the time of the Enlightenment (*Lumières, Aufklärung, Illuminismo*) in the relationship between the political and the theological or, rather, the religious, though still un-even, unfulfilled, relative, and complex, will have left in European political space absolutely original marks with regard to religious doctrine (notice I'm not saying with regard to religion or faith but with regard to the authority of religious doctrine over the political).[16] Such marks can be found neither in the Arab world nor in the Muslim world, nor in the Far East, nor even, and here's the most sensitive point, in American democracy, in what *in fact* governs not the principles but the predominant reality of American political culture. This final point is complex and tricky. For such a philosophical "deconstruction" would have to operate not against something we would call the "United States" but against what today constitutes a certain American hegemony, one that actually dominates or marginalizes something in the U.S.'s own history, something that is also related to that strange "Europe" of the more or less incomplete Enlightenment I was talking about.

B O R R A D O R I :   What role do you see religion playing in this context?

D E R R I D A :   We have been speaking of a strange "war" without war. It often takes the form, at least on the surface, of a confrontation between two groups with a strong religious identification. On the one side, the only great European-style "democratic" power in the world that still has at once the death penalty in its judicial system and, despite the separation in principle between church and state, a fundamental biblical (and primarily Christian) reference in its official political discourse and the discourse of its political leaders: "God Bless America," the reference to "evildoers" or to the "axis of evil," and the first rallying cry (which was later retracted) of "infinite justice," would be but a few signs among so many others. And facing them, on the other side, an "enemy" that identifies itself as Islamic, Islamic extremist or fundamentalist, even if this does not necessarily represent authentic Islam and all Muslims are far from identifying with it. No more, in fact, than all Christians in the world identify with the United States's fundamentally Christian professions of faith.

I'm oversimplifying, but such oversimplification provides, I believe, at least the general outline of the overall situation. There would thus be a confrontation between two political theologies, both, strangely enough, issuing out of the same stock or common soil of what I would call an "Abrahamic" revelation. It is highly significant that the

epicenter, at least metonymically, of all these "wars" is the confrontation between the state of Israel (another "democracy" that has not cut
the umbilical cord with religious, indeed with ethnoreligious, authority
and that is strongly supported, though in a complicated way, by the
United States) and a virtual Palestinian state (one that, in preparing its
constitution, has not yet given up on declaring Islam the official state
religion and that is strongly supported, though in a complicated and
often perverse way, by Arab Muslim states).

I would like to hope that there will be, in "Europe" or in a certain
modern tradition of Europe, at the cost of a deconstruction that is still
finding its way, the possibility of another discourse and another politics, a way out of this double theologico-political program. "September
11"—whatever is ultimately put under this title—will thus have been at
once a sign and a price to pay, a very high price, to be sure, without any
possible redemption or salvation for the victims, but an important stage
in the process.

BORRADORI :   So you see an important role for Europe?

DERRIDA :   I hope for it, but I do not see it. I have not seen anything in the facts that would give rise to any certainty or knowledge.
Only a few signs to interpret. If there are responsibilities to be taken
and decisions to be made, responsibilities and decisions worthy of
these names, they belong to the time of a risk and of an act of faith. Beyond knowledge. For if I decide because *I know,* within the limits of
what *I know* and *know I must do,* then I am simply deploying a foresee-
able program and there is no decision, no responsibility, no event. As
for what I have just risked on the subject of "Europe," let's say that I'm
raising a few questions, in the midst of a certain night and on the basis
of a certain number of signs. I decipher, I wager, I hope. If I put so
many cautionary quotation marks around these proper names, beginning with "Europe," it is because I am not sure about anything. Especially not about Europe or the European community *such as it exists* or
announces itself *de facto.* It is a matter of thinking the "perhaps" of
which I spoke at such length in *Politics of Friendship* on the subject of
the *democracy to come.*

BORRADORI :   Sticking for a moment with Europe in its current state, how do you see Europe's political role and the possibilities
for it to exercise a real influence?

DERRIDA :   Right now, the French and German governments

are trying, timidly, to slow down or temper the hastiness or overzealousness of the United States, at least with respect to certain forms this "war on terrorism" might take. But little heed is taken here to voices coming from Europe. The major television networks speak only of the unconditional and enthusiastic support of England and Tony Blair beside the United States. France should do more and do better, it seems to me, to make an original voice heard. But it's a small country, even if it has nuclear weapons and a vote on the Security Council. As long as Europe does not have a unified military force sufficient for autonomous interventions, interventions that would be motivated, calculated, discussed, and deliberated in Europe, the fundamental premises of the current situation will not change, and we will not get any closer to the transformation I alluded to earlier (a new international law, a new international force in the service of new international institutions, a new concept and a new concrete figure of sovereignty, as well as other names, no doubt, for all these things to come).

I do not wish to grant too great a privilege to the juridical sphere, to international law and its institutions, even if I believe more than ever in their importance. Among the international institutions that matter most today, there's not only the UN but the International Monetary Fund and the G8, to name just two. Recall what happened recently in Genoa,[17] for example. Some have said, not without exaggeration but also not without some plausibility, that between the forces that are being mobilized today against globalization and those of international terrorism (in two words, "September 11") there is a common cause, a *de facto* alliance or collusion, if not an intentional conspiracy. Enormous effort will be required to introduce here all the necessary distinctions (both conceptual and practical), which will have to take into account the contradictions, that is, the autoimmunitary overdeterminations on which I've been insisting. Despite their apparently biological, genetic, or zoological provenance, these contradictions all concern, as you can see, what is beyond living being pure and simple. If only because they bear death in life.

BORRADORI: The question of international sovereignty appears to me extremely complicated. When the role of international organizations and of international law is pushed to its extreme, don't we end back up with a state model: a meta-state, a meta-law?

DERRIDA: This is an enormous problem, to be sure. The

major references to discuss here would be, for me, Kant and Hannah Arendt. Both of these thinkers called for an international law and yet excluded, indeed rejected, the hypothesis of a superstate or world government. It is not a question of going through, as is the case today, more or less temporary crises of sovereignty to end up at a world state. This absolutely new and unprecedented form of de-state-ification would allow us to think, beyond what Kant and Arendt formulated in a determined way, the new figure to come of an ultimate recourse, of a sovereignty (or rather, and more simply, since this term "sovereignty" is still too equivocal, still too theologico-political: a force or power, a -*cracy*), of a -*cracy* allied to, or even one with, not only law but justice. That is what I wished to bring out in the phrase "democracy to come (*la démocratie à venir*)." "Democracy to come" does not mean a future democracy that will one day be "present." Democracy will never exist in the present; it is not presentable, and it is not a regulative idea in the Kantian sense. But *there is the impossible,* whose promise democracy inscribes—a promise that risks and must always risk being perverted into a threat. There is the impossible, and the impossible remains impossible because of the aporia of the demos: the demos is *at once* the incalculable singularity of anyone, before any "subject," the possible undoing of the social bond by a secret to be respected, beyond all citizenship, beyond every "state," indeed every "people," indeed even beyond the current state of the definition of a living being as living "human" being, *and* the universality of rational calculation, of the equality of citizens before the law, the social bond of being together, with or without contract, and so on. And this impossible that *there is* remains ineffaceable. It is as irreducible as our exposure to what comes or happens. It is the exposure (the desire, the openness, but also the fear) that opens, that opens itself, that opens us to time, to what comes upon us, to what arrives or happens, to the event. To history, if you will, a history to be thought completely otherwise than from a teleological horizon, indeed from any horizon at all. When I say "the impossible that there is" I am pointing to this other regime of the "possible-impossible" that I try to think by questioning in all sorts of ways (for example, around questions of the gift, forgiveness, hospitality, and so on), by trying to "deconstruct," if you will, the heritage of such concepts as "possibility," "power," "impossibility," and so on. But I cannot develop this any further here.[18]

Of all the names grouped a bit too quickly under the category "political regimes" (and I do not believe that "democracy" ultimately designates a "political regime"), the inherited concept of democracy is the only one that welcomes the possibility of being contested, of contesting itself, of criticizing and indefinitely improving itself. If it were still the name of a regime, it would be the name of the only "regime" that presupposes its own perfectibility, and thus its own historicity—and that is responsive in as responsible a fashion as possible, I would say, to the aporia or the undecidability on the basis of which—a basis without basis—this regime gets decided. I'm quite aware that such formulations remain obscure, but if democracy is also a thing of the reason to come, this reason can present itself today, it seems to me, only in this penumbra. Yet I can already hear in it so many intractable injunctions.

B O R R A D O R I : What is your position concerning the concept of globalization and what is the relationship between globalization and cosmopolitanism?

D E R R I D A : As for globalization, or what I prefer to refer to in French, for reasons I give elsewhere, as *mondialisation,* the violence of "September 11" seems once again to attest to a series of contradictions.[19] Contradictions that are, in fact, destined to remain; for they are aporias that have to do, once again, it seems to me, with that autoimmunitary inevitability whose effects we are constantly registering. First, globalization does not take place in the places and at the moment it is said to take place. Second, everywhere it takes place without taking place, it is for better and for worse. Let me try to clarify these two points.

1. *It does not take place.* In an age of so-called globalization, an age where it is in the interest of some to speak about globalization and celebrate its benefits, the disparities between human societies, the social and economic inequalities, have probably never been greater and more spectacular (for the spectacle is in fact more easily "globalizable") in the history of humanity. Though the discourse in favor of globalization insists on the transparency made possible by teletechnologies, the opening of borders and of markets, the leveling of playing fields and the equality of opportunity, there have never been in the history of humanity, in absolute numbers, so many inequalities, so many cases of malnutrition, ecological disaster, or rampant epidemic (think, for example, of AIDS in Africa and of the millions of people we allow to die

and, thus, kill!). As for technological inequalities, think of the fact that less than 5 percent of humanity has access to the Internet, though in 1999 half of all American households did, and that the majority of servers are in English. At the very moment when the "end of work" is being touted, unprecedented numbers of people are being oppressed by work conditions or, inversely, are unable to find the work they desire.[20] Only certain countries, and in these countries only certain classes, benefit fully from globalization. Wealthy, northern countries hold the capital and control the instruments of economic decisions (G8, IMF, World Bank, and so on). If the organized perpetrators of the "September 11" attack are themselves among those who benefit from this so-called globalization (capitalist power, telecommunication, advanced technology, the openness of borders, and so on), they nonetheless claimed (unfairly, no doubt, though to great effect) to be acting in the name of those doomed by globalization, all those who feel excluded or rejected, disenfranchised, left by the wayside, who have only the means of the poor in this age of globalization (which is, today, television, an instrument that is never neutral) to witness the spectacle of the offensive prosperity of others.

A special place would have to be reserved here for Islamic cultures and populations in this context. In the course of the last few centuries, whose history would have to be carefully reexamined (the absence of an Enlightenment age, colonialization, imperialism, and so on), several factors have contributed to the geopolitical situation whose effects we are feeling today, beginning with the paradox of a marginalization and an impoverishment whose rhythm is proportional to demographic growth. These populations are not only deprived of access to what we call democracy (because of the history I just briefly recalled) but are even dispossessed of the so-called natural riches of the land, oil in Saudi Arabia, for example, or in Iraq, or even in Algeria, gold in South Africa, and so many other natural resources elsewhere. They are dispossessed at once by the owners, that is, the sellers, and by the exploiters and clients, in truth, by the nature of the game whereby the two parties engage in these more or less peaceful alliances or transactions. These "natural" riches are in fact the only nonvirtualizable and nondeteritorializable goods left today; they are the cause of many of the phenomena we have been discussing. With all these victims of supposed globalization, dialogue (at once verbal and peaceful) is not taking place.

Recourse to the worst violence is thus often presented as the only "response" to a "deaf ear." There are countless examples of this in recent history, well before "September 11." This is the logic put forward by all terrorisms involved in a struggle for freedom. Mandela explains quite well how his party, after years of nonviolent struggle and faced with a complete refusal of dialogue, resigned itself to having to take up arms. The distinction between civilian, military, and police is thus no longer pertinent.

From this point of view, globalization is not taking place. It is a simulacrum, a rhetorical artifice or weapon that dissimulates a growing imbalance, a new opacity, a garrulous and hypermediatized noncommunication, a tremendous accumulation of wealth, means of production, teletechnologies, and sophisticated military weapons, and the appropriation of all these powers by a small number of states or international corporations. And control over these is becoming *at once* easier and more difficult. The power to appropriate has such a structure (most often deterritorializable, virtualizable, capitalizable) that, at the very moment when it seems controllable by a small number (of states, for example), it escapes right into the hands of international nonstate structures and so tends toward dissemination in the very movement of its concentration. Terrorism of the "September 11" sort (wealthy, hypersophisticated, telecommunicative, anonymous, and without an assignable state) stems in part from this apparent contradiction.

2. And yet wherever it is believed *globalization is taking place, it is for better and for worse.* For better: discourses, knowledge, and models are transmitted better and faster. Democratization thus has more of a chance. Recent movements toward democratization in Eastern Europe owe a great deal, almost everything perhaps, to television, to the communication of models, norms, images, informational products, and so on. Nongovernmental institutions are more numerous and better known or recognized. Look at the efforts to institute the International Criminal Tribunal.

You spoke of "cosmopolitanism"—a formidable question, to be sure. Progress of cosmopolitanism, yes. We can celebrate it, as we do any access to citizenship, in this case, to world citizenship. But citizenship is also a limit, that of the nation-state; and we have already expressed our reservations with regard to the world state. I believe we should thus, beyond the old Greco-Christian cosmopolitical ideal (the Stoics, Saint Paul, Kant), see the coming of a universal alliance or solidarity that extends beyond the internationality of nation-states and thus beyond citizenship. This was one of the major themes of *Specters of Marx* and other texts. We are always led back to the same aporia: how to decide between, on the one hand, the positive and salutary role played by the "state" form (the sovereignty of the nation-state) and, thus, by democratic citizenship in providing protection against certain kinds of international violence (the market, the concentration of world capital, as well as "terrorist" violence and the proliferation of weapons) and, on the other hand, the negative or limiting effects of a state whose sovereignty remains a theological legacy, a state that closes its borders to noncitizens, monopolizes violence,[21] controls its borders, excludes or represses noncitizens, and so forth? Once again the state is both self-protecting and self-destroying, at once remedy and poison. The *pharmakon* is another name, an old name, for this autoimmunitary logic.[22] One can see it at work in the inevitable perversion of technoscientific advances (mastery over living beings, aviation, new informational teletechnologies, e-mail, the Internet, mobile phones, and so on) into weapons of mass destruction, into "terrorisms" of all kinds. Perversions that are all the more quick to occur when the progress in question is first of all a progress in speed and rhythm. Between the two supposed war leaders, the two metonymies, "bin Laden" and "Bush," the war of images and of discourses proceeds at an ever quickening pace over the airwaves, dissimulating and deflecting more and more quickly the truth that it reveals, accelerating the movement that substitutes dissimulation for revelation—and vice versa. For worse *and* for better, therefore; for the worst *and* the best, the worst that, it seems, *is* also the best. That is what remains terrible, terrifying, terrorizing; that is, on earth, *in terra,* in and beyond territories, the ultimate resource of all terrorisms.

B O R R A D O R I :   What is the relationship between globalization—or what you call *mondialisation*—and tolerance?

D E R R I D A :   If the term and theme of tolerance have come back of late, it is perhaps to accompany what is called in a rather simplistic and confused fashion the "return of the religious." The stakes of the violence we have been discussing are often, in fact, territorial, ethnic, and so on. Whether religion is being used as an alibi or not, it is commonly invoked, explicitly and literally on the side of "bin Laden" and in an implicit, disguised, but profound and fundamental fashion on the side of "Bush." Intolerance, then: how old is that concept? Can one still ask the question, "What is tolerance?" as Voltaire did in the first sentence of his article on the subject in the *Philosophical Dictionary*?[23] How would this article be written today? Who would write it, with and without Voltaire?

If we must be faithful to the memory of the Enlightenment, if we must not forget certain exemplary models in the struggle against intolerance, models that are part of our legacy, must we not today, and precisely out of fidelity, question anew without, however, contesting the very concept of tolerance? Considering everything that has marked this concept historically, would it be sufficient to inspire, enlighten, and guide our resistance to the violence being unleashed throughout the world today, in conditions that are in part unprecedented (but what part?—that is the ineluctable question), against all those who do not unconditionally respect certain orthodoxies? These dogmatic persecutions all wear the face of intolerance, to be sure, but is that enough to define them? Is tolerance, that "appurtenance of humanity" (Voltaire), the essence of what we must oppose to them?

It is once again a question of the Enlightenment, that is, of access to Reason in a certain public space, though this time in conditions that technoscience and economic or telemedia globalization have thoroughly transformed: in time and *as space,* in rhythms and proportions. If intellectuals, writers, scholars, professors, artists, and journalists do not, before all else, stand up together against such violence, their abdication will be at once irresponsible and suicidal.

Since not all figures of intolerance are new (anathema, excommunication, censorship, marginalization, distortion, control, programming, expulsion, exile, imprisonment, hostage taking, death threats, execution, and assassination, to name just a few), since they have never been separable from the very movement of culture, of tradition, of processes of legitimation, and of communities in general, and particularly ecclesiastical or state institutions, isn't one of our first responsibilities (intellectual, ethical, political, and even beyond those responsibilities attached to the citizen-subject of a particular nation-state or democracy) at once to analyze the laws of such recurrences and the emergence of what is new or unprecedented? Only by rigorously taking into account this novelty will we be able to adjust our ripostes and our acts of resistance. If we must, in order to carry this out, do a kind of historical genealogy of the concept of tolerance, if we must celebrate, study, and teach the admirable examples of all the struggles against intolerance, in Europe and elsewhere, from Voltaire to Zola to Sartre and so many others, if we must also take inspiration and draw lessons from them, a no less urgent task consists in trying to analyze that which today *no longer depends* on the same conditions or on the same axiomatic. An earthquake has completely transformed the landscape in which the ideal of tolerance took its first form a few centuries ago. We would have to analyze every mutation in the structure of public space, in the interpretation of democracy, theocracy, and their respective relations with international law (in its current state, in that which compels or calls it to transform itself and, thus, in that which remains largely to come within it), in the concepts of the nation-state and its sovereignty, in the notion of citizenship, in the transformation of public space by the media, which at once serve and threaten democracy, and so on.

Our acts of resistance must be, I believe, at once intellectual and political. We must join forces to exert pressure and organize ripostes, and we must do so on an international scale and according to new modalities, though always by analyzing and discussing the very foundations of our responsibility, its discourses, its heritage, and its axioms. The concept of tolerance would here constitute a prime example.

The article "Tolerance" in the *Philosophical Dictionary* is a tour de force, a kind of fax for the eighteenth century. It contains such a wealth of historical examples and analyses, so many axioms and principles to reflect upon, today, word by word. Yet this message calls for so many questions in return. We would have to be extremely vigilant, it seems to me, in interpreting this heritage. I would be tempted to say "yes and no" to each sentence, "yes but no," "yes, although, however," and so forth, swearing in a form that is other than that of the Christian apostles, the disciples, or the Quakers: "The apostles and disciples," writes Voltaire, "swore by yea and nay; the Quakers will not swear in any other form." The word "tolerance" is first of all marked by a religious war between Christians, or between Christians and non-Christians. Tolerance is a *Christian* virtue, or for that matter a *Catholic* virtue. The Christian must tolerate the non-Christian, but, even more so, the Catholic must let the Protestant be. Since we today feel that religious claims are at the heart of the violence (you will notice that I keep saying, in a deliberately general fashion, "violence," so as to avoid the equivocal and confused words "war" and "terrorism"), we resort to this good old word "tolerance": that Muslims agree to live with Jews and Christians, that Jews agree to live with Muslims, that believers agree to tolerate "infidels" or "nonbelievers" (for this is the word "bin Laden" used to denounce his enemies, and first of all the Americans). Peace would thus be tolerant cohabitation. In the United States, everything is done so as not to identify the enemy as the religious foreigner, the Muslim (and this is clearly better than the alternative, no matter the motivations). It is said over and over: "We are not fighting Islam; the three monotheistic religions have always taught tolerance." We know, of course, that this is largely inaccurate, but little matter, it's certainly better than the contrary. These official declarations of tolerance also obey a strategy: there are many, indeed more and more, Muslims in America and in Europe; it is thus necessary to reassure them, to gain assurance of their support, to dissociate them from "terrorism," to divide the enemy camp. Fair enough, that's part of fighting the good fight. Though I clearly prefer shows of tolerance to shows of intolerance, I nonetheless still have certain reservations about the word "tolerance" and the discourse it organizes. It is a discourse with religious roots; it is most often used on the side of those with power, always as a kind of condescending concession . . .

B O R R A D O R I :   You seem to understand tolerance as a form of charity . . .

D E R R I D A :   Indeed, tolerance is first of all a form of charity. A Christian charity, therefore, even if Jews and Muslims might seem to appropriate this language as well. Tolerance is always on the side of the "reason of the strongest," where "might is right"; it is a supplementary mark of sovereignty, the good face of sovereignty, which says to the other from its elevated position, I am letting you be, you are not insufferable, I am leaving you a place in my home, but do not forget that this is my home . . .

B O R R A D O R I :   Would you agree with the claim that tolerance is a condition of hospitality?

D E R R I D A :   No. Tolerance is actually the opposite of hospitality. Or at least its limit. If I think I am being hospitable because I am tolerant, it is because I wish to limit my welcome, to retain power and maintain control over the limits of my "home," my sovereignty, my "I can" (my territory, my house, my language, my culture, my religion, and so on). In addition to the religious meaning of tolerance whose origin we have just recalled, we should also mention its biological, genetic, or organicist connotations. In France, the phrase "threshold of tolerance" was used to describe the limit beyond which it is no longer decent to ask a national community to welcome any more foreigners, immigrant workers, and the like. François Mitterrand once used this unfortunate expression as a self-justifying word of caution: beyond a certain number of foreigners or immigrants who do not share our nationality, our language, our culture, and our customs, a quasi-organic and unpreventable—in short, a natural—phenomenon of rejection can be expected. I had at the time, in an article published in the newspaper *Libération,* condemned this organicist rhetoric and the "naturalist" politics it attempted to justify. It is true that Mitterrand later retracted this language, which he himself deemed unfortunate. But the word "tolerance" there ran up against its limit: we accept the foreigner, the other, the foreign body *up to a certain point,* and so not without restrictions. Tolerance is a conditional, circumspect, careful hospitality.

B O R R A D O R I :   Tolerance thus amounts to granting someone permission to continue living on?

D E R R I D A :   Indeed, and so a limited tolerance is clearly preferable to an absolute intolerance. But tolerance remains a scrutinized hospitality, always under surveillance, parsimonious and protective of its sovereignty. In the best of cases, it's what I would call a conditional hospitality, the one that is most commonly practiced by individuals, families, cities, or states. We offer hospitality only on the condition that the other follow our rules, our way of life, even our language, our culture, our political system, and so on. That is hospitality as it is commonly understood and practiced, a hospitality that gives rise, with certain conditions, to regulated practices, laws, and conventions on a national and international—indeed, as Kant says in a famous text, a "cosmopolitical"—scale.[24] But pure or unconditional hospitality does not consist in such an *invitation* ("I invite you, I welcome you into *my home,* on the condition that you adapt to the laws and norms of my territory, according to my language, tradition, memory, and so on"). Pure and unconditional hospitality, hospitality *itself,* opens or is in advance open to someone who is neither expected nor invited, to whomever arrives as an absolutely foreign *visitor,* as a new *arrival,* nonidentifiable and unforeseeable, in short, wholly other. I would call this a hospitality of *visitation* rather than *invitation.* The visit might actually be very dangerous, and we must not ignore this fact, but would a hospitality without risk, a hospitality backed by certain assurances, a hospitality protected by an immune system against the wholly other, be true hospitality? Though it's ultimately true that suspending or suppressing the immunity that protects me from the other might be nothing short of life-threatening.

An unconditional hospitality is, to be sure, practically impossible to live; one cannot in any case, and by definition, organize it. Whatever happens, happens, whoever comes, comes (*ce qui arrive arrive*), and that, in the end, is the only event worthy of this name. And I well recognize that this concept of pure hospitality can have no legal or political status. No state can write it into its laws. But without at least the thought of this pure and unconditional hospitality, of hospitality *itself,* we would have no concept of hospitality in general and would not even be able to determine any rules for conditional hospitality (with its rituals, its legal status, its norms, its national or international conventions). Without this thought of pure hospitality (a thought that is also, in its own way, an experience), we would not even have the idea of the other, of the alterity of the other, that is, of someone who enters into our lives without having been invited. We would not even have the idea of love or of "living together (*vivre ensemble*)" with the other in a way that is not a part of some totality or "ensemble." Unconditional hospitality, which is neither juridical nor political, is nonetheless the condition of the political and the juridical. For these very reasons, I am not even sure whether it is ethical, insofar as it does not even depend on a decision. But what would an "ethics" be without hospitality?[25]

Paradox, aporia: these two hospitalities are at once heterogeneous and indissociable. Heterogeneous because we can move from one to the other only by means of an absolute leap, a leap beyond knowledge and power, beyond norms and rules. Unconditional hospitality is transcendent with regard to the political, the juridical, perhaps even to the ethical. But—and here is the indissociability—I cannot open the door, I cannot expose myself to the coming of the other and offer him or her anything whatsoever without making this hospitality effective, without, in some concrete way, giving *something determinate.* This determina-

tion will thus have to re-inscribe the unconditional into certain conditions. Otherwise, it gives nothing. What remains unconditional or absolute (*unbedingt,* if you will) risks being nothing at all if conditions
(*Bedingungen*) do not make of it some thing (*Ding*). Political, juridical,
and ethical responsibilities have their place, if they take place, only in
this transaction—which is each time unique, like an event—between
these two hospitalities, the unconditional and the conditional.

B O R R A D O R I :   The fact that these two poles are at once heterogeneous and indissociable is, philosophically, very difficult to think.
How can political discourse assimilate it? Might the modern ideal of
cosmopolitanism be the solution?

D E R R I D A :   The idea of cosmopolitanism emerges out of a very
old tradition that goes back, as we have already noted, to Saint Paul in
his letter to the Ephesians, to the Stoics, and to Kant. In his short treatise *Perpetual Peace,* Kant explains why we should probably give up
the idea of a "world republic" (*Weltrepublik*) but not the idea of a cosmopolitical law, "the idea of a law of world citizenship," which is "no
high-flown or exaggerated notion."[26] It would be, on the contrary, the
condition for continually approaching perpetual peace. But if we must
in fact cultivate the spirit of this tradition (as I believe most international institutions have done since World War I), we must also try to
adjust the limits of this tradition to our own time by questioning the
ways in which they have been defined and determined by the ontotheological, philosophical, and religious discourses in which this cosmopolitical ideal was formulated. This is no small task, and we do not
have time even to begin the discussion here.[27] What I call "democracy
to come" would go beyond the limits of cosmopolitanism, that is, of a
world citizenship. It would be more in line with what lets singular beings (anyone) "live together," there where they are not yet defined by
citizenship, that is, by their condition as lawful "subjects" in a state or
legitimate members of a nation-state or even of a confederation or
world state. It would involve, in short, an alliance that goes beyond the
"political" as it has been commonly defined (a designation usually reserved for the state or citizen body in a nation linked to a territory, even
if, as Schmitt reminds us, the state is not the only form of the political).
This does not, however, lead to a depoliticization—quite the contrary.
Yet it does require another thought and another putting into practice of
the concept of the "political" and the concept "world"—which is not

the same as "cosmos." That said, and because all of this will remain for some time out of reach, I believe that everything must be done to extend the privilege of citizenship in the world: too many men and women are deprived of citizenship in so many ways. Even when they are not outright refused the title of citizen, the "human rights and citizens' rights" to which they might lay claim are severely limited.

B O R R A D O R I : It seems to me that this deconstruction of the concept of cosmopolitanism implies a deconstruction of the idea of the state.

D E R R I D A : Cosmopolitanism as it is classically conceived presupposes some form of state sovereignty, something like a world state, whose concept can be theologico-political or secular (that is, secular in its filiation, though secretly theologico-political). For a deconstruction to be as effective as possible, it should not, in my view, oppose the state head on and in a unilateral fashion. In many contexts, the state might be the best protection against certain forces and dangers. And it can secure the citizenship of which we have been speaking. The responsibilities to be taken with regard to the state thus differ according to the context, and there is no relativism in recognizing this. But, ultimately, these necessary transactions must not obstruct a deconstruction of the state form, which should, one day, no longer be the last word of the political. This movement of "deconstruction" did not wait for us to begin speaking about "deconstruction"; it has been underway for a long time, and it will continue for a long time. It will not take the form of a suppression of the sovereign state at one particular moment in time but will pass through a long series of still unforeseeable convulsions and transformations, through as yet unheard-of forms of shared and limited sovereignty. The idea and even the practice of shared sovereignty, that is, of a limitation of sovereignty, has been accepted for a long time now. And yet such a divisible or shared sovereignty already contradicts the pure concept of sovereignty. As Bodin, Hobbes, and others have pointed out, sovereignty has to be and must remain indivisible. The deconstruction of sovereignty has thus already begun, and it will have no end, for we neither can nor should renounce purely and simply the values of autonomy or freedom, or those of power or force, which are inseparable from the very idea of law. How are we to reconcile unconditional *auto-nomy* (the foundation of any pure ethics, of the sovereignty of the subject, of the ideal of emancipation and of freedom, and

so on) and the *hetero-nomy* that, as I recalled a moment ago, imposes itself upon all unconditional hospitality worthy of this name, upon every
welcoming of the other as other? The decision, if there is one, is always
a decision of the other, as I have tried to show elsewhere.[28] Responsibility for a decision, if there is any and if one must answer for it,
amounts each time, in an irreducibly singular way, without any normative program and without any assured knowledge, to a transaction between the imperative for autonomy and the imperative for heteronomy,
the two being equally imperious.

B O R R A D O R I : We have spoken about tolerance, hospitality,
and cosmopolitanism. How do you see the problem of human rights?
What is the relationship between the notion of right and that of hospitality? A right presupposes someone who avails him- or herself of that
right in relationship to another, that is, more precisely, in a social context, in an organized community. If the concept of state, which is the
concept of a juridically organized community, is no longer the last
word of the political, how are you going to maintain the idea of human
rights?

D E R R I D A : Actually, it is today more and more often in the
name of human rights and their universality that the sovereign authority of the state is called into question, that international courts of justice
are established, that heads of state or military leaders are judged after
having been removed from the judicial institutions of their own state.
The concept of a crime against humanity or of a war crime no longer
falls under the authority of national judicial institutions and sovereign
states. At least in principle. You know about the enormous problems
we are now facing in this regard.

We must (*il faut*) more than ever stand on the side of human
rights. *We need (il faut) human rights.* We are in need of them and they
are in need, for there is always a lack, a shortfall, a falling short, an in-
sufficiency; human rights are never sufficient. Which alone suffices to
remind us that they are not natural. They have a history—one that is recent, complex, and unfinished. From the French Revolution and the
first Declarations right up through the declaration following World
War II, human rights have been continually enriched, refined, clarified,
and defined (women's rights, children's rights, the right to work, rights
to education, human rights beyond "human rights and citizens' rights,"
and so on). To take this historicity and this perfectibility into account

in an affirmative way we must never prohibit the most radical questioning possible of all the concepts at work here: the humanity of man (the "proper of man" or of the human, which raises the whole question of nonhuman living beings, as well as the question of the history of recent juridical concepts or performatives such as a "crime against humanity"), and then the very concept of rights or of law (*droit*), and even the concept of history.

For justice does not end with law.[29] Nor even with duties (*devoirs*), which, in a still wholly paradoxical way, "must," "should" go beyond obligation and debt. I tried to show elsewhere that any pure ethics must begin beyond law, duty, and debt. Beyond law, that's easy to understand. Beyond duty, that's almost unthinkable. Recall what Kant says: a moral action must be accomplished not only "according to duty (*pflichtmässig*)" but "from duty (*eigentlich aus Pflicht*)," "out of pure duty (*aus reiner Pflicht*)."[30] Once we have followed Kant this far, as we no doubt ought to do, a leap is still required. If I act out of pure duty, *because I must do so, because I owe it,* because there is a debt I must repay, then two limits come to taint any pure ethicity or pure morality. On the one hand, I subordinate my action to a knowledge (I am supposed to know what this pure duty is in the name of which I must act). Yet an action that simply obeys knowledge is but a calculable consequence, the deployment of a norm or program. It does not engage any decision or any responsibility worthy of these names. On the other hand, by acting out of pure duty, I acquit myself of a debt and thus complete the economic circle of an exchange; I do not exceed in any way the totalization or reappropriation that something like a gift, hospitality, or the event itself should exceed. We must thus be dutiful beyond duty, we must go beyond law,[31] tolerance, conditional hospitality, economy, and so on. But to go beyond does not mean to discredit that which we exceed. Whence the difficulty of a responsible transaction between two orders or, rather, between order and its beyond. Whence all these aporias, and the inevitability of an autoimmunitary risk.

B O R R A D O R I : This sounds like a regulative idea, though I know you do not like this expression . . .

D E R R I D A : That's true. But my reservations are not straightforward objections. They are precisely reservations. For lack of anything better, if we can say this about a regulative idea, the regulative idea remains perhaps an ultimate reservation. Though such a last recourse

risks becoming an alibi, it retains a certain dignity; I cannot swear that
I will not one day give in to it.

I have, in short, *three sorts* of reservations. Some concern first of all
the very loose way this notion of a regulative idea is currently used, outside its strictly Kantian context. In this case, the regulative idea remains
in the order of the *possible,* an ideal possible, to be sure, one that is infinitely deferred, but one that participates in what at the end of an infinite history would still fall into the realm of the possible, the realm of
what is virtual or potential, of what is within the power of someone,
some "I can," to reach, in theory, in a form that is not wholly freed from
all teleological ends.

To all this I would oppose, in the first place, everything I placed
earlier under the title of the im-possible, of what must remain (in a non-
negative fashion) foreign to the order of my possibilities, to the order of
the "I can," to the theoretical, descriptive, constative, and performative
orders (inasmuch as this latter still implies a power guaranteed for
some "I" by conventions that neutralize the pure eventfulness of the
event). That is what I meant earlier by heteronomy, by a law come from
the other, by a responsibility and decision of the other—of the other in
me, an other greater and older than I am. This im-possible is not priv-
ative. It is not the inaccessible, and it is not what I can indefinitely
defer: it is announced to me, sweeps down upon me, precedes me, and
seizes me *here now,* in a nonvirtualizable way, in actuality and not po-
tentiality. It comes upon me from on high, in the form of an injunction
that does not simply wait on the horizon, that never leaves me in peace
and will not let me put it off until later. Such an urgency cannot be *ide-
alized,* no more than the other as other can. This im-possible is thus
not a regulative *idea* or *ideal.* It is what is most undeniably *real.* Like
the other. Like the irreducible and nonappropriable difference of the
other.

Then, in the second place, the responsibility of what remains to be
decided or done (in actuality) cannot consist in following, applying, or
realizing a norm or rule. When there is a determinable rule, I know
what must be done, and as soon as such knowledge dictates the law, action follows knowledge as a calculable consequence: one *knows* what
path to take, one no longer hesitates; the decision then no longer decides anything but simply gets deployed with the automatism attributed to machines. There is no longer any place for justice or responsi-

bility (whether juridical, political, or ethical). Finally, in the third place, if we come back this time to the strict meaning Kant gave to the *regulative* use of ideas (as opposed to their *constitutive* use), we would, in order to say anything on this subject and, especially, in order to appropriate such terms, have to subscribe to the entire Kantian architectonic and critique. I cannot do this or even decide to do this with any seriousness here. We would have to begin by asking about what Kant calls "those differences in the interest of reason,"[32] the *imaginary* (the *focus imaginarius*, that point toward which all the lines directing the rules of understanding—which is not reason—tend and converge, the point they thus indefinitely *approximate*), the necessary *illusion*, which need not necessarily deceive us, the figure of an approach or approximation (*zu nähern*) that tends indefinitely toward rules of universality, and especially the indispensable use of the *as if* (*als ob*).[33] We cannot treat this here, but you can imagine how circumspect I would be to appropriate in any rigorous way this idea of a regulative idea. Let us not forget, since we have been talking so much about the world and about worldwide movements, that the very idea of *world* remains a *regulative idea* for Kant,[34] the second one, between two others that are themselves, so to speak, two forms of sovereignty: the "myself" (*Ich selbst*), as soul or as thinking nature, and God.

These are a few of the reasons why, without ever giving up on reason and a certain "interest of reason," I hesitate to use the expression "regulative idea" when speaking of the to come or of the democracy to come.

BORRADORI: You thus follow Kierkegaard in this regard.

DERRIDA: No doubt, as always. But a Kierkegaard who would not necessarily be Christian, and you can imagine how difficult that is to think. I tried to explain myself on this subject elsewhere.[35] I always make *as if* I subscribed to the *as if*'s of Kant (which I am never quite able to do), or *as if* Kierkegaard helped me to think beyond his own Christianity, *as if* in the end he did not want to know that he was not Christian or refused to admit that he did not know what being Christian means. (In the end, I cannot quite bring myself to believe this, indeed I cannot quite bring myself to believe in general, that is, what is normally called "to believe.")

But what makes the rule of such an interview impossible, impracticable, is a law of the genre that orders us always *to make as if: as if* everything we are speaking about in a quasi-spontaneous fashion had not already been treated elsewhere, by others or by ourselves, in already published writings and with more developed arguments. As you can see, I believe I must, at each moment, make as if I were at once honoring and breaking our contract.

DECONSTRUCTING
TERRORISM

Derrida

While Habermas's work has been almost exclusively in social and political philosophy, Derrida has contributed to an array of philosophical
fields: from the philosophy of literature to linguistics, from the philosophy of history to ethics and politics. His ethical and political views are
contained in several treatises that started to appear in the 1980s,
roughly twenty years after he composed his first philosophical works.
For this reason, it is commonly believed that Derrida came to these
topics late in life, perhaps like Locke, Kant, Spinoza, and Hegel, for
whom discussions of ethics and politics gained center stage only in the
second half of their careers. But this is not an entirely accurate impression, for Derrida has been implicitly engaging ethical and political considerations as long as he has been writing. The reason why his contribution to these fields was not readily detected before it was presented
in a more explicit and systematic fashion is that, from very early on,
Derrida transformed the outlook of these disciplines to such a degree

that his readers often did not even recognize them anymore. "Deconstruction" is the name Derrida has given to such transformation.

Deconstruction seeks to disassemble any discourse standing as a "construction."[1] Given that philosophy is about ideas, beliefs, and values constructed within a conceptual scheme,[2] what is being deconstructed is the way in which they hold together in a given scheme. Unlike a general method or analytical procedure, deconstruction is a highly individualized type of intervention aimed at destabilizing the structural priorities of each particular construction. The reason why Derrida pursues destabilization rather than, say, consolidation is that philosophical constructions seem to him to depend on seemingly clear-cut oppositions and irreducible conceptual pairs: spiritual and material, universal and particular, eternal and temporal, male and female are just some examples. These pairs raise two problems: on the one hand, as a result of their extreme rigidity, all that does not fit neatly within their oppositional relation tends to be marginalized or even suppressed; on the other hand, these oppositions impose a hierarchical order. For example, in the Platonic framework later appropriated by Christian thought, truth and goodness coincide with the spiritual, universal, eternal, and male side of the opposition at the expense of the material, particular, temporal, and female side.

Deconstruction first sets out to identify the conceptual construction of a given theoretical field, whether it is religion, metaphysics, or ethical and political theory, which usually makes use of one or more irreducible pairs. Second, it highlights the hierarchical ordering of the pairs. Third, it inverts or subverts their ordering by showing that the terms placed at the bottom—material, particular, temporal, and female, in this example—could with justification be moved to the top—in place of the spiritual, universal, eternal, and male. While the inversion reveals that the hierarchical arrangement reflects certain strategic and ideological choices rather than a description of features intrinsic to the pairs, the fourth and final move is to produce a third term for each oppositional pair, which complicates the original load-bearing structure beyond recognition. If the first two moves take on the description of a given conceptual construction, the final two are aimed at deforming it, reforming it, and eventually transforming it. Because deconstruction's work is so minutely tailored to the specificity of its object, Derrida likes to refer to it as "intervention."

Under the pressure of deconstruction, classical philosophical constructions assume the semblance of baroque façades: no longer linear, they now look twisted and deformed, internally complicated by overlapping patterns and an endless play of perspectives. Ultimately, they are transformed beyond recognition, their original motif stretched to its limits and possibly extended beyond them. For Derrida experiencing the limits of philosophy positively changes the way we think. The acknowledgment of limits protects thought from dogmatism as well as from excessive self-assurance and injects into it a healthy sense of systematic incompleteness and doubt. Socrates used to enrage his fellow Athenians by exposing them to the limits of their own thinking: all of a sudden, in the course of their dialogues with him, scholars, rhetoricians, poets, generals, and even self-proclaimed philosophers felt paralyzed by dilemmas, paradoxes, and aporias. Socrates' distinctive dedication to philosophy shows how much he treasured the encounter with those limits—the sense of challenge, the risk, and surprise that they propagate, as soon as we meet them. Deconstruction follows Socrates in this human and inhuman tradition of testing the limits of thought.

In our dialogue, Derrida engaged the themes of terror as a psychological and metaphysical state as well as terrorism as a political category. Again in Socratic fashion, he laid out a number of seeming conceptual dead ends that at first plainly disoriented me. In the present essay, my aim is to unravel the productive aspects of these apparent conceptual dead ends, or aporias, in which resides the extreme originality of Derrida's thought. This dialogue is a quintessential example of his unique style of thinking: a fascinating mix of erudition and exuberance, conceptual rigor and linguistic genius, existential depth and intellectual sophistication, timelessness and timeliness.

I would like to begin by framing Derrida's approach to ethics and politics, examining a topic that consistently underscored our dialogue but never quite made it to the surface. This is the concept of forgiveness, which is crucial both theoretically and practically to questions surrounding war crimes, genocide, and terrorism. Exploring Derrida's notion of forgiveness will also provide the reader with a clear example of deconstruction at work, illuminating a path similar to the one Derrida took in commenting on the attacks of 9/11 and global terrorism. As we shall see, Derrida defines forgiveness as the impossible task of forgiving the unforgivable. This is why, for him, forgiveness cannot be reduced to any legal or moral boundaries but only appreciated whenever and however it arises.

Derrida's conclusion on forgiveness will give me the opportunity to explore the significance of boundaries and limits in deconstruction alongside the relations of inclusion and exclusion that they establish. I will then clarify the role of boundaries, which is essential to understanding Derrida's interpretation of 9/11 as an unnamable event. I will then examine Derrida's interpretation of terrorism as a symptom of an autoimmune crisis, whose cause he attributes in part to the complex heritage of the Cold War as well as to the unhappy marriage between religion and the global information network.

A salient moment of the dialogue is Derrida's critique of tolerance, where he sharply disagrees with Habermas. Derrida's views on the inadequacy of tolerance will allow me to identify some key elements of Derrida's relationship with Kant and Enlightenment philosophy. As I will show, Derrida opposes Kant on the ground that tolerance is anything but a neutral moral demand. Yet it is precisely from Kant that Derrida takes off in his rejection of tolerance in favor of hospitality.

I shall conclude with a discussion of Derrida's thinking about the nature of violence, a concept that is essential to any appraisal of terrorism. The discussion of violence will open the way to the crucial issue of secularism in today's politics. Derrida believes that the post-9/11 geopolitical scenario consists of two theologically infused political entities: the United States and its declared enemy. This situation raises new possibilities for the most secularized political interlocutor Derrida sees available: Europe. Beyond the alternative programs of Eurocentrism and anti-Eurocentrism, which Derrida declares both unforgettable and exhausted, he points to a third way. This way does not involve the European Community as it exists but the memory of a European promise that is yet to be fulfilled: democracy and emancipation for all. This means, for Derrida as it does for Habermas, that the Enlightenment is not dead. However, in order to be effective against terrorism, Derrida demands an endless updating of the Enlightenment agenda: for we need to work "on this Enlightenment of this time, this time that is ours—*today.*"[3]

Forgiveness Deconstructed

In the face of the bloody traumas of history, from the betrayals arising during civil wars to the terrorist slaughters of civilians, Derrida calls for a rigorous reflection on the notion of forgiveness. The rigor he is invoking concerns the study of this concept not as an abstract entity but as it is employed in concrete historical and cultural contexts.

> In all the scenes of repentance, confession, forgiveness, or apology which have multiplied on the geopolitical scene since the last war, and in an accelerated fashion in the past few years, one sees not only individuals, but also entire communities, professional corporations, the representatives of ecclesiastical hierarchies, sovereigns, and heads of state ask for "forgiveness." They do this in an Abrahamic language which is not (in the case of Japan and Korea, for example) that of the dominant religion of their society, but which has already become the universal idiom of law, of politics, of the economy, or of diplomacy: at the same time the agent and the symptom of this internationalization.[4]

Without the presence of an almighty god of Abrahamic ancestry, the two essential questions of forgiveness would not find an answer: namely, what calls for forgiveness and who calls upon forgiveness. In ancient Greek polytheism or Native American animism, just to name two different structures of religious belief, forgiveness does not occupy a prominent place. Whenever the Greek gods were angered by human arrogance or bad judgment they would mercilessly take it out on individuals, entire cities, and even the progeny of the culprit. A deeply felt communion with nature rather than the emendation of improper behavior is at the center of Native American animism, where the figure of the shaman does not ask the individual or the community for acts of confession or repentance.

No matter where forgiveness appears, it belongs to a specific religious heritage, which Derrida defines as Abrahamic "in order to bring together Judaism, the Christianities, and the Islams."[5] A remarkable occurrence in the late twentieth century geopolitical scene is that contexts geographically and culturally very distant from the Abrahamic roots of Western monotheism have absorbed it to the point of molding their international profile in accordance with it. This is the case of Japan, which publicly apologized to South Korea for the sexual enslavement of thousands of women during World War II.

Derrida's first deconstructive move is to locate the Abrahamic root in the meaning of forgiveness, which links forgiveness to the possibility of expiation. This quickly leads him to expose several pairs of opposites: finite and infinite, immanent and transcendent, temporal and eternal, reparable and irreparable, expiable and inexpiable, possible and impossible. Unearthing these oppositional pairs is Derrida's second move. His third deconstructive move consists in showing that these pairs are hierarchically arranged. For punishment to be calculable, it needs to be finite, immanent, and temporally delimited; accordingly, forgiveness is bestowed limitedly to expiable and reparable cases. Only under such conditions does forgiveness become the ground for salvation, reconciliation, redemption, and atonement. His fourth and final move is to upset the workings of the pairs by suggesting that the Abrahamic axiom, according to which forgiveness applies only to what is reparable, is founded on a paradox. If forgiveness forgives what can be expiated, is it really forgiveness that we are discussing? If not, can we forgive the unforgivable?

Forgiveness, in the Abrahamic sense, has significantly influenced Western political discourse, which Derrida renames the geopolitics of forgiveness. In this regard, he cites a declaration made by Jacques Chirac, then prime minister of France, about anti-Semitic crimes under the collaborationist Vichy Republic: "France that day performed the irreparable." Several theorists of the Holocaust agree with the position voiced by Chirac: if no punishment proportionate to a crime can be found, the crime remains indeed unforgivable.[6] Clearly, the Holocaust is the quintessential example. Derrida flatly opposes the symmetry between punishing and forgiving as well as the binary conceptual organization that underlies it.

> If I say, "I forgive you on the condition that, asking forgiveness, you would thus have changed and would no longer be the same," do I forgive? What do I forgive? And whom? . . . Does one forgive *something*, a crime, a fault, a wrong, that is to say, an act or a moment which does not exhaust the person incriminated, and at the limit does not become confused with the guilty, who thus remains irreducible to it? Or rather, does

one forgive *someone,* absolutely, no longer marking the limit between the injury, the moment of the fault, and on the other side the person taken as responsible or culpable? And in the latter case (the question *"whom?"*) does one ask forgiveness of the victim, or some absolute witness, of God, of such a God, for example, who prescribed forgiving the other (person) in order to merit being forgiven in turn?[7]

What are we to do with forgiveness? Derrida believes that what can be authentically forgiven is in fact only the unforgivable, whether we are talking about the act of whoever is guilty or the guilty agent herself. Forgiveness, for him, forgives both the evil intention (who) and the evil action (what) for exactly what they are: evil. And this is an evil that, insofar as it is unredeemable, can repeat itself in the future. Evil, writes Derrida, "is capable of repeating itself, unforgivably, without transformation, without amelioration, without repentance and promise."[8]

Two types of forgiveness can thus be distinguished. The first is "conditional forgiveness," whose condition is the calculability of the punishment. This type of forgiveness often follows an act of repentance in which the guilty party will promise not to engage ever again in whatever demanded forgiveness. The second type of forgiveness is termed "unconditional" because it consists in forgiving the unforgivable without conditions. And yet, can unconditional forgiveness really exist? Can we possibly forgive what cannot be forgiven?

> If I say, as I think, that forgiveness is mad, and that it must remain a madness of the impossible, this is certainly not to exclude or disqualify it. It is even, perhaps, the only thing that arrives, that surprises, like a revolution, the ordinary course of history, politics and law. Because that means that it remains heterogeneous to the order of politics or of the juridical as they are ordinarily understood. One could never, in the ordinary sense of the words, found a politics or law on forgiveness.[9]

The unconditional type of forgiveness belongs to the realm of the incalculable, the immeasurable, and maybe even the impossible. In principle, it is impossible or at least inconceivable to forgive the unforgivable. This could sound like the epitaph to the whole question of forgiveness: a concept that makes sense only in self-contradiction. Yet, this is not Derrida's conclusion. He does admit that unconditional forgiveness belongs to "madness" but also stresses that it "arrives," in the strong sense of something unexpected that arrives as a surprise, upsetting the "ordinary course of history, politics and law." Without the experience of unconditional forgiveness there would be no forgiveness at all.

Whenever conditions are put on forgiveness, a proportionate, calculable punishment corresponds to whomever or whatever is being forgiven. In this sense, conditional forgiveness concurs with law and politics, but it gets reduced to a therapy of reconciliation. If, instead, forgiveness is to be kept distinct from reconciliation, as Derrida thinks it should, it ends up becoming unconditional. The conditional and the unconditional are two sharply separate and yet corollary meanings of forgiveness. Conditional forgiveness belongs to the order of law and politics, of pragmatic negotiations and calculable debts. Unconditional forgiveness, which is the act of forgiving the unforgivable, cannot be reconciled with law and politics because it allows no pragmatic negotiation or equal exchange.

> The secret of this experience remains. It must remain intact, inaccessible to law, to politics, even to morals: absolute. But I would make of this transpolitical principle a political principle, a political rule or position taking: it is necessary also in politics to respect the secret, that which exceeds the political or that which is no longer in the juridical domain.[10]

We know all too well that there is a distinction between legal reconciliation and proper (and perhaps only private) forgiveness. It is very easy to imagine a case of a victim who has already forgiven the criminal at whose hands she suffered even as she is demanding legal prosecution. By the same token, it is very plausible that a victim may never forgive, even after a process of acquittal or amnesty. The conclusion is that the meaning of forgiveness remains enigmatic: we cannot reduce it to a simple or univocal definition. Its oscillation between the two orders of the conditional and the unconditional hints at its reach as well as its ineffability.

By indicating a territory beyond history, politics, and law, Derrida accomplishes two concurrent goals: he exposes the concept of forgiveness to the boundaries imposed on it by its heritage—Christian, Judaic, and Islamic monotheism—and pushes forgiveness beyond its limits, transforming it from within while complicating it in order to expose its multiple implications.

The Limits of Intervention

Intervening at the limits of a concept means to redefine it, as well as the network of relations in which it is inscribed. Geography can serve as an example to clarify the role played by limits and boundaries in the definition of a concept. In geography a political or physical entity, such as a desert or an ocean, is demarcated by drawing boundaries around it. A boundary is the line where one thing ends and another begins. Like geography, the philosophical job of clarifying the meaning of concepts, categories, and values as well as theoretical fields such as ethics and politics consists in drawing boundaries around them.[11]

Derrida's reflection on the notion of boundary focuses on the fact that a boundary is as much about identification as it is about exclusion. Sometimes the implications of this double function are trivial; sometimes they are not. Take for instance Mont Blanc, the highest mountain in Europe, which is half French and half Italian. The line of separation between France and Italy is the product of a benign convention, which is not only recognized by everyone *as* convention but bears innocuous consequences: nobody really cares about which rocks and blades of grass are to be included or excluded from each country. By contrast, sometimes conventions are not as benign and highlight the pain that inclusions and exclusions may cause. The Berlin Wall is an example where exclusion did not apply to rocks and blades of grass but rather to people who were suddenly separated from families and friends.

Derrida's contention is that traditional philosophy tends to evade the double function of boundaries by downplaying their contingency. In its search for ultimate truth and infallible knowledge, the Western philosophical tradition denies the potential instability intrinsic to any contingent boundary. The suppression of the contingency of boundaries and of the structural ambiguity that pertains to their double function carries with it a substantial political import.

Believing in the contingency of boundaries was certainly not a small matter for family members separated by the Berlin Wall; for to affirm it was probably the only way to survive an absurd and unjust separation. By contrast, think about a high official of the former Democratic Republic of Germany who firmly believed, as the Berlin Wall was being built in August 1961, that it simply materialized the Iron Curtain, namely, the idea of an essential and not contingent separation between justice and injustice, future and past, progress and decadence. Siding with either the conventionalist or the essentialist interpretation of the Berlin Wall would have meant to implicitly subscribe to the relations of inclusion and exclusion that depended on it. Engaging philosophy as it is presented to us by a certain tradition inclines us to buy into the normative assumptions behind its conceptual organization: its categories, distinctions, oppositions, and demarcation of areas such as ethics and politics. In Derrida's mind, there is thus an ethical and political urgency to understand what we are subscribing to and making ourselves responsible for.

Yet, assuming philosophical responsibility is not limited to disclosing the political import of what a boundary includes or excludes but extends to calling into question the way in which we understand the identity of what it encircles. The example of the Berlin Wall is again useful. In the East German official's mind, the Wall symbolically encircled the essence of the egalitarian and emancipatory promise of communism. The way in which the Wall established what is within it—communism—is through the exclusion of what lay beyond it—capitalism. A relation of mutual exclusion would thus be in place between the two worlds understood as self-contained totalities.

This conception of identity entails that it be internally homogeneous, which is what Derrida deems to be the fault of traditional metaphysics. On one side of the Wall lay corruption, injustice, and bourgeois civilization; on the other side, the emancipated communist utopia. In this picture, one side is perfectly immune to the other.[12] By contrast, Derrida objects, traces of what a totality explicitly excludes are always silently contained within it. Following a Derridean line of argument one could illustrate this point by highlighting the presence of separated family members living on either side of the Wall, for they represented an instance of those traces. Where did they belong? How far back would family ties have justified a policy of family reunification? The great monuments of the Prussian Empire as well as the urban grid of most Eastern German cities raise similar questions: wouldn't they reveal the sedimentation of a bourgeois social structure? Might they be still silently affecting the way in which even orthodox communists relate to each other, both in private and in public situations?

For Derrida, reflecting critically on the nature of limits and boundaries transforms our well-established way of thinking about identity as a homogeneous and self-enclosed totality. As the example of the Berlin Wall shows, a given identity may not be perfectly homogeneous because it includes traces of what it explicitly excludes. Deconstruction searches for these traces and uses them to give voice to that which doesn't fit the dominant set of inclusions and exclusions. Deconstructive interventions detotalize self-enclosed totalities by placing them face to face with their internal differentiation.

Why Do We Call "It" 9/11?

The traces deconstruction insists on are disseminated first and foremost in language. In his reading of the terrorist attack of 9/11, Derrida starts from reflecting upon the significance of naming such an occurrence with a date. What does it mean to name an event with a date, he asks, while the place and meaning of the event remain ineffable? The date, 9/11, gets repeated over and over again as if its singularity were so absolute that it could not be matched by any generalization. To him, 9/11 sounds like an intuition without a concept, a species without a genus.

For Derrida, by pronouncing 9/11 we do not use language in its obvious referring function but rather press it to name something that it cannot name because it happens beyond language: terror and trauma.

Trauma for Freud is the effect of an experience whose intensity cannot be matched by the subject's usual response mechanism.[13] A traumatic experience entails terror because it designates a danger that is both unpredictable and beyond the subject's control. Repetition is a common reaction to trauma: by repeating any fragment of the traumatic situation the victim tries retrospectively to dominate it. Derrida suggests that we similarly repeat 9/11 without ever asking ourselves what it names.

Yet, we not only repeat it to ourselves as if it were a soothing mantra or ritual incantation, but we are also incessantly exhorted to repeat it "by means of a prodigious techno-socio-political machine," the same machine responsible for the original christening of the terrorist attacks as 9/11. The reason for this exhortation is to consolidate the impression that a major event has taken place. Referring to an event with a date automatically gives it historical stature: it monumentalizes it. Naming the terrorist attacks against the World Trade Center and the Pentagon "9/11" alleviates the sense of responsibility for the failure to prevent them as well as the sense of vulnerability that such failure inevitably provokes.

Derrida developed this argument by subjecting the two terms I used in my first question, "event" and "impression," to a deconstructive intervention. Neither one of these two terms, he warned me, is self-evident.

For Heidegger, the notion of "event" indicates something that offers itself to being experienced but also resists being wholly comprehended and appropriated.[14] An event exposes us to a situation in which we are unable to wholly appropriate what happens. Utter unpredictability is one feature of events, for if something cannot be predicted it cannot be entirely explained either. This causes the event to remain irreproducible, singular, and somewhat free-floating. Death, forgiveness, and poetry are all events in this strong sense: they befall us unexpectedly.

Was 9/11 truly unpredictable? Not for Derrida. After all, he reminded me, the World Trade Center had been the object of an earlier attack in 1993. Also, the kind of attack that the terrorists launched in 2001 had already been prefigured in detail by the technocinematic culture of our days. For some time now, films and videogames had been anticipating the gutting (*éventrement*) and collapse (*effondrement*) of the two immense towers in downtown Manhattan. Plus, Derrida added, not only did they literally visualize the attacks, but they also conjured up the feelings that these two unmistakably phallic objects elicited in the collective imagination: love and hate, admiration and envy, sublimity and shame.

For all these reasons, 9/11 does not fit the description of an event and, perhaps, if we go by the number of the victims or by the amount of destruction on the ground, it does not seem to be a major one, either.[15] This may all follow. And yet, Derrida admitted, the impression that it was a major event remains. A closer look at the concept of impression explains this apparent contradiction. In the vocabulary of the Western philosophical tradition, the notion of impression carries the illustrious signature of David Hume, the eighteenth-century empiricist who made it the center of his thought. He believed that the raw materials of thinking are indeed impressions, understood as the imprint left by the external world on our nervous system.[16] If I am in the proximity of a flame, for example, I seem to receive a number of vivid impressions: the color of the flame, its temperature, its shape, and its movement. According to Hume, only after we have collected all these impressions can we form them into the idea of the flame.

For Derrida, the impressions that 9/11 imprinted on the global audience as well as on the victims and the bystanders fall under two headings: the indignation over the killings and the drumbeat of the media that obsessively declared the attacks as a "major event." The first set, he said to me, struck us as the shape and the temperature of a flame: revulsion toward the blind violence of the attacks coupled with human compassion and infinite sadness in the face of loss and pain. Because of their direct impact on the global audience these are to be considered authentic impressions in the Humean sense. In contrast, the second set encompasses our responses to the media construction of 9/11 as a major event. Even though we term these as impressions in the generic sense, from a Humean standpoint they would be inauthentic impressions, as they do not meet his requirement of immediacy.

Pursuing Hume's argument about how ideas form from impressions, Derrida thus distinguished two different sets of ideas deriving from the two sets of impressions. The first set of impressions crystallized into the idea that 9/11 is an absolutely singular event in all respects: unframeable, unpredictable, and ultimately incomprehensible. This idea coincides with the strong notion of event advanced by Heidegger: a happenstance that resists appropriation and understanding. For Derrida, what distinguishes 9/11 as an event of this kind is that, in the end, it resists virtualization and media reproduction. Instead, the cluster of inauthentic impressions imposed by the media onto the global audience formed into the idea that 9/11 is a world event of major importance. Because these are strategically organized data, we mistake them for impressions, whereas, in fact, they are acts of propaganda. We, the global audience, tend to collapse real and immediate impressions and media-constructed impressions. Even though Derrida concedes that it is impossible to keep them neatly separate experientially, he believes it is our moral duty to keep them apart at least conceptually.

By reciting 9/11 as a litany, we repeat to ourselves what needs to remain silent: the unconditional sorrow for the loss of human life and the vulnerability of the system that was supposed to protect us. This system is embodied by a paternal figure: the United States of America, which is both the site of the attacks and the repository of the world order. The United States, in its role as the greatest technoscientific, capitalist, and military power, symbolizes the world order, the legitimacy of international law and diplomacy, and the power of the media. The world order, said Derrida, is based on the solidity, reliability, and credibility of American power. Exposing the fragility of the superpower means exposing the fragility of the world order.

Trauma and Autoimmunity

In Derrida's reading, 9/11 is the symptom of an autoimmune crisis occurring within the system that should have predicted it. Autoimmune conditions consist in the spontaneous suicide of the very defensive mechanism supposed to protect the organism from external aggression. This is a mechanism by which, as Derrida noted, a living organism "works to destroy its own protection, to immunize itself against its 'own' immunity."

Derrida counted three phases (*temps*) in the autoimmune crisis of which 9/11 is a symptom. The first phase is the Cold War, a war that was fought "in the head" more than on the ground or in the air. If we look at 9/11 from the standpoint of its continuity with the Cold War, it is easy to see that the hijackers who turned against the United States had been trained by the United States during the era of the Soviet invasion of Afghanistan. American weapons and intelligence have made an essential contribution to the Islamic Afghan fighters since the early 1980s, some of whom became the Taliban political elite that ruled Afghanistan under perhaps the most extreme implementation of shari'a ever advanced. Possibly, said Derrida, 9/11 could be interpreted as the implosive finale of the Cold War, killed by its own convolutions and contradictions.

The second phase of the autoimmune crisis is what Derrida calls "worse than the Cold War" both historically and psychologically. While the Cold War was characterized by the possibility of balance between two superpowers, it is impossible to build a balance with terrorism because the threat does not come from a state but from incalculable forces and incalculable responsibilities. The dissemination of the nuclear arsenal and the relative availability of bacteriological and chemical weapons is the reality on which terrorism impinges. George W. Bush's proclamation that all the nations he accuses of harboring terrorism constitute an "axis of evil" speaks to the United States' denial of the elusiveness of the forces of terror.

Psychologically, "what is worse than the Cold War" foregrounds the temporality of trauma, which is oriented toward the future. Any traumatic experience wounds the future as much as the present. Playing on the French word for future, *avenir,* Derrida claims that since the threat haunts the future, in a sense, it is still to come (*à venir*). This pointing to the temporality of trauma is a direct follow-up to his discussion of the significance of the choice of 9/11 as a name for the attacks. Like the fourth of July, recognized as Independence Day in the United States, or the first of May, recognized as Labor Day in Europe as well as in most countries around the world, 9/11 has the scope of monumentalizing the attacks. Since this monumentalization is in the interest of *both* the Western media *and* the terrorists, it adds another fold to the autoimmune reaction.

This second phase of autoimmunity displays another important feature. By monumentalizing the terrorist attacks, the date 9/11 also declares that they are over. In so doing, it denies precisely the futurity of the threat, the possibility that the worst might still be to come. For Derrida, the massive media reporting acted in sync with the naming of the attacks as 9/11. As the tragedy was still unfolding, he said, calling it 9/11 revealed the illusion that it was already over.

The third and last phase of the autoimmune crisis is what Derrida calls "the vicious circle of repression." It is the most obviously suicidal of the three because it describes the way in which, by declaring war against terrorism, the Western coalition engenders a war against itself.

One function of the concept of autoimmunity is to act as a third term between the classical opposition of friend and foe. As we have seen, to identify a third term is a characteristically deconstructive move aimed at displacing the traditional metaphysical tendency to rely on irreducible pairs. Although the explicit discussion of autoimmunity is limited to three, it implicitly continues as Derrida sets out to call into question the distinction between war and terrorism.

Wars have always been contaminated by terrorism through the intimidation of civilians. Yet, even at the theoretical level, the distinction is impossible to draw. Suppose, he said in reference to Carl Schmitt, the German legal scholar,[17] that a war can only be declared between two states, whereas terrorism is a conflict between forces other than a sovereign state. The political history of the term "terrorism" would easily contradict this definition, since terror has always been inflicted by sovereign states on their population or other populations, in peacetime as well as in wartime. The current usage of the term "terrorism" derives from the late phase of the French Revolution, when Robespierre's Reign of Terror engaged in mass executions and purges of civilians. Robespierre inflicted terror in the name of a sovereign state; also, given that his declared objective was to rid France of all its internal enemies, this early instance of terrorism seems to point precisely to the autoimmune element theorized by Derrida. This is not to deny that the terrorists justify themselves by presenting their attacks as responses to previous acts of terrorism conducted against them by a state. "Every terrorist in the world," Derrida observed, "claims to be responding in self-defense to a prior terrorism on the part of a state, one that simply went by other names and covered itself with all sorts of more or less credible justifications."

To complicate the matter further, terrorists can be liberation fighters in one context and plain criminals in the very same context at a different point in time. The Islamic guerrillas who fought against the Soviet invasion in the 1980s and became the new political leaders is an example. Another is the recent history of Algeria, Derrida's home for the first nineteen years of his life.

> No one can deny that there was state terrorism during the French repression in Algeria from 1954 to 1962. The terrorism carried out by the Algerian rebellion was long considered a domestic phenomenon insofar as Algeria was supposed to be an integral part of French national territory, and the French terrorism of the time (carried out by the state) was presented as a police operation for internal security. It was only in the 1990s, decades later, that the French Parliament retrospectively conferred the

status of "war" (and thus the status of an international confrontation) upon this conflict so as to be able to pay the pensions of the "veterans" who claimed them.

In Derrida's mind, it is impossible to draw any distinctions regarding terrorism—between war and terrorism, state and nonstate terrorism, terrorism and national liberation movements, national and international terrorism. If it is so hard to meaningfully attach any predicates to it, it simply means that terrorism *is* irreducibly ineffable and enigmatic. This truth is hard to accept but even more dangerous to reject.

Politically speaking, the more slippery a concept the easier it is to appropriate it opportunistically. Derrida did not hesitate to declare that the most powerful and destructive appropriation of terrorism is precisely its use as a self-evident concept by all the parties involved. These include what he calls the "technoeconomic media," the U.S. State Department, and national governments as well as relevant international institutions. Obviously, nobody means to cause harm—but this does not erase responsibility, which means that all political, economic, and military interlocutors on the post-9/11 global scene are in dire need to use language very carefully.

Derrida was also somber about the difficulty of beating the perverse dynamics of autoimmunity. None of the parties involved in the struggle against terrorism can afford to refrain from talking about it, but the more they do so the more they help the terrorist cause, by giving it status, visibility, and a sense of purpose. This is how both the information and political systems, which are supposed to protect civilians from the threat of global terrorism, progressively weaken in the face of danger.[18]

Another devastating aspect of the autoimmune crisis started by 9/11 is being constantly reminded of the futurity of the terrorist threat. According to the interpretation of terror as the essence of trauma that I already mentioned, victims of a traumatic experience need to endlessly play the trauma back for themselves in order to feel reassured that they have withstood it. This *self-destructive* tendency becomes a *destructive* weapon in the hands of the media and the political leadership. Imagine, said Derrida, if we told the American public and the world that what has happened is no doubt an unspeakable crime, but it's over. Everyone would then begin their own period of mourning, the preliminary step to turning the page. All responsible parties need to facilitate this turning of the page and stop hindering it. This is an urgent responsibility, the evasion of which transforms the enemies of terrorism into its allies.

The need for both the political leadership and the media to act responsibly will intensify in the future in light of what Derrida fears is the future of terrorism: virtual attacks. In his reading, "technoscience" has transformed the relation between terror, terrorism, and territory, three terms sharing a root—the Latin word *terra*. From this angle, Derrida exclaimed

> September 11 is still part of the archaic theater of violence aimed at striking the imagination. One day it might be said: "September 11"—those were the ("good") old days of the last war. Things were still of the order of the gigantic: visible and enormous!

Derrida's ominous suspicion is that the virtualization of terrorism will erase the remnants of the distinction between terrorism and war and between war and peace. There are worse scenarios, he said, than two commercial planes crashing into skyscrapers and causing their collapse. At least, the attacks of 9/11 were conducted against determinate places, at determinate times. We know exactly when they began and when they ended. In contrast,

> [N]anotechnologies of all sorts are so much more powerful and invisible, uncontrollable, capable of creeping in everywhere. They are the micrological rivals of microbes and bacteria. Yet our unconscious is already aware of this; it already knows it, and that's what's scary.

Religious Responsibilities

During the winter of 1994, some eight years before the catastrophe of 9/11, Derrida began his reflection on the mechanism of autoimmunization. His interest in it emerged in connection with a study of the concept of religion, which frames his discussion of religious fundamentalism and its role in global terrorism.

On the basis of the work of French linguist Emile Benveniste, who discovered that there is "no 'common' Indo-European term for what we call 'religion,'"[19] Derrida claims that there has not always been, nor should there always be, "*something, a thing that is one and identifiable,* identical with itself, which, whether religious or irreligious, all agree to call 'religion.'"[20]

Religion, in Derrida's reading, is an ancient Roman creation subsequently appropriated by Christianity. His discussion of the Latin matrix of religion starts from its etymology, which has been the subject of some debate since antiquity. In the first century B.C., Cicero pointed out that *religio* comes from *relegere,* a slight modification of the Latin verb *legere* meaning to harvest or to gather. In the second century A.D., Tertullian, a later Roman writer from North Africa and convert to Christianity, suggested instead that the etymology of religion is *religare,* meaning to tie, which for him came to signify the bond of obligation, the debt between man and God.

In light of this etymological duplicity, Derrida insists that two distinct but inextricable elements are intrinsic to the Western religious experience: sacredness and indebtedness.[21] Eventually, with the expansion of Christianity religion became progressively more focused on indebtedness and obligation and moved farther apart from a sense of sacredness over and beyond any exchange. In Derrida's opinion, this new focus injects juridical issues into religion, binding religion to the sphere of law.

Continuing in the genealogy of *religio,* Derrida sees another salient aspect in the fact that it contains the prefix "re-," a mark of repetition and self-reference, "a resistance or a reaction to dis-junction. To absolute alterity."[22] Derrida sees the presence of the prefix "re-" in both *re-legere* and *re-ligare* as etymological evidence for his argument that religion in the Abrahamic definition tends to resist true openness toward the other.

For Derrida, the deconstruction of the Latin and Christian limits of religion, wrongly taken to be a neutral descriptive term, may open the gates of a new, and more properly "religious," sensibility. This is what he means when he writes that "A Christian—but also a Jew or a Muslim—would be someone who would harbor doubts about this limit; about the *existence* of this limit or about its reducibility to any other limit."[23] Only by deconstructing religion as it is now conceived will we be able to really engage it by reaching out to the other and breaking the circle of obligation and deliverance. This singular opening to the other is very close to the notion of unconditional forgiveness, the act of forgiving the unforgivable. "The coming of the other can only emerge as a singular event when no anticipation sees it coming, when the other and death—and radical evil—can come as a surprise at any moment."[24]

No doubt, there is a "messianic quality" in Derrida's longing for this encounter. However, as he himself warns, it is essential that there be no messiah, no ultimate word from a messiah that can be repeated, taken as a promise, or interpreted as an obligation. As unconditional forgiveness, this "messianicity without messianism"[25] would entail taking risks, for the other can be the best as well as the worst—we can be greeted by the other or we can be killed by the other. Yet, for Derrida, without a sense of what it means to await the other in this way, we cannot even begin to discuss ethics and politics.

> This messianic dimension does not depend on any messianism, it follows no determinate revelation, it belongs properly to no Abrahamic religion . . . An invincible desire for justice is linked to this expectation . . . This justice, which I distinguish from right, alone allows the hope, beyond all "messianisms," of a universalizable culture of singularities, a culture in which the abstract possibility of the impossible translation could nevertheless be announced. This justice inscribes itself in advance in the promise, in the act of faith or in the appeal to faith that inhabits every act of language, every address to the other.[26]

The openness to the other urged by Derrida points at a religious community in which membership is not tied to fulfilling an obligation but rather established by the simple relation between differences.[27] Derrida admits that a community of this kind would not provide a common platform on which to establish religious identity.

In a community without mutual obligations, the concept of responsibility would have to be reconceived on new grounds. Again, Derrida turns to etymology for guidance. The resistance to disjunction revealed by the prefix "re-" present in "religion" as well as its two Latin etymological sources, *relegere* and *religare*, emerges in a parallel fashion in "responsibility" and "response." Derrida notes that both come from the

Latin verb *spondeo*, which means to guarantee or to promise, which is close in meaning to *religare*, or to tie, the verb that Tertullian identifies as the origin of the word "religion": "*Respondeo, responsum*, is said of the interpreters of the gods, of priests, notably of the haruspices, *giving a promise in return for the offering*, depositing a security in return for a gift; it is the 'response' of an oracle, of a priest."[28]

In Derrida's reading, this etymological analysis reveals that response and responsibility share with religion a concern with economic exchange whereby promises are made in return for offerings and securities are deposited in return for gifts. This is the same complaint that Derrida voices about forgiveness, which in its conditional form forgives only what can be quantified in terms of punishment. To understand response and responsibility only in the context of an economic exchange, which usually goes together with the juridical guarantee that the exchange has been fair, does not address what Derrida believes is the core of responsibility: responsibility in the face of the incalculable.

Deconstructing the familiar sense of religion and responsibility has a political urgency determined by what Derrida describes as the unhappy marriage between religion and digital technology. There is no question, in Derrida's mind, that religion affirms itself globally because of its alliance with the digital highways, but he has no doubt that it is an alliance full of tensions and contradictions. All the constitutive components of religion—the respect for the sacredness of the harvest, a sense of obligation to God, and the promise of absolute truthfulness—speak to religion's profound wariness of displacement, fragmentation, and disembodiment, which are instead the conditions of existence of digital technology. While the global information network and its technological underpinning represent the forces of abstraction and dissociation, religion remains anchored in the need for inscription and embodiment. If information circulates in the language of bits, religion propagates itself in human idioms, be it English, Arabic, Spanish, or Japanese. Religion, writes Derrida, which is inextricably linked to the body and to linguistic inscription, feels dominated, suffocated, expropriated by the global information system. This feeling of expropriation and self-estrangement explains the primitive modality of the new wars fought in its name.

Revenge is taken against the decorporealizing and expropriating machine by resorting—reverting—to bare hands, to the sexual organs or to primitive tools, often to weapons other than firearms. What is referred to as "killings" and "atrocities"—words never used in "clean" or "proper" wars, where, precisely, the dead are no longer counted (guided and "intelligent" missiles directed at entire cities, for instance)—is here supplanted by tortures, beheadings and mutilations of all sorts. What is involved is always vengeance, often declared as sexual revenge: rapes, mutilated genitals or severed hands, corpses exhibited, heads paraded, as not too long ago in France, impaled on the end of stakes (phallic processions of "natural religions").[29]

Derrida's description applies to the majority of wars declared and undeclared in the last decade, among them the genocide in Rwanda, the Bosnian and Kosovo conflicts, the civil war in Algeria, and the fundamentalist interpretations of Islamic law in Iran, Afghanistan, Pakistan, Yemen, Sudan, and Saudi Arabia. They suggest, in his reading, that the body itself took revenge on its own expropriation, identified in the global dissemination of the market and the Western capitalistic hegemony. One would be justified in thinking of the attacks of 9/11 as a mutilation of this kind.

If it is true that a desire for the reinstitution of the living being over and beyond its mechanical reproducibility lies behind the primitive features of contemporary religious wars, what many refer to as the "return of the religious" is instead, for Derrida, the unprecedented expansion of the Roman heritage of *religio,* with the help and under the threat of what he calls tele-technoscience, the global information system. Derrida's use of alternative names for globalization—"*mondial-*Latinization" or the French *mondialisation*—highlights his belief that a crucial element in what we call globalization is the unhappy marriage of religion and tele-technoscience, imperialistically exported throughout the world. In this perspective, whenever we think of globalization, we have to think of the spread of a certain way of construing religion according to the Latin and Christian imprint.

In spite of all the tensions characterizing the alliance between religion and the global information system, there is no doubt that their link is an incredibly powerful one. To have reached such a planetary scale of expansion, this link must count on a strong immune system that protects it against external aggression. And yet as Derrida points out, there is no immunity without autoimmunity, which is the self-destruction of one's own defenses. Globalization shows both immunitary strength and an autoimmune weakness. This is the mark of our time.

The Conditions of Tolerance

Tolerance is one of the key concepts of globalization. Propounded as a neutral moral and political call for hospitality and friendliness among different people, ethnicities, traditions, and religious beliefs, it is in fact, according to Derrida, profoundly marked by a normative frame of reference: Christianity.

The modern-day sense of tolerance has its heritage in the Enlightenment. Kant understood tolerance as the emancipatory promise of the modern age. In Derrida's reading, the problematic implications of tolerance begin with Kant's project of relocating religion "within" the limits of reason in order to neutralize its irrationalist potential. A classic text by Kant, *Religion within the Limits of Reason Alone,*[30] illustrates this effort. Derrida's deconstructive reading of this essay shows that Kant's attempt to provide religion with a rational justification ends up with the paradoxical result of having reason founded on religion, and more specifically, Christianity. Exploring Derrida's intervention on Kant's text will not only show the reach of Derrida's involvement with the legacy of the Enlightenment but also dispel any suspicion that his reading of global terrorism as autoimmune crisis may be affirming a nihilistic stance.

Derrida's intervention on Kant's text begins with the title. While Kant's treatise reads *Religion within the Limits of Reason Alone,* Derrida's response, which comes in the subtitle of his own treatise *Faith and Knowledge,* reads *Religion at the Limits of Reason Alone.* To say that religion does not arise *within* the limits of reason (as in Kant's title) but *at* its limits (as in Derrida's appropriation of Kant's title) points to the interdependence of what is included and what is excluded by this limit. In the same way that the geographical identity of two countries, say, Canada and the United States, depends on their sharing a border, which serves the double function of including one country and excluding the other, the line of demarcation between reason and religion has for him the same role, inextricably intertwining them.

Kant distinguished between two types of religion: one is the "religion of cult alone," which teaches prayer and does not demand the believer to find her own way out of sin by pursuing the moral life. The other is "moral religion," which prescribes that the individual improve herself by acting on her own moral ground, which Kant expresses in an axiomatic form: "It is not essential and hence not necessary for everyone to know what God does or has done for his salvation but it is essential to know *what man himself must* do in order to become worthy of his assistance."[31]

In correspondence with these two types of religion, Kant describes two different kinds of faith: "dogmatic faith," which does not operate on this principle and does not recognize the distinction between revelation and knowledge; and "reflecting faith," for which the way out of sin does not depend on historical revelation but on human rationality and goodwill. Reflecting faith mandates that we "suspend" our belief in God and pretend that God did not exist in order to prove our moral commitment. In this text, our philosophical, secular, and moral responsibility appears to be bound to the experience of abandonment: the death of God, silent and inexplicable, beyond any Scriptural narrative.

After laying out this classification, Kant identifies in Christianity the archetype of the only moral religion. Christianity has liberated reflecting faith from the paralyzing expectation of the Messiah: the historical revelation has already occurred in Christianity, so the process of self-edification can start based on the individual strength of the believer, her character, and dedication. This "strong, simple and dizzying" conclusion, in Derrida's words, entails that pure morality and Christianity are indistinguishable: if this is true, the whole apparatus of Kantian moral theory, including "the unconditional universality of the categorical imperative," is evangelical. "The moral law inscribes itself at the bottom of our hearts like the memory of the Passion. When it addresses us, it either speaks the idiom of the Christian—or is silent."[32] The process of secularization of religion, which is Kant's objective, is thus inseparable from the essence of Christianity, the religion that understands itself in terms of the death of God.[33] Kant's effort to moralize

religion has pushed him, according to Derrida, to the paradoxical result of having transformed morality into a religious endeavor. The concept of tolerance is the quintessential example of this Kantian double
bind: it presents itself as being religiously neutral and yet it contains a
strong Christian component. The case of tolerance is almost too easily
shaped by Christian history to serve as evidence for Derrida's argument. As he recalled in our dialogue,

> The word "tolerance" is first of all marked by a religious war between
> Christians, or between Christians and non-Christians. Tolerance is a
> *Christian* virtue, or for that matter a *Catholic* virtue. The Christian must
> tolerate the non-Christian, but, even more so, the Catholic must let the
> Protestant be. Since we today feel that religious claims are at the heart of
> the violence (you will notice that I keep saying, in a deliberately general
> fashion, "violence," so as to avoid the equivocal and confused words
> "war" and "terrorism"), we resort to this good old word "tolerance": that
> Muslims agree to live with Jews and Christians, that Jews agree to live
> with Muslims, that believers agree to tolerate "infidels" or "nonbelievers"
> (for this is the word "bin Laden" used to denounce his enemies, and first
> of all the Americans). Peace would thus be tolerant cohabitation.

The history of the concept reveals that tolerance "is always on the
side of the 'reason of the strongest,'" firmly tied to the figure of the sovereign that Habermas also mentions in our dialogue. From this point of
view, being tolerant is not going to make those who feel excluded any
more included or understood. This was certainly a blunt statement to
make in the immediate aftermath of the attacks of 9/11, when Western
countries were relying on tolerance as their unifying moral commitment.

While in Derrida's mind there is no way to overcome the one-sidedness of tolerance, hospitality is a much more flexible concept. "If I
think I am being hospitable because I am tolerant, it is because I wish
to limit my welcome, to retain power and maintain control over the limits of my 'home,' my sovereignty, my 'I can' (my territory, my house, my
language, my culture, my religion, and so on)." Tolerance is "a scrutinized hospitality, always under surveillance, parsimonious and protective of its sovereignty. In the best of cases, it's what I would call a con-

ditional hospitality, the one that is most commonly practiced by individuals, families, cities, or states."[34]

The advantage of hospitality over tolerance is that it lends itself, as forgiveness does, to being posited in the double register of the conditional and the unconditional. In fact, tolerance is, for Derrida, conditional hospitality. By being tolerant one admits the other under one's own conditions, and thus under one's authority, law, and sovereignty. Derrida hopes instead for a new conception of hospitality that is, in a sense, much more tolerant than tolerance. Surprisingly for those who believe that Derrida is a counter-Enlightenment thinker, Kant is his point of reference. Derrida's articulation of unconditional hospitality hinges on Kant's distinction between two kinds of rights: right of invitation and right of visitation.

> But pure or unconditional hospitality does not consist in such an *invitation* ("I invite you, I welcome you into *my home,* on the condition that you adapt to the laws and norms of my territory, according to my language, tradition, memory, and so on"). Pure and unconditional hospitality, hospitality *itself,* opens or is in advance open to someone who is neither expected nor invited, to whomever arrives as an absolutely foreign *visitor,* as a new *arrival,* nonidentifiable and unforeseeable, in short, wholly other. I would call this a hospitality of *visitation* rather than *invitation.* The visit might actually be very dangerous, and we must not ignore this fact, but would a hospitality without risk, a hospitality backed by certain assurances, a hospitality protected by an immune system against the wholly other, be true hospitality?

As no sense of forgiveness would exist without unconditional forgiveness, no sense of true hospitality and openness to the other would exist without unconditional hospitality.

Excessive Violence

Conditional hospitality, or tolerance, is fundamentally the right of invitation and as such lays the conditions for international and cosmopolitan conventions. Unconditional hospitality, by contrast, corresponds to the right of visitation. As such, it exposes the host to the maximum risk, as it does not allow for any systematic defense or immunity against the other. Derrida admits that unconditional hospitality cannot have a political or juridical status. States cannot include it in their laws, because hospitality without conditions is irreconcilable with the very idea of a sovereign state. And yet, it is only from the standpoint of unconditional hospitality, or the right of visitation, that we gain a critical perspective on the limits of cosmopolitan right, tolerance, conditional hospitality, and the right of invitation.

In his treatise *Perpetual Peace,* Kant backs the idea of cosmopolitan right without the support of a world government. Not only, since World War I, did international institutions operate in line with Kant's legacy, but this is Derrida's as well as Habermas's political dream. However, while Habermas sees it as a program, Derrida understands it as an ideal that can best be pursued by continually having it face its limits. For, as we have seen, cosmopolitanism expresses only conditional hospitality, or what Kant calls the right of invitation.

For Derrida, the ideal of democracy lies beyond cosmopolitanism and world citizenship, over and beyond the economy of sovereignty, politics, and jurisdiction. Cosmopolitanism applies to a world viewed as cosmos, which since the Greeks means an orderly whole regulated by principles and laws. Even though Derrida explicitly stands by cosmopolitanism and world citizenry, he feels that commitment to justice cannot be fully exercised within the boundaries of law and cosmopolitanism. For justice, as well as democracy, is not just about our conduct within the framework of the state or under the obligations of citizenship but also in the face of a stranger.

I want to underline that Derrida's belief that room needs to be left for something located somewhere *beyond* politics and law, cosmopolitanism and world citizenry, is firmly anchored in a formal scheme: the distinction between the conditional and unconditional registers. The conceptual formalism of this gesture allows him to avoid reactionary and nostalgic revivals as well as an essentialist reading of tradition and identity. The quality of what is beyond politics and law is never spelled out in terms of any specific content or value but simply indicated as the condition of possibility for what politics and law articulate.[35]

As forgiveness in the hands of politics and the juridical domain becomes a therapy of reconciliation, and hospitality in the hands of cos-

mopolitanism becomes the simple right of invitation, justice in the
hands of law is reduced to law's simple enforceability.

> Applicability, "enforceability," is not an exterior or secondary possibility
> that may or may not be added as a supplement to law. It is the force es-
> sentially implied in the very concept of *justice as law* (*droit*), of justice as
> it becomes *droit*, of the law as "*droit*" (for I want to insist right away on
> reserving the possibility of a justice, indeed of a law that not only exceeds
> or contradicts "law" (*droit*) but also, perhaps, has no relation to law, or
> maintains such a strange relation to it that it may just as well command
> the "*droit*" that excludes it). The word enforceability reminds us that
> there is no such thing as law (*droit*) that doesn't imply *in itself, a priori,
> in the analytic structure of its concept,* the possibility of being "enforced,"
> applied by force.[36]

The notions of excess and supplement are central to Derrida's conception of politics and expose a key difference between his thinking and
that of Habermas, since they imply that politics has to admit the existence of something located beyond its limits. For Derrida, justice is
andwhat is beyond law; otherwise, it would be reduced to law's enforceability. Law and justice belong to two different dimensions. Because law is the product of social and political dynamics, it is finite, relative, and historically grounded. By contrast, justice transcends the
sphere of social negotiation and political deliberation, which makes it
infinite and absolute. Justice, for Derrida, stands beyond the boundaries of politics as its inexhaustible demand.

Let us examine more closely how Derrida reaches this conclusion.
His point of departure is the English expression "to enforce the law."
Unlike the French phrase "appliquer la loi," the English "to enforce
the law" reveals a decisive assumption concerning the nature of law,
namely, that its enforceability demarcates the authorized use of force.
In a constitutional democracy law is authorized because it represents
the will of the citizens. In the case of a nondemocratic political system,
authorization corresponds to the uncontestable authority of an absolute ruler or ruling party. However, in both cases the link between enforceability and law allows for the distinction between law as authorized force and violence as unauthorized force.

Insisting on the idiomatic element in language, Derrida turns to the German noun *Gewalt*, which means both violence, in the sense of unauthorized force, and legitimate power or public force. Derrida makes the argument that the semantic oscillation displayed by *Gewalt* is not an isolated oddity but a window onto the structural instability of the conceptual distinction between authorized and unauthorized force, which is usually construed as an oppositional pair. Derrida pursues his argument through a close reading of Benjamin's difficult essay "Zur Kritik der Gewalt," commonly translated as "Critique of Violence," which revolves precisely around the ambivalence of *Gewalt*.[37] As the distinction between authorized and unauthorized use of force clearly exhibits, Benjamin's take is that the evaluation of violence is traditionally approached through its use or application, leaving the discussion of what it is, in and of itself, unexplored.

What is *Gewalt?* An earthquake, a tsunami, or any other natural event is violent only in the figurative sense. Violence is a concept that belongs to the symbolic order of law, politics, and morals. Granted that this is the case, for Benjamin the relevant distinction is not between authorized and unauthorized force, but between "law-making force," which refers to the founding moment of the legal system, and "law-conserving force," which corresponds to the enforceability of the law. Derrida picks up this distinction from Benjamin and employs it to deconstruct the more traditional distinction between authorized and unauthorized force that Benjamin seems to cavalierly set aside.[38]

In Derrida's reading, what Benjamin calls law-making force, the act of founding a new system of law, cannot possibly be carried out within legal boundaries. "The origin of authority, the foundation or ground, the position of the law can't by definition rest on anything but themselves."[39] This pronouncement sounds trivial if applied to the position of an absolute monarch, say, Louis XIV of France, who famously declared, "L'etat, c'est moi." However, from Derrida's striking perspective the case of Thomas Jefferson and the Founding Fathers of American parliamentary democracy is no different because even the principles of the U.S. Constitution lack prior legal justification.[40]

All revolutionary situations, all revolutionary discourses, on the left or on the right . . . justify the recourse to violence by alleging the founding, in progress or to come, of a new law. As this law to come will in return legit-imate, retrospectively, the violence that may offend the sense of justice, its future anterior already justifies it. The foundation of all states occurs in a situation that we can thus call revolutionary. It inaugurates a new law, it always does so in violence. Always, which is to say even when there haven't been those spectacular genocides, expulsions or deportations that so often accompany the foundation of states, big and small, old or new, right near us or far away . . . These moments, supposing we can iso-late them, are terrifying moments. Because of the sufferings, the crimes, the tortures that rarely fail to accompany them, no doubt, but just as much because they are in themselves, and in their very violence, uninter-pretable or indecipherable.[41]

The foundation of a new system of law occurs in the absence of any legal parameters. This fact makes it, literally, lawless. Since law re-tains the monopoly of both authorized and unauthorized force, the consequence is that even the most amicable inauguration of a new legal order happens over and beyond the distinction between authorized and unauthorized use of force.

Derrida is careful to underline that the foundation of law *exceeds* the boundaries of legality rather than offends them. This is why he be-lieves all revolutionary moments are fundamentally uninterpretable and undecipherable. The legitimacy of the legal order cannot be of-fered except retroactively, namely, once the system of law is established and enforceable. To this extent Derrida thinks that the moral justifica-tion of law, namely, justice, is always *à venir,* to come. The irreducible futurity of justice is what Derrida, borrowing an expression from six-teen-century French philosopher Michel Montaigne, calls the "mysti-cal foundation of authority."

The acknowledgment of the peculiar condition that accompa-nies the foundation of all laws is terrifying not only because it often happens in bloodshed of various sorts but also because it makes it possible to conceive of one's actions beyond the opposition between legal and illegal. What category would these actions belong to? If legal action corresponds to authorized violence and illegal action cor-responds to unauthorized violence would, an action that is neither legal nor illegal correspond to pure violence? Derrida does not be-lieve that this impasse is solvable but considers it productive to the extent that it reveals that violence is internal rather than external to the order of law.

Under this premise, terrorism would seem to be the quintessential expression of founding violence. "Even on the grand scale of the Mafia or heavy drug trafficking," crime transgresses the law in view of particular benefits, so that the legal system and the state that depends on it are not threatened at their foundations. But terrorism creates a different situation because what it attacks is the founding moment of law and, through it, the legitimacy of the state. The difficulty of prosecuting terrorism as terrorism is in the fact that it poses the same challenge to the system of law as a revolution or a war. This is why Derrida suggests that the distinction between terrorism and war is very slippery.

Alongside the juridical questions concerning the prosecution of terrorism is the moral question regarding the parameters of judgment. How are we to judge terrorism if, in fact, its violence is neither legal nor illegal? This is what Derrida said in our dialogue.

> What appears to me unacceptable in the "strategy" (in terms of weapons, practices, ideology, rhetoric, discourse, and so on) of the "bin Laden effect" is not only the cruelty, the disregard for human life, the disrespect for law, for women, the use of what is worst in technocapitalist modernity for the purposes of religious fanaticism. No, it is, above all, the fact that such actions and such discourse open onto no future and, in my view, have no future. If we are to put any faith in the perfectibility of public space and of the world juridico-political scene, of the "world" itself, then there is, it seems to me, *nothing good* to be hoped for from that quarter.

What terrorism lacks is the projection onto the future and the interest in the perfectibility of the present, which Derrida identifies with the inexhaustible demand of justice. In this sense, terrorism simply lacks justice.

> That is why, in this unleashing of violence without name, if I had to take one of the two sides and choose in a binary situation, well, I would. Despite my very strong reservations about the American, indeed European, political posture, about the "international antiterrorist" coalition, despite all the de facto betrayals, all the failures to live up to democracy, international law, and the very international institutions that the states of this

"coalition" themselves founded and supported up to a certain point, I would take the side of the camp that, in principle, by right of law, leaves a perspective open to perfectibility in the name of the "political," democracy, international law, international institutions, and so on.

Derrida's view of justice leads him to interpret law as universal and justice as uniquely particular. While the legal realm presupposes the generality of rules, norms, and universal imperatives, justice concerns individuals, the uniqueness of their lives and situations. Insofar as law is organized around the demand for universality—rules and imperatives—it operates in the domain of what is possible, often predictable, and certainly calculable. Justice presents us instead with a series of impossible demands: judging what is absolutely singular, relating to the other in her full alterity, and coming to decisions in the face of the infinite perfectibility of any decision. Justice requires us to calculate the incalculable and to decide the undecidable. In short, justice requires the experience of aporia, indeed an impossible experience. And yet, Derrida insists, "there is no justice without this experience, however impossible it may be."[42] Maintaining the rift between justice and law helps keep open the impossible promise of utopia.

Derrida's conception of justice requires revising the familiar conception of responsibility. For if justice cannot be constrained within the boundaries of law, the calculable and the universal, responsibility cannot be conceived under the aegis of the autonomous moral agent, defined as each individual's ability to legislate for herself. This classical conception of autonomy, laid out by Kant, understands responsibility as the founding moment of a separate legal order. By contrast, Derrida believes that such a foundational moment exceeds the law that it establishes. In the same way that justice exceeds law, there needs to be a concept of responsibility that exceeds the self-legislation of free will. Like justice, a radically unconditional responsibility is an impossible experience, without which, however, there cannot be ethics and morality. To be responsible is to respond to the call of the other: another individual, another culture, another time. Such a response also makes one responsible for the other "in oneself."

> To be just, the decision of a judge, for example, must not only follow the rule of law or a general law but must assume it, approve it, confirm its

value, by a reinstituting act of interpretation, as if ultimately nothing previously existed of the law, as if the judge himself invented the law in every case ... In short, for a decision to be just and responsible, it must, in its proper moment if there is one, be both regulated and without regulation: it must confirm the law and also destroy it or suspend it enough to have to reinvent it in each case, to rejustify it, at least to reinvent it in the affirmation of the new and free confirmation of its principle.

The European Promise

In Derrida's view, after 9/11 international politics and diplomacy would benefit enormously from working alongside philosophers. More than ever, today's challenge is to develop a critical framework from which to evaluate and reinvent the language of international relations. Philosophy can play a unique role at this juncture because it knows how to examine the links between the juridico-political system and the philosophical heritage that produced it. Only by appropriating this complex network of explicit and implicit links will the transformation of the system occur. With its privileged access to these links, philosophy could help to evaluate the language that is used in international politics and eventually pose the question of the accountability of those who manage it.

A number of large and difficult issues need to be addressed anew after 9/11. One of them, according to Derrida, is sovereignty, which constitutes the special aporia of cosmopolitanism: how to establish international right without a world government. World politics seems to hinge on this. For example, the issue of sovereignty dominates the discussion on the legitimacy of declaring war against terrorism. Derrida calls it "a war without war." Following in Schmitt's path, Derrida maintains that a war can only occur between two sovereign states. Not only has no aid or support for terrorism been formally offered by any states, but the Bush administration's thesis that there are nations "harboring" terrorist activity is hard to prove, given that London, Madrid, and Hamburg have all hosted terrorist cells where individuals were dispatched, trained, and indoctrinated.

The issue of sovereignty, Derrida said in our dialogue, affects international relations at yet another level: the incompleteness of the process of secularization in today's politics. Derrida's view is that 9/11 has revealed the conflict between two political theologies. On the one hand, there is the United States, the only great democratic power that maintains the death penalty and cultivates a Biblical Christian imprint in its political discourse. On the other, is its enemy, which identifies itself as Islamic. Derrida observes that not only do these two political theologies spring from the same Abrahamic source, but the epicenter of their conflict, at least symbolically, is the state of Israel (a Jewish state) and the virtual state of Palestine.

The front, as Derrida sees it, is not East versus West as it is commonly configured. Rather, it is between the United States and a Europe that he identifies as the only secular actor on the world stage. In naming Europe, Derrida refers to a "new figure of Europe" or the Europe-to-come rather than to the European Community, which nevertheless he credits with one of the most advanced nontheological political cultures.

Derrida's reflection on the Europe-to-come began in 1990 when he was asked by the Italian philosopher Gianni Vattimo to respond to the question of European cultural identity. It was just a few months after the fall of the Berlin Wall. Surprisingly, given his usual tendency to refrain from axiomatic statements, on that occasion Derrida did offer one: "What is proper to a culture is not to be identical with itself."[43] This assertion confirms his belief in the ethical value of heterogeneity and difference, which I addressed by discussing the exclusive and inclusive function of geographical boundaries, including the Berlin Wall, in the second section of this essay. For Derrida, identity entails internal differentiation or, in his formulation, "difference with itself." Indeed, self-relation produces culture; but there is no culture without a relation to the other. No culture has a single origin: it is in the very nature of culture to explore difference and to develop a systematic openness toward others within one's culture as well as in other cultures.

On the one hand, European cultural identity cannot be dispersed . . . It cannot and must not be dispersed into a myriad of provinces, into a multiplicity of self-enclosed idioms or petty little nationalisms, each one jealous and untranslatable. It cannot and must not renounce places of great circulation or heavy traffic, the great avenues or thoroughfares of translation and communication, and thus, of mediatization. But, *on the other hand,* it cannot and must not accept the capital of a centralizing authority that, by means of its trans-European mechanisms . . . would control and standardize.[44]

Beyond Eurocentrism and anti-Eurocentrism, two programs that Derrida characterizes as "unforgettable" but "exhausted," what is the cultural identity that we are responsible for? What memory and what promise does the name Europe evoke? For whom and before whom are we responsible? Derrida lists two kinds of responsibility. There is responsibility toward memory and responsibility toward oneself. While responsibility toward oneself underlines the need for a personal and unconditional commitment to the process of decision-making, responsibility towards memory calls for a historical self-understanding based on difference and heterogeneity.[44] To be responsible *for* this memory of Europe, we need to transform it to the point of reinventing it. In this way, we won't simply either repeat or abhor its name. This transformation will occur only if we accept the possibility of an impossibility, the experience of aporia.

> It is necessary to make ourselves the guardians of an idea of Europe, of a difference of Europe, *but* of a Europe that consists precisely in not closing itself off in its identity and in advancing itself in an exemplary way towards what it is not, toward the other heading or the heading of the other.[46]

The notion of capital features in the title that Derrida gave to his short book on Europe: *The Other Heading.* The book is meant to respond to the political promise of a unified Europe by taking responsibility for Europe's past—a past that Derrida hopes will both protect and redirect Europe to another heading, another destination. Geographically, Europe has understood itself as a promontory, a cape or a headland: the extreme portion of Eurasia and the point of departure for discoveries and colonization. Even though the need for a physical capital, a single metropolis that has the function of the heart of a nation, has considerably aged, the "discourse of the capital" is still intact. This discourse is intertwined with the question of European identity. European culture is responsible for the emergence of the ideal of the nation-state "headed" by a capital city. Paris, Berlin, Rome, Brussels, Amsterdam, Madrid, are all capitals in this very strong sense. The word capital comes from the Latin for head, *caput,* which also appears in a variety of other expressions, such as the headlines of a newspaper or the heading, the title, of a book. Europe, for Derrida, is the name for the heading of culture, the exemplary heading of all cultures.

Taking responsibility for Europe means responding to the complexity constituting its past, present, and future, and reinventing their relations. Sovereignty, which Derrida renames "discourse of the capital" is first on the list. In order to reinvent Europe and, at the same time, taking responsibility for its heritage, we need to believe in paradoxical contaminations, such as "the memory of a past that has never been present," or "the memory of the future." After all, Derrida points out, the movement of memory is not necessarily tied to the past. Memory is not only about preserving and conserving the past, it is always already turned toward the future, "toward the promise, toward what is coming, what is arriving, what is happening tomorrow."[47]

This other heading is the direction in which Europe, the actual Europe, should be traveling. This is also the direction toward a new form of sovereignty, urgently demanded if cosmopolitanism is to become a political reality in the post-9/11 world. This destination is neither new nor old but the memory of a past that has never been present. This is the memory of the promise of the Enlightenment: freedom and equality for all.

Notes

Preface

1. Immanuel Kant, "On Perpetual Peace," in *Kant's Political Writings,* ed. Hans Reiss, trans. H. B. Nisbet (Cambridge University Press, 1970), p. 106.

2. Kant, "On Perpetual Peace," p. 108.

Introduction

1. Aristotle, *Poetics,* trans. and with an intro. Gerald F. Else (University of Michigan Press, 1967), p. 33.

2. There are some notable exceptions to the predominant view initiated by Aristotle. An outstanding example is the eighteenth-century Italian philosopher Giambattista Vico, who defends the priority of history and memory over reason, assumed as a faculty independent from time. Underlying his thought is the principle that "the true and the made are the same," *verum ipsum factum.* If by "made" we understand the realm of human-produced facts and events, what Vico endorses is the idea that historical knowledge can aspire to absolute certainty. Contrary to Descartes's rationalist standpoint, Vico's thesis is that the human sciences can offer exact knowledge because societies as well as historical events are our own creation. See Giambattista Vico, *The New Science: Unabridged Translation of the Third Edition,* rev. ed., trans. Thomas Goddard Bergin and Max Harold Fisch (Cornell University Press, 1984).

3. John Stuart Mill's treatise *On Liberty* is a manifesto of the principle of negative freedom. "The object of this Essay is to assert one very simple principle . . . that the sole end for which mankind are warranted, individually or collectively, in

interfering with the liberty of any of their number, is self-protection. That the only purpose for which power can be rightfully exercised over any member of the civilized community, against his will, is to prevent harm to others. His own good, either physical or moral, is not a sufficient warrant." John Stuart Mill, *On Liberty* (Norton, 1975), p. 48.

4. When asked to reflect on models of political commitment among twentieth-century philosophers, many readers may think of Jean-Paul Sartre rather than of Russell and Arendt. I want to underline that my focus here is the *contrast between* two different ways of understanding the relationship between philosophy and politics. Such a contrast seems to me to be most visible in the juxtaposition of these two figures. Also, the ground on which I line up Arendt, Habermas, and Derrida is the experience of history as trauma. Arendt's articulation of philosophy as response to historical trauma provides a model for what is common in the trajectories of Habermas and Derrida.

5. Bertrand Russell, *Philosophy and Politics* (Cambridge University Press, 1947), p. 20.

6. Russell, *Philosophy and Politics*, p. 26.

7. Russell, *Philosophy and Politics*, p. 8.

8. Noam Chomsky, *9–11* (Seven Stories Press, 2001).

9. There are many aspects of Arendt's anatomy of totalitarianism that I won't be able to discuss here. Perhaps my greatest ommission is her description of the installation of totalitarian regimes in the middle of the twentieth century as the result of the progressive impoverishment of the Western conception of citizenship. Symbolically, this means the triumph of the *bourgeois,* the greedy individual in search of wealth and power at any cost, over the *citoyen,* a believer in the value of political life. In her reading, nineteenth-century imperialism, with its pursuit of global conquest outside the boundaries of the nation-state, opens the stage for political movements whose concern is the self-assertion of national, ethnic, or racial identity rather than the care of a stable and self-contained public world. See Hannah Arendt, *The Origins of Totalitarianism* (Allen and Unwin, 1967).

10. "If we want to be at home on this earth, even at the price of being at home in this century, we must try to take part in the interminable dialogue with the essence of totalitarianism." Hannah Arendt, "Understanding and Politics (The Difficulties of Understanding)," in *Essays in Understanding, 1930–1954,* ed. Jerome Kohn (Harcourt, Brace & Co., 1994), p. 323.

11. Arendt, *The Origins of Totalitarianism,* p. 457.

12. Hannah Arendt, *Eichmann in Jerusalem: A Report on the Banality of Evil* (Viking Press, 1963).

13. The first point that is made repeatedly through the book is that criminal, moral, and political justice involves the particular actions of particular people, so that rendering a judgment is corrupted as soon as this key point is forgotten. One of her main indictments of the proceedings in Jerusalem is that the trial was deliberately engineered, in spite of the attempts of the judges, to deal with group inter-

ests—both during the events being judged and at the time of the trial, which took place fifteen years after the end of the war. She found it problematic that during the trial the question of Jewish collaborationism did not get properly foregrounded. Also, in her reading, the Israeli government wanted a trial that would remind the entire world of the sufferings of the Jewish people and that would at last allow the Jewish survivors an official hearing. The fact that a political agenda would drive this trial was for her a perversion of justice, no matter how sympathetic she was to the motives. The controversy became so bitter that it led Gershom Scholem, the eminent Zionist, to cruelly declare that Arendt's report on the Eichmann trial lacked "Ahabath Israel," or love for the Jewish people. See Seyla Benhabib, "Arendt's *Eichmann in Jerusalem,*" in *The Cambridge Companion to Hannah Arendt,* ed. Dana R. Villa (Cambridge University Press, 2000), pp. 65–85. Excellent treatments of this topic can be found in Richard J. Bernstein, *Hannah Arendt and the Jewish Question* (MIT Press, 1996); and Dana R. Villa, *Politics, Philosophy, Terror: Essays on the Thought of Hannah Arendt* (Princeton University Press, 1999).

14. Jürgen Habermas, "Ideologies and Society in Post-War World," in *Autonomy and Solidarity: Interviews with Jürgen Habermas,* ed. with an intro. by Peter Dews (Verso, 1986), p. 43.

15. The expression "unmastered past" (*unbewältige Vergangenheit*) arose in the context of post–World War II German intellectual history. It was coined to describe German attempts to come to terms with the Nazi past. It regained central stage during the *Historikerstreit* on the normalization of the German past. See, Charles S. Maier, *The Unmasterable Past: History, Holocaust, and German National Identity* (Harvard University Press, 1988).

16. Ernst Nolte, "Vergangenheit, die nicht vergehen will. Eine Rede, die geschrieben, aber nicht gehalten werden konnte," *Frankfurter Allgemeine Zeitung,* June 6, 1986.

17. Jürgen Habermas, "On the Public Use of History," in Habermas, *The New Conservatism: Cultural Criticism and the Historians' Debate,* ed. and trans. Shierry Weber Nicholsen, with an intro. by Richard Wolin (MIT Press, 1989), p. 229.

18. Habermas, "On the Public Use of History," p. 233.

19. See Jürgen, Habermas, "Yet Again: German Identity—A Unified Nation of Angry DM-Burghers," in *When the Wall Came Down: Reactions to German Unification,* eds. Harold James and Marla Stone (Routledge, 1992), pp. 86–102.

20. Jacques Derrida, "Circumfession," in Geoffrey Bennington and Jacques Derrida, *Jacques Derrida,* trans. Geoffrey Bennington (University of Chicago Press, 1993), p. 58.

21. Derrida, "Circumfession," p. 73.

22. In addition, the notion of species itself has a specific history that dates back to Aristotle, who used *eidos* for the species, in contrast to both the particular (i.e., an individual) and the genus (the animal realm). See Aristotle, "Categories,"

2a14, in *The Categories; On Interpretation*, trans. Harold P. Cooke (Harvard University Press, 1973).

23. The paper in which Derrida works out this line of argument is "The Ends of Man" and was delivered at the conference entitled "Philosophy and Anthropology" held in New York City in October 1968. Derrida was specifically asked to comment on the state of the debate on humanism in post–World War II French philosophy. From the outset, he declares the political implications of his intervention. "It will be recalled that these were the weeks of the opening of the Vietnam peace talks and of the assassination of Martin Luther King. A bit later, when I was typing this text, the universities of Paris were invaded by the forces of order—and for the first time at the demand of a rector—and then reoccupied by the students in the upheaval you are familiar with . . . I have simply found it necessary to mark, date and make known to you the historical circumstances in which I prepared this communication. These circumstances appear to me to belong, by all rights, to the field and the problematic of our colloquium." Jacques Derrida, "The Ends of Man," in *Margins of Philosophy*, trans. Alan Bass (University of Chicago Press, 1982), p. 113.

24. See Jean Paul Sartre, *Being and Nothingness. An Essay on Phenomenological Ontology,* special abridged ed., trans. and with an intro. by Hazel E. Barnes (Citadel Press, 1956), and *The Emotions: Outline of a Theory,* trans. Bernard Frechtman (Philosophical Library, 1948).

25. Derrida is profoundly critical of the French existentialist appropriation of the German tradition, including Hegel, Husserl, and Heidegger, which he sees as less dependent on the anthropological ideal of the essential unity of man. "The anthropological reading of Hegel, Husserl, and Heidegger was a mistake in one respect, perhaps the most serious mistake. And it is this reading which furnished the best conceptual resources to postwar French thought." Derrida, "The Ends of Man," p. 117.

26. Derrida, "The Ends of Man," p. 116.

27. Habermas, "On the Public Use of History," p. 234.

28. Immanuel Kant, "An Answer to the Question: 'What Is Enlightenment?'" in *Kant's Political Writings,* ed. Hans Reiss, trans. H. B. Nisbet (Cambridge University Press, 1970), p. 54.

29. Kant, "An Answer to the Question: 'What Is Enlightenment?'" p. 58.

30. Ayatollah Ruhollah Khomeini, radio announcement, 14 February 1989, in "Fiction Fact, and the *Fatwa,*" in *The Rushdie Letters. Freedom to Speak, Freedom to Write,* ed. Steve MacDonogh (University of Nebraska Press, 1993), p. 130.

31. Kant had firsthand experience with religious prejudice when, with the publication of a treatise on religion, he offended Frederick William II, king of Prussia. Unlike his predecessor, Frederick the Great, William II was not a supporter of religious tolerance. While Salman Rushdie received a worldwide death threat by Iran's theocratic government that included his publishers and translators, Kant was formally asked in a letter to promise that he would never again write on religion. Re-

luctantly, he agreed to the request as "His Majesty's Most Loyal Subject." This qualification allowed him to resume writing on religion after the king's death, which occurred only three years later. The king's death, Kant later explained, absolved him from his promise since he was not that specific king's subject anymore. See Immanuel Kant, *Gesammelte Schriften* (G. Reimer, 1900), 7: 7–10

32. Christopher Norris most lucidly affirmed the need to acknowledge the heterogeneity of postmodernism, warning scholars about the danger of confusing serious and carefully thought out positions with philosophical muddle. Jean Baudrillard is, for Norris, a quintessential representative of the counter-Enlightenment strain that Derrida is wrongly accused to belong to. From Norris's perspective, Baudrillard equates "what is currently, and contingently, 'good in the way of belief' with the limits of what can possibly be known from a critical or truth-seeking standpoint. Of course, this goes along with the wider-fashion for pragmatist, anti-foundationalist or consensus-based theories of knowledge, theories which take it pretty much for granted that 'truth' in any given situation can only be a matter of values and beliefs that happen to prevail among members of some existing 'interpretive community.'" From *Uncritical Theory: Postmodernism, Intellectuals and the Gulf War* (University of Massachusetts Press, 1992), p. 16. On the contrary, Derrida's deconstructive orientation does not repudiate criteria of reference, validity, and truth. Norris's position, which I fully endorse, is that one of the virtues of Derrida's work is that "it raises issues of ethical accountability (along with epistemological questions) which are rendered invisible by the straightforward appeal to reference, intentions, textual authority, right reading, authorial warrant and so forth" (18). This is what allows Norris to make the important claim that Derrida "sustains the impulse of enlightenment critique even while subjecting that tradition to a radical reassessment of its grounding concepts and categories" (17).

33. "Critical theory" was coined by Max Horkheimer in an article entitled "Traditional and Critical Theory" (see Max Horkheimer, *Critical Theory: Selected Essays*, trans. Matthew J. O'Connell and others [Continuum, 1986], pp. 188–252). Published in 1930 when he was director of the Institute for Social Research in Frankfurt, this article presents the views circulating among a group of philosophers and social theorists, including Theodor W. Adorno, Herbert Marcuse, and Walter Benjamin. Habermas is the greatest second-generation interpreter of this line of thinkers, which came to be known as the Frankfurt School. The positions associated with the general heading "Frankfurt School" are anything but homogeneous, both among its various representatives and across time. Furthermore, Habermas's philosophical evolution is marked by different assessments of the positions of the main Frankfurt School theorists. A discussion of this complexity of relations within the general orientation of critical theory would go beyond the scope of this introduction. The literature on this topic is vast. I will just mention two essays by Habermas dedicated to the first generation of critical theorists associated with the Frankfurt School: "The Entwinement of Myth and Enlightenment: Max Horkheimer and Theodor Adorno," in Jürgen Habermas, *The Philosophical*

Discourse of Modernity: Twelve Lectures, trans. Frederick Lawrence (MIT Press, 1987), pp. 106–130, and "Psychic Thermidor and the Rebirth of Rebellious Subjectivity," in *Habermas and Modernity,* ed. Richard J. Bernstein (MIT Press, 1985), pp. 67–77. Also, the reader may gain a general initial orientation from the essay by Albrecht Wellmer, "Reason, Utopia, and the *Dialectic of the Enlightenment,*" in *Habermas and Modernity,* pp. 35–66. Finally, as Adorno was the first-generation critical theorist closest to Habermas, the reader may want to consult, Romand Coles's excellent essay entitled "Identity and Difference in the Ethical Positions of Adorno and Habermas," in *The Cambridge Companion to Habermas,* ed. Stephen K. White (Cambridge University Press, 1995), pp. 19–45.

34. Tolerance, or toleration as some philosophers prefer to define it (see Michael Walzer, *On Toleration* [Yale University Press, 1997]), has also been discussed as an attitude and a virtue rather than a political concept inscribed in modern European history. See *Toleration: An Elusive Virtue,* ed. David Heyd (Princeton University Press, 1996).

35. In the dialogue Derrida extends his rejection of the universality of tolerance to the notion of religion, which, because of its Abrahamic demarcation, cannot be indiscriminately used in all contexts around the world (pp. 117–118, 124–127).

36. In the section of this essay entitled "The Conditions of Tolerance" (pp. 159–162), I explicate Derrida's complex relationship with Kant on matters of tolerance and hospitality.

37. For Derrida, tolerance is a principle that cannot be reduced to an applicable rule. As justice cannot be defined in terms of law since there can be unjust laws, tolerance needs to be kept distinct from specific policy choices or norms. Kant seems to hint at a similar position when he recalls the enlightened attitude of Fredrick the Great of Prussia: "A prince who does not regard it as beneath him to say that he considers it his duty, in religious matters, not to prescribe anything to his people, but to allow them complete freedom, a prince who thus even declines to accept the presumptuous title of *tolerant,* is himself enlightened." See Kant, "An Answer to the Question: 'What Is Enlightenment?'" p. 58.

38. Derrida's critique of tolerance was anticipated by one of the major representatives of critical theory, Herbert Marcuse, in a short essay entitled "Repressive Tolerance" (1965). Along the same lines as Derrida's reservations concerning the notion of tolerance, Marcuse writes, "What is proclaimed and practiced as tolerance today is in many of its most effective manifestations serving the cause of oppression." Herbert Marcuse, "Repressive Tolerance," in Robert Paul Wolff, Barrington Moore, Jr., and Herbert Marcuse, *A Critique of Pure Tolerance* (Beacon Press, 1965), p. 81. Against the classical, liberalistic understanding of tolerance Marcuse advocates "the practice of discriminating tolerance. . . The tolerance which is the life element, the token of a free society, will never be the gift of the powers that be; it can, under the prevailing conditions of tyranny by the majority,

only be won in the sustained effort of radical minorities willing to break this tyranny and to work for the emergence of a free and sovereign majority—minorities intolerant, militantly intolerant and disobedient to the rules of behavior which tolerate destruction and suppression" (123).

Fundamentalism and Terror—A Dialogue with Jürgen Habermas

1. This dialogue took place in December 2001, three months after the attacks of 9/11—*GB.*

2. On November 12, 2001, only two months and one day after the 9/11 attacks, a commercial plane crashed in the Queens section of New York City, killing 260 people aboard and 5 on the ground. The city was completely shut down in fear that the crash was the result of another terrorist attack. Habermas, who was then visiting New York, lived that moment firsthand—*GB.*

3. Here, Habermas refers to the peace talks that took place in late November 2001 near Bonn, Germany. These brought together the political leaders of the Northern Alliance, made up mostly of ethnic Tajiks, Uzbeks, and Hazaras, and three ethnic Pashtun-dominated factions of exiles known as the Rome, Cyprus, and Peshawar groups. The Rome group represented allies of the former king, whose return as even a figurehead leader was rejected by the Northern Alliance—*GB.*

4. See *Süddeutsche Zeitung,* December 19, 2001—*GB.*

5. This is Habermas's acceptance speech for the Peace Prize of the German Publishers and Booksellers Association, which he received in Paulskirche, Frankfurt, in October 2001. The topic of the speech was to be biotechnology. However, as it was delivered a month after the attacks of 9/11, Habermas frames the original topic within the larger issue of the rivalry between what he calls "organized science" and "organized religion": "If one side feared obscurantism and the revival of an atavistic suspicion against science, the other accused the scientistic belief in progress of a crude naturalism that undermines morality. But after 11 September, the tension between secular society and religion exploded in an entirely different way." *Süddeutsche Zeitung,* 15 October 2001—*GB.*

6. Habermas refers to the debate opened by Samuel P. Huntington's article, "The Clash of Civilizations?" published in *Foreign Affairs* in 1993. Huntington's argument is that world politics is being reconfigured along cultural lines so that future conflicts will not be fought for economic or political motives but for the sake of different cultural values. The Islamic, Western, and Asian "cultures" are the ones that Huntington seems to be most worried about. See Samuel P. Huntington et al., *The Clash of Civilizations? The Debate* (Foreign Affairs, 1993); *Many Globalizations. Cultural Diversity in the Contemporary World,* ed. Peter L. Berger and Samuel P. Huntington (Oxford University Press, 2002)—*GB.*

7. Association of South East Asian Nations—*GB.*

Reconstructing Terrorism—Habermas

1. Jürgen Habermas, "What Theories Can Accomplish," in *The Past as Future*, p. 103.

2. Habermas, "What Theories Can Accomplish," p. 102

3. From a communicative perspective, the Gulf War was presented to the public as a media-produced montage; by contrast, 9/11 was narrated and televised in real time. The notion of historic world event, which Habermas uses to specify the uniqueness of 9/11, refers to the simultaneity of reality and representation at the global or world level.

4. Jürgen Habermas, "The Gulf War," in *The Past as Future*, interview by Michael Haller, ed. and trans. Max Pensky (Nebraska University Press, 1994), p. 6.

5. Habermas, "The Gulf War," p. 7.

6. Hans Georg Gadamer defines this interplay "fusion of horizons." With it he states the impossibility of approaching or accounting for a tradition in an immediate or simply neutral way, for the present is the unique angle from which access to the past becomes available. See Hans-Georg Gadamer, *Truth and Method*, translated by Garrett Barden and John Cumming (Seabury Press, 1975).

7. Habermas, "Europe's Second Chance," in *The Future of the Past*, p. 96.

8. Kant, "An Answer to the Question: What Is Enlightenment?" p. 55

9. The social context in which the "public use" of reason is more obviously crucial is the academic setting, which Kant indicates as the ideal model of all political exchanges. "By the public use of one's reason I mean that use which anyone may make of it *as a man of learning* addressing the entire reading public. What I term private use of reason is that which a person may make of it in a particular *civil* post or office with which he is entrusted" (Kant, "An Answer to the Question: What Is Enlightenment?" p. 55). The private use of freedom, which Kant also qualifies with the term "civil," is what we often call "individual discretion," the exercise of individual judgment within the limits set by the legal system as well as by the circumstances of one's own social responsibilities. For Kant, thinking freely in the theoretical sense as well as acting freely at the practical level are distinct and yet structurally interdependent functions: "A high degree of civil freedom seems advantageous to a people's *intellectual* freedom, yet it also sets up insuperable barriers to it. Conversely, a lesser degree of civil freedom gives intellectual freedom enough room to expand to its fullest extent" (59).

While it might appear that a higher degree of civil freedom stimulates intellectual freedom, Kant warns us that this is not always the case. Civil freedom, or discretionary power, requires the exercise of rules. In the absence of rules it becomes a matter of personal preference and not the result of the rational argumentation of one's choice or position. Intellectual freedom or the force of the better argument can thus only flourish in a democratically regulated context in which individuals feel empowered enough to discuss the validity of the rules by which they abide. Kant's point, which Habermas shares, is that if the constraints of legislation allow the citizens to make "public" use of their reason, enlightenment will follow. This way, men and women will fulfill their human nature, whose "original destiny," says Kant, lies "in enlightenment" (59).

10. Habermas, "Yet Again: German Identity—A Unified Nation of Angry DM-Burghers," pp. 86–102.

11. Despite his political affiliation with the Nazis, which clearly affects many of his views, Carl Schmitt remains the subject of a productive debate among young political theorists and philosophers of law. See, for example, Gershon Weiler, *From Absolutism to Totalitarianism: Carl Schmitt on Thomas Hobbes* (Hollowbrook Publishers, 1994); Heinrich Meier, *Carl Schmitt and Leo Strauss: The Hidden Dialogue*, trans. J. Harvey Lomax (University of Chicago Press, 1995) and *The Lesson of Carl Schmitt: Four Chapters on the Distinction between Political Theology and Political Philosophy*, trans. Marcus Brainard (University of Chicago Press, 1998); John P. McCormick, *Carl Schmitt's Critique of Liberalism: Against Politics as Technology* (Cambridge University Press, 1997).

12. If British colonialism delayed the development of this model of sovereign nations around the world, the imperialist tendencies that Schmitt ascribes to both the USSR and to the United States did exactly the same. To gain a sense of the role Schmitt ascribed to Europe, see John McCormick, "Carl Schmitt's Europe: Cultural, Imperial and Spatial Proposals for European Integration, 1923–1955," paper presented at the European University Institute, Florence, 1999, 2000. See also McCormick, *Carl Schmitt's Critique of Liberalism*, chapter 2.

13. Immanuel Kant, *Perpetual Peace*, in *Kant's Political Writings*, ed. Hans Reiss, trans. H. B. Nisbet (Cambridge University Press, 1970), p. 102.

14. Kant, *Perpetual Peace*, p. 105.

15. Kant, *Perpetual Peace*, p. 106.

16. Kant, *Perpetual Peace*, p. 107.

17. In 1974, Pinochet took power in Chile as a result of a coup d'état, after which more than three thousand political opponents were rounded up, interrogated, tortured, and murdered, and a million Chileans went into exile. In 1998, he retired from politics and appointed himself "senator for life." While in London on his annual shopping spree, the general developed serious back pains and was hospitalized. It was there that he was arrested immediately after surgery. He spent the next 503 days under house arrest at an estate outside London while the House of Lords debated whether he should be extradited to Spain to face trial for his crimes. Former prime minister Margaret Thatcher's courtesy visits to Pinochet, who had been Britain's ally during the Falkland Islands campaign, were criticized. Although the House of Lords eventually divested him of the legal immunity that has traditionally protected heads of state from prosecution for crimes against humanity, the general was still allowed to return to Chile for medical reasons. Although deemed

too ill to stand trial in Santiago, he was stripped of his immunity by the Chilean supreme court, declared a criminal, and kept under house arrest.

18. As I point out in the introduction, this is one of the points of maximum disagreement between Habermas and Derrida.

19. This elitist quality, which shines through Kant's conception of the public sphere, is consistent with his reliance on the academic setting as the ideal model of all political exchanges (see fn. 9).

20. Habermas's line of argument intersects a wide-ranging field of discussion on the spectacularization of politics. A classical text in this field is the 1967 book by French sociologist Guy Debord, *Society of the Spectacle* (Black & Red, 1977).

21. This is in contrast to the book's rejection by the two godfathers of Critical Theory, Horkheimer and Adorno, when it was submitted as *Habilitationschrift*, the dissertation for the postdoctoral qualification required of German professors. They both found it insufficiently critical of the potentially destructive forces entailed by Enlightenment thought as well as of its overall illusory character. In this sense, *The Structural Transformation of the Public Sphere* is in line with the "original" theoretical orientation of Critical Theory, not its later post–World War II development, to which Adorno and Horkheimer were adhering at that time. The book was eventually accepted as *Habilitationschrif* at the University of Marburg.

22. See Theodor Wiesegrund Adorno, *Aesthetic Theory*, trans. C. Lenhardt, ed. Gretel Adorno and Rolf Tiedemann (Routledge & Kegan Paul, 1984).

23. Jürgen Habermas, "Further Reflections on the Public Sphere," in Craig Calhoun, ed., *Habermas and the Public Sphere* (MIT Press, 1992), p. 441.

24. Unlike the large majority of European leftist intellectuals, who in 1968 expressed a strong disillusionment toward the democratic institutions in their respective countries, Habermas's appreciation of them never dwindled. Habermas's critical approach to the student movement of 1968 revolved around its ability and willingness to address the trauma of twentieth-century German history. When Inge Marcuse suggested to him that the student movement was confronting for the first time the heritage of fascism in a critical manner, Habermas was outraged because he felt that "for the most part the left-wing students had a rather clichéd notion of fascism. At the time it cost a real effort to assert in public that the organs of state also carried out functions that helped to secure freedom, or that, in spite of everything, the *Bundesrepublik* was one of the six or seven most liberal countries in the world. It was difficult for me to find an audience for such statements, which were intended to introduce a sense of historical proportion." From "The Role of the Student Movement in Germany," in *Autonomy and Solidarity*, ed. Peter Dews (Verso, 1986), p. 231.

25. Jürgen Habermas, *Communication and the Evolution of Society*, trans. and with an intro. by Thomas McCarthy (Beacon Press, 1979), p. 93.

26. See Jürgen Habermas, "What Is Universal Pragmatics?" in *Communication and the Evolution of Society*, trans. and with an intro. by Thomas McCarthy

(Beacon Press, 1979), pp. 1–68. Habermas is not the only philosopher seeking to develop this approach. Karl Otto Apel is another important theorist of universal pragmatics. See his *Understanding and Explanation. A Transcendental Pragmatic Perspective,* trans. Georgia Warnke (MIT Press, 1984). An excellent exploration of universal pragmatics is John P. Thomson's essay, "Universal Pragmatics," in *Habermas. Critical Debates,* eds. John P. Thompson and David Held (MIT Press, 1982), pp. 116–133.

27. Here Habermas follows Wittgenstein's private language argument (see Ludwig Wittgenstein, *Philosophical Investigations,* trans. G. E. M. Anscombe [Blackwell, 1953], sections 243–264). Wittgenstein's and Habermas's point of departure is that for anyone to follow a rule meaningfully, she must be capable of following that rule correctly or incorrectly. "A linguistic expression can only have an identical meaning for a subject who is capable, together with at least one additional subject, of following a rule that is *valid for both of them.* A monadically isolated subject can no more employ an expression with identical meaning than a rule can be followed privately." Jürgen Habermas, *Postmetaphysical Thinking. Philosophical Essays,* trans. William Mark Hohengarten (MIT Press, 1996), p. p. 68.

28. Since "a speaker simultaneously does something in saying something, pronouncing a phrase is neither describing what I am saying that I am doing while I do it, nor declaring that I am doing it: it is simply doing it." Habermas, *Postmetaphysical Thinking,* p. 62. See also J. L. Austin, *How to Do Things with Words* (Harvard University Press, 1962), p. 49.

29. The idea that there is always a better argument clearly presupposes a fundamental epistemological unity—namely, the existence of a single scheme within which all-possible positions can be ranked according to a unity of measurement. Whether there exists, in practice, such unity, is the subject of debate. In believing that this is the case Habermas makes a strong cognitivist claim that pervades his articulation of discourse ethics. This is the ground on which he rejects all brands of moral skeptics, for whom practical reason cannot be decided on rational grounds. While Habermas's take is that even moral problems are capable of being solved in a rational and cognitive way, he does not intend to assimilate the specific phenomenon of "morality" to the domain of cognitivism. There is an obvious difference between "You ought not to be a racist" and "This snow is white." Hence the term "moral truth" presents intrinsic difficulties, as Habermas himself recognizes. For normative sentences he endorses only the redemption of "weaker" validity claims.

30. Jürgen Habermas, "A Reply to My Critics," in John B. Thompson and David Held, eds., *Habermas: Critical Debates* (Macmillan, 1983), pp. 221, 227.

31. Habermas, "Further Reflections on the Public Sphere," p. 442

32. In this sense, Habermas's notion of consensus is sharply distinguished from that espoused by neopragmatists such as Richard Rorty for whom consensus is assumed, quite literally, as the deliberate agreement reached by two or more participants in a discussion or members of a community. See Richard Rorty, "Haber-

mas and Lyotard on Postmodernity," in *Essays on Heidegger and Others. Philosophical Papers, Volume 2* (Cambridge University Press, 1991), pp. 164–176.

33. Habermas specifies the ideal speech situation as a set of formal properties that discursive argumentations should possess if the consensus they produce is to be sharply distinguished from a mere compromise or agreement of convenience. The ideal speech situation has four binding conditions: "First, each participant must have an equal chance to initiate and to continue communication; second, each must have an equal chance to make assertions, recommendations, and explanations and to challenge justifications. Third, all must have equal chances as actors to express their wishes, feelings, and intentions. Fourth, the speaker must act *as if* in contexts of action there is an equal distribution of chances 'to order and to resist orders, to promise and to refuse, to be accountable for one's own conduct and to demand accountability from others.'" Jürgen Habermas, "Wahrheitstheorien," in *Wirklichkeit und Reflexion: Walter Schulz zum 60. Geburtstag*, ed. Helmut Fahrenbach (Neske, 1973), p. 256; see also Seyla Benhabib, "The Utopian Dimension in Communicative Ethics," in *New German Critique* 35 (spring–summer 1985): 83–96, subsequently included in *Critique, Norm and Utopia: A Study of the Foundations of Critical Theory* (Columbia University Press, 1985). The four conditions of the ideal speech situation are, in Habermas's theory of communicative action, the guiding parameters for the formation of beliefs and will in the public sphere.

34. See Samuel P. Huntington, *The Clash of Civilizations and the Remaking of the World Order* (Simon and Schuster, 1998).

35. Habermas, "Further Reflections on the Public Sphere," p. 444.

36. See Jürgen Habermas, *Legitimation Crisis*, trans. Thomas McCarthy (Beacon Press, 1975). Habermas's debate with Luhmann first peaked with the publication of *Legitimation Crisis;* it later rekindled in the 1990s over the new emphasis on law and the legal community vis-à-vis the issue of democratic legitimation that emerges in Habermas's *Between Facts and Norms. Contributions to a Discourse Theory of Law and Democracy*, trans. William Rehg (MIT Press, 1996).

37. Habermas, "Further Reflections on the Public Sphere," p. 446

38. Habermas, *Theory of Communicative Action*, 2: 393–396.

39. Jürgen Habermas, "New Social Movements," in *Telos* 49 (1981): 33–37.

40. See Emile Benveniste, *Problems in General Linguistics*, trans. Mary Elisabeth Meek (University of Miami Press, 1971).

41. The hypothesis that modernity is inoculated with a self-destructive virus was an integral part of a certain section of conservative German culture at the turn of the century, which is not necessarily associated with Weber. See, for example, Oswald Spengler, *The Decline of the West*, trans. Charles F. Atkinson (Knopf, 1926–1928).

42. Jürgen Habermas, "The Dialectics of Rationalization: An Interview with Jürgen Habermas," *Telos* 49 (fall 1981): 7.

43. Habermas, *Between Facts and Norms*, p. 117

44. Max Weber, *The Protestant Ethic and the Spirit of Capitalism* (Scribner, 1958), p. 25.

45. "Emile Durkheim and George Herbert Mead saw rationalized lifeworlds as characterized by the reflective treatment of traditions that have lost their quasi-natural status; by the universalization of norms of action and the generalization of values, which set communicative action free from narrowly restricted contexts and enlarge the field of options; and finally, by patterns of socialization that are oriented to the formation of abstract geoidentities and force the individuation of the growing child." Jürgen Habermas, *The Philosophical Discourse of Modernity,* trans. Frederick G. Lawrence (MIT Press, 1987), p. 2.

46. Habermas, *The Philosophical Discourse of Modernity,* p. 16.

47. Habermas, *The Philosophical Discourse of Modernity,* p. 7.

48. Whether a culture can make this choice without any historical support remains an open question. The example of Islamic cultures, which cannot count on the historical experience of democratic revolutions or anything comparable to an Enlightenment-type moment in their recent history—a point that Derrida makes in this volume—speaks directly to the question I am raising, although it does not provide a definitive answer.

49. Habermas's acceptance speech for that prize, entitled "Modernity: An Incomplete Project" (in *Postmodern Culture,* ed. Hal Foster [Pluto, 1883], pp. 3–15), exhibits an interesting and almost eerie relationship with the scope of this book: not only did the city of Frankfurt decide twenty-two years later to award the very same prize to Derrida, but the date of his own acceptance was September 22, 2002, only eleven days after the attacks against the World Trade Center and the Pentagon.

50. Habermas, preface, *The Philosophical Discourse of Modernity,* p. ix.

51. This is a highly idiosyncratic definition, conflating postmodernism and poststructuralism, used only in the German context. Habermas and Manfred Frank seem to remain faithful to it even after repeated criticism. See Frank, *What Is Neostructuralism?* trans. Sabine Wilke and Richard Gray with an intro. by Martin Schwab (University of Minnesota Press, 1989).

52. There are only a few but excellent sources to explore the complexity of the relationship between Habermas and Derrida as political thinkers. See Christopher Norris, "Deconstruction, Postmodernism and Philosophy: Habermas and Derrida," in *Derrida: A Critical Reader,* ed. David Wood (Blackwell, 1992), pp. 167–192; idem, "Deconstruction and the Unfinished Project of Modernity," in *Deconstruction and the Unfinished Project of Modernity* (Routledge, 2000), pp. 48–74. Another very thoughtful and balanced assessment of the relationship between Derrida and Habermas as political thinkers can be found in the work of Bill Martin, "What Is at the Heart of Language? Habermas, Davidson, and Derrida," in *Matrix and Line. Derrida and the Possibilities of Postmodern Social Theory* (SUNY Press, 1992), pp.65–124; idem, "Transformations of Humanism," in *Humanism and Its Aftermath. The Shared Fate of Deconstruction and Politics,* (Hu-

manities Press, 1995), pp. 47–137, esp. pp. 47–72. Tightly aligned on the Habermasian side lies Thomas McCarthy, *Ideals and Illusions: On Reconstruction and Deconstruction in Contemporary Critical Theory* (MIT Press, 1991).

53. My general indication that Benjamin is a key figure for the relation between Derrida's and Habermas's political frameworks is supported by Beatrice Hanssen in her excellent book *Critique of Violence Between Poststructuralism and Critical Theory* (Routledge, 2002).

54. Habermas, *The Philosophical Discourse of Modernity*, p. 11. Habermas quotes from Walter Benjamin, "Theses on the Philosophy of History," in *Illuminations* (New York, 1969), p. 263.

55. Habermas, *The Philosophical Discourse of Modernity*, p. 14.

56. In our dialogue, Derrida confirms Habermas's reading: this call cannot be articulated discursively at all; but, unlike Habermas, Derrida thinks that this is its very virtue.

Autoimmunity: Real and Symbolic Suicides— *A Dialogue with Jacques Derrida*

1. In English in the original—*trans.*

2. Although I have modified a few formulations and tried to clarify or develop an argument or two, I have followed as faithfully as possible the transcript of a conversation that took place in New York on October 22, 2001. I thought it important to respect not only, of course, the order in which the questions were asked, but also the tone and everything related to the constraints of oral improvisation. All the references and notes were obviously added after the fact. They seemed to me necessary to help the reader develop further, should he or she so desire, the analyses that the time and genre of the interview forced me to cut short—*JD.*

3. In English in the original—*trans.*

4. Derrida is referring to the address he delivered on September 22, 2001, in Frankfurt when he accepted the Adorno Prize. See *Fichus: Discours de Francfort* (Éditions Galilée, 2002)—*GB.*

5. The Japanese attack on Pearl Harbor, Hawaii, on December 7, 1941, was not conducted on the continental soil of the United States. Because Hawaii was a U.S. territory it could be said that the attack was not technically speaking an attack on U.S. "national territory." Hence, 9/11 was the first attack on U.S. national territory since the War of 1812—*GB.*

6. In fact, the reflections of certain architects about the Twin Towers had already taken into account the possibility (premonitory, fateful, spectral, engraved in the stone of the unconscious) of a "terrorist" attack several years before September 11, 2001. In his remarkable (and as yet unpublished) article, "Target Architecture: Destination and Spectacle before and after 9–11," Terry Smith speaks of an "architecture of trauma" and cites the commentary of Joseph B. Juhas on Yamasaki, in *Contemporary Architects*, 3d ed., ed. Muriel Emanuel (St. James Press, 1994). The

text is from 1994! "The WTC had been our Ivory Gates to the White City . . . Though, at least when viewed from a distance, the WTC still shimmers—it is at the moment thoroughly besmirched by its unfortunate role as a target for Middle-East terrorism." And further: "Of course, any 'stability' based on the suppression of open systems becomes an element in a drama which in its own term *must* terminate in cataclysm. In an allegorical sense, the vast, twinned doubled ghostly presence of WTC presents a sepulchre from which ghosts will not rise on the day of cataclysm as the resurrected dead: rather as a tombstone it prophecies the raising of Golems and Zombies."

Without considering the architectural problems (urban, technical, political, aesthetic) posed by the World Trade Center, we must at least recognize this: the affect, indeed the affection, the love that it inspires (a love whose double specter has invaded my own memory, for example, for more than ten years) cannot exclude the at least unconscious feeling of a terrible vulnerability, the fascinating exposure of these two enormous vertical bodies to heinous or loving aggression. How can one not "see" these two towers without "seeing" them in advance, without foreseeing them, slashed open? Without imagining, in an ambiguous terror, their collapse? That is to say, their sublime sublation in the filmed archive, a film more unforgettable than ever for the grieving, idealizing memory of the worldwide-ization (*mondialisation*) of the world.

In addition to so many other necessary analyses, must we not reconstruct the phantasms—both conscious and unconscious—of those who decided and then put into action, in their heads and in their airplanes, right up to suicide, the slashing open and collapse of this double tower? Archaic and forever puerile, terribly childish, these masculine phantasms were in fact fed by an entire technocinematographic culture, and not only the genre of science fiction. Which is obviously not enough, indeed quite the contrary, to make of the September 11 attack a "work of art," as Stockhausen had the very bad taste to do in order to lay claim, through this cheap provocation, to a pittance of originality—*JD*.

7. For example, in "Faith and Knowledge: The Two Sources of 'Religion' at the Limits of Reason Alone," trans. Samuel Weber, in *Religion*, ed. Jacques Derrida and Gianni Vattimo (Stanford University Press, 1998). In analyzing "this *terrifying* but inescapable logic of the *autoimmunity of the unscathed* that will always associate Science and Religion," I there proposed to extend to life *in general* the figure of an autoimmunity whose meaning or origin first seemed to be limited to so-called natural life or to life pure and simple, to what is believed to be the purely "zoological," "biological," or "genetic":

> It is especially in the domain of biology that the lexical resources of immunity have developed their authority. The immunitary reaction protects the "*indemn-ity*" of the body proper in producing antibodies against foreign antigens. As for the process of auto-immunization, which interests us particularly here, it consists for a living organism, as is well known and in short, of protecting itself against its self-protection by de-

stroying its own immune system. As the phenomenon of these antibodies is extended to a broader zone of pathology and as one resorts increasingly to the *positive* virtues of immuno-depressants destined to limit the mechanisms of rejection and to facilitate tolerance of certain organ transplants, we feel ourselves authorized to speak of a sort of general logic of *autoimmunization.* It seems indispensable to us today for thinking the relations between faith and knowledge, religion and science, as well as the duplicity of sources in general. (73 n.27)

I underscored "terrifying" in the above in order simply to suggest a hypothesis: since we are speaking here of terrorism and, thus, of terror, the most irreducible source of absolute terror, the one that, by definition, finds itself most defenseless before the worst threat would be the one that comes from "within," from this zone where the worst "outside" lives with or within "me." My vulnerability is thus, by definition and by structure, by situation, without limit. Whence the terror. Terror is always, or always becomes, at least in part, "interior." And terrorism always has something "domestic," if not national, about it. The worst, most effective "terrorism," even if it seems external and "international," is the one that installs or recalls an interior threat, *at home* [in English in the original—*GB*]—and recalls that the enemy is *also always* lodged on the inside of the system it violates and terrorizes.

8. The figure of the "loop" suggests itself here for at least *three reasons*:

1. The re-productive re-transmission "loops," as we say, the same televised images of a "live transmission" (the slashing open and then collapse of the two towers, a film that runs and reruns ceaselessly on screens across the entire world; this repetition compulsion at once confirms and neutralizes the effect of this reality insofar as a frightening, frightened, terrified pain becomes bound up with an unavowable elation [jouissance], one that is all the more unavowable, uncontrollable, and irrepressible insofar as it operates at a distance, neutralizing the reality and thus keeping it at bay.

2. The loop is also meant to refer to the circular and narcissistic specularity of this painful elation, of this climax, terrified by the other and terrified to discover that there is something we are elated about seeing here, terrified to find ourselves allaying our terror by our voyeurism.

3. Finally, the loop is the vicious circle of a suicide that avows itself in denial, that detests itself by attesting to itself, that gets carried away in its own testament, that bears witness to what will remain, on the side of the "suicides" (the hijackers and the "missing" cadavers), *without witness—JD.*

9. The evil of this traumatism has to do with the fact that the *aggression is not over.* It's not all over and done with, that's the first conclusion. Of all the reflections that might be inspired by the televisual media coverage of the event, I would like to underscore the following, which I don't think has really been discussed. By

establishing a complete and continuously accessible archive, reproducible at every moment, in a loop, we give ourselves the comforting feeling that "it's over." It's over because it's archived, and anyone can visit the archive! The archive, the archive effect, reassures (the matter is closed! it's all on record! it's all been recorded!), and we then do everything to monumentalize the recordings, thereby reassuring ourselves that the dead are dead; it won't happen again because it already took place. We thus deny the irresistible foreboding that the worst has not taken place, not yet. Thus to the visual archive there have recently been added the recordings made by an amateur radio operator in San Francisco of all the messages exchanged by police and firemen during the collapse of the Twin Towers. The only testimonies that escape archivization are those of the victims, not of the dead or of the cadavers (there were so few) but of the missing. By definition, the missing resist the work of mourning, like the future, just like the most recalcitrant of ghosts. The missing of the archive, the ghost, the phantom—that's the future—*JD.*

10. In English in the original—*trans.*

11. In Thomas Hobbes, *Leviathan*, ed. with an intro. by C. B. Macpherson (Penguin, 1968), 11: 27—*GB.*

12. See Walter Benjamin, "Critique of Violence," in *Reflections,* trans. Edmund Jephcott (Schocken Books, 1978), pp. 277-300—*GB.*

13. See, for example, Noam Chomsky, *9-11* (New York: Seven Stories Press, 2001), pp. 43-54. These pages contain some interesting comparative statistics concerning the number of victims of "September 11" and the number of victims of other relatively recent "state terrorist" attacks.

The official definitions of terrorism by American institutions never define the *status* (individual or collective, national or international, state or nonstate related) of the *origin* or the *author* of acts of terrorism. The author can thus be an individual, a group of individuals—or a state. The American government defines not terrorism but what it calls "terrorist activity" as

any activity which is unlawful under the laws of the place where it is committed (or which, if committed in the United States, would be unlawful under the laws of the United States or any State) and which involves any of the following: 1. The hijacking or sabotage of any conveyance (including an aircraft, vessel, or vehicle) [in other words, terrorism would begin with auto theft; the fact that this is clearly not what the text means suggests that the concept is confused]. 2. The seizing or detaining, and threatening to kill, injure, or continue to detain, another individual in order to compel a third person (including a governmental organization) to do or abstain from doing any act as an explicit or implicit condition for the release of the individual seized or detained. 3. A violent attack upon an internationally protected person (as defined in section 1116(b)(4) of title 18, United States Code) or upon the liberty of such a person. 4. An assassination. 5. The use of any (a) biological agent, chemical agent, or nuclear weapon or device, or (b) explosive or firearm (other than for mere personal monetary gain), with intent to endanger, directly or indirectly, the safety of one or more individuals or to cause substantial damage to property. 6. A threat, attempt, or conspiracy to do any of the foregoing." (cited in Chomsky, 123–124)

This legal "definition" (which includes nuclear weapons, I note, in support of my earlier argument) is loose enough to include practically any crime, any "assassination." It is thus hardly rigorous. One can no longer see the difference between a nonterrorist crime and a terrorist one, national terrorism and international terrorism, an act of war and an act of terrorism, military and civilian. If the restriction specifying "other than for mere personal monetary gain" seems to exclude from terrorism armed robbery, bank holdups, or mob activities, it is in contradiction with what defines as terrorist anything that aims to "cause substantial damage to property."

The definition given by the *United States Code Congressional and Administrative News*, 98th Cong., 2d sess., Oct. 19 1984, vol. 2, par. 3077, 98 STAT.2707 [West, 1984]) is shorter but essentially the same, with one important difference: it speaks of violent acts intended to intimidate or coerce a "civilian" population or intended to influence the policy of a government by intimidation or coercion. The "civilian" population is also named in the definition given by the FBI. And the international dimension is explicitly mentioned in the definitions published by the CIA and the Departments of State and Defense—*JD*.

14. The meaning I have attached here to the words "utopia" and "aporia" suggest to me, as I reread this, an ironic and somewhat playful interpretation of a particular statement made by Heidegger in the *Der Spiegel* interview. ("Only a God Can Save Us," trans. Maria P. Alter and John D. Caputo in *Philosophy Today* 20, no. 4 [winter 1976]: 267–284).

How could anyone deny that the name "god to come" just might be suitable for an ultimate form of sovereignty that would reconcile absolute justice with absolute law and thus, like all sovereignty and all law, with absolute force, with an absolute saving power? One will always be able to call "god to come" the improbable institution I just invoked above by speaking of a "faith in the possibility of this impossible thing." This "faith" is not foreign to that universal structure I referred to elsewhere as a "messianicity without messianism" (in *Specters of Marx: The State of the Debt, the Work of Mourning, and the New International* [Routledge, 1994], for example, and in numerous other places). Of course, such a fanciful interpretation would have shocked Heidegger. This is certainly not what he "meant." And he would have seen (though wrongly, in my view) the irony of my discourse as symptomatic of everything he denounced under the categories of the juridical and the technological, indeed of the "technological state." In the same interview, he in fact answered with a brief "yes," without further comment, without leaving any room for discussion, firmly and clearly, the following question of the journalist: "You obviously envisage, and this is what you have already said, a world movement which either leads up to or has already led up to the absolute technological state?—Yes" (277).

It goes without saying that nothing resembles an "absolute technological state" less than that which I have spoken about under the terms *faith, messianicity, democracy to come,* the untenable promise of a *just international institution,* an institution that is strong in its justice, *sovereign without sovereignty,* and so on—*JD.*

15. Allow me to refer to a couple of texts that develop this theme: *Of Spirit: Heidegger and the Question,* trans. Geoffrey Bennington and Rachel Bowlby (University of Chicago Press, 1991); *The Other Heading,* trans. Pascale-Anne Brault and Michael Naas (Indiana University Press, 1992); "Khôra," trans. Ian McLeod, in *On the Name,* ed. Thomas Dutoit (Stanford University Press, 1995), pp. 87–127; and "Faith and Knowledge."—*JD.*

16. To complicate and refine my use here of these words, allow me to refer once again to "Faith and Knowledge."—*JD.*

17. Derrida here refers to a G8 meeting that took place in Genoa, Italy, July 20–22, 2001. The countries involved in the meeting were Italy, Canada, France, Germany, Japan, Russia, the United Kingdom, and the United States. The summit was called to discuss topics such as poverty reduction and environmental protection. Violent protests were held by the anti-globalization movement, which resulted in extensive damage to buildings, cars, and shops. Several protesters were wounded, some critically, and one died—*GB.*

18. See, for example, "As If It Were Possible, 'Within Such Limits,'" in *Negotiations: Interventions and Interviews, 1971–2001,* ed. and trans. Elizabeth Rottenberg (Stanford University Press, 2002), pp. 343–370; *Papier machine: Le ruban de machine à écrire et autres réponses* (Galilée, 2001); "The University Without Condition," in *Without Alibi,* ed. and trans. Peggy Kamuf (Stanford University Press, 2002), pp. 202–237—*JD.*

19. In "The University Without Condition," Derrida writes: "I am keeping the French word *mondialisation* in preference to 'globalization' or *Globalisierung* so as to maintain a reference to the world—*monde, Welt, mundus*—which is neither the globe nor the cosmos" (23). Despite the reservations expressed by Derrida in this and other texts, *mondialisation* has sometimes been translated here as "globalization" when the discussion concerns what is commonly called, in the English-speaking world and even beyond, "globalization"—*trans.*

20. See "The University Without Condition"; and Jeremy Rifkin, *The End of Work: The Decline of the Global Labor Force and the Dawn of the Post-Market Era* (G. P. Putnam's Sons, 1995)—*JD.*

21. See Walter Benjamin, "Critique of Violence"; and Jacques Derrida, "Force of Law: The 'Mystical Foundation of Authority,'" trans. Mary Quintance, in *Cardozo Law Review* 11, nos. 5–6 (1990): 920–1045—*JD.*

22. See "Plato's Pharmacy," in *Dissemination* (University of Chicago Press, 1981), pp. 61–171—*JD.*

23. Voltaire, "Tolerance," in *The Philosophical Dictionary* (E. R. Dumont, 1901), 10: 100–112; *la tolérance* has been translated throughout as "tolerance" rather than "toleration," this latter being the term used in the standard English translation of Voltaire, because while Derrida begins, like Voltaire, with the more restrictive notion of "religious toleration," he invokes other registers of "tolerance" that "toleration" does not usually cover—*trans.*

24. See Jacques Derrida and Anne Dufourmantelle, *Of Hospitality*, trans. Rachel Bowlby (Stanford University Press, 2000); and Jacques Derrida, *On Cosmopolitanism and Forgiveness*, trans. Mark Dooley and Michael Hughes (Routledge, 2001)—*JD.*

25. Jacques Derrida, *Adieu to Emmanuel Levinas*, trans. Pascale-Anne Brault and Michael Naas (Stanford University Press, 1999)—*JD.*

26. ". . . keine phantastische und überspannte Vorstellungsart des Rechts." From Immanuel Kant, *Perpetual Peace*, trans. Lewis White Beck (Bobbs-Merrill Co., 1957), pp. 20, 23—*JD.*

27. See Derrida, *On Cosmopolitanism and Forgiveness* and *Politics of Friendship*, trans. George Collins (Verso, 1997), in particular, on the theme of fraternity —*JD.*

28. Derrida, *Politics of Friendship*—*JD.*

29. See Derrida, "Force of Law: The 'Mystical Foundation of Authority'" —*JD.*

30. See book 1, chapter 3, "Of the Drives of Pure Practical Reason," in Immanuel Kant, *Critique of Practical Reason*, trans. Lewis White Beck (Macmillan Publishing Co., 1993), esp. pp. 84–85—*JD.*

31. In this sentence, Derrida plays with the French word *devoir*, which is repeated three times: "Il faut donc devoir au-delà du devoir, devoir aller au-delà du droit . . . "—GB.

32. " . . . differences in the interest of reason [ein verschiedenes Interesse der Vernunft]," in Immanuel Kant, *Critique of Pure Reason*, "Appendix to the Transcendental Dialectic: The Regulative Employment of the Ideas of Pure Reason," trans. Norman Kemp Smith (St. Martin's Press, 1965), p. 547—*JD.*

33. Kant, *Critique of Pure Reason*, p. 533. We know the decisive and enigmatic role played by the *als ob* in all of Kant's thought; but this is especially true of the regulative idea. It is a matter of considering the connections between phenomena "*as if* they were the ordinances of a supreme reason, of which our reason is but a faint copy [als ob sie Anordnungen einer höchsten Vernunft waren, von der die unsrige ein schwaches Nachbild ist]," *Critique of Pure Reason*, p. 555; "*as if* this being, as supreme intelligence, acting in accordance with a supremely wise purpose, were the cause of all things [als ob diese als höchste Intelligenz nach der weisesten Absicht die Ursache von allem sei]," (561). "For the regulative law of systematic unity prescribes that we should study nature *as if* systematic and purposive unity, combined with the greatest possible manifoldness, were everywhere to be met with, *in infinitum* [als ob allenthalben ins Unendliche systematische

und zweckmässige Einheit bei der grossmöglichen Mannigfaltigkeit angetroffen wurde]" (568).

To continue in the direction I indicated above by distinguishing a "reservation" from an "objection," I would say that I am sometimes tempted to make "as if" I had no objections to Kant's "as ifs." See "The University Without Condition," where I treat the difficult question of the "as if" in Kant—*JD*.

34. "The second regulative idea of merely speculative reason is the concept of the world in general [Die zweite regulative Idee der bloss speculativen Vernunft ist der Weltbegriff überhaupt]," *Critique of Pure Reason*, p. 558—*JD*.

35. See Jacques Derrida, *The Gift of Death*, trans. David Wills (University of Chicago Press, 1995), p. 8off—*JD*.

Deconstructing Terrorism—Derrida

1. Derrida's choice for the term "deconstruction" emerges out of his dialogue with Martin Heidegger. As Derrida vividly remembers, "When I chose that word, or when it imposed itself on me . . . I think it was in *Of Grammatology*, I wished to translate and adapt to my own ends the Heideggerian word *Destruktion* or *Abbau*. Each signified in this context an operation bearing on the structure or traditional architecture of the fundamental concepts of ontology or of Western metaphysics. But in French *destruction* too obviously implied an annihilation or a negative reduction much closer perhaps to Nietzschean "demolition" than the Heideggerian interpretation or to the type of reading that I proposed." Jacques Derrida, "A Letter to a Japanese Friend," in *Derrida and Différance*, ed. David Wood and Robert Bernasconi (Northwestern University Press, 1988), p. 1.

2. See Donald Davidson, "On the Very Idea of a Conceptual Scheme," in *Inquiries into Truth and Representation* (Clarendon Press, 1984). The possibility that Davidson's notion of a conceptual scheme may be connected to the project of deconstruction, as defined by Nietzsche, Heidegger, and Derrida, has been advanced by Rorty. See Richard Rorty, "The Contingency of Language," in *Contingency, Irony, Solidarity* (Cambridge University Press, 1989), pp. 3–22.

3. Jacques Derrida, *The Other Heading: Reflections on Today's Europe*, trans. Pascale-Anne Brault and Michael B. Naas (Indiana University Press, 1992), p. 79.

4. Jacques Derrida, "On Forgiveness," in *Cosmopolitanism and Forgiveness*, trans. Michael Collins Hughes (Routledge, 2001), p. 28.

5. Derrida, "On Forgiveness," p. 28.

6. As an example of this orientation among theorists of the Holocaust, Derrida mentions Vladimir Jankélévitch. See the latter's *L'Imprescriptible: Pardonner? Dans l'honneur et la dignité* (Éditions du Seuil, 1986).

7. Derrida, "On Forgiveness," p. 38.

8. Derrida, "On Forgiveness," p. 39.

9. Derrida, "On Forgiveness," p. 39.

10. Derrida, "On Forgiveness," p. 55.

11. Boundaries are more central to philosophy than to most other disciplines, since drawing conceptual boundaries is not just what philosophy does but what philosophy is about. The boundaries of philosophy itself have been the main philosophical question since the Greeks. Throughout the twenty-five hundred years of its history, philosophy has never stopped examining and justifying its boundaries, drawing them over and over again in different ways. The incessant negotiation about the demarcation of their field of inquiry has made some philosophers suspect that it is wrong to presume that philosophy, indeed, names "something." For these thinkers philosophy is not to be understood as a field but as a method of analysis applicable to various things, material and conceptual. This was how René Descartes in the seventeenth century hoped to solve the question of philosophy's fuzzy boundaries. He conceived philosophy as a sound "constructive" technique, granting the edifice of knowledge to be erected on rock-solid foundations. This, of course, did not dispense him from having to draw boundaries between genuinely secure foundations and shaky ones. Descartes's way to solve this further step was to apply "methodic doubt" to all beliefs after which he invited us to retain only those that are indubitable. Descartes was convinced that methodic doubt of the sort that he presented in the *Meditations* would make the distinction self-evident, thus relieving us from the burden of having to draw the boundary between dubitable and indubitable beliefs: if I think, I exist, because whether I am awake, asleep and dreaming, or intoxicated and hallucinating, I am still involved in some kind of thought. As has been incessantly discussed since Descartes, this argument is less definitive than it seems. First, it has an oddly temporary quality in that I can be sure that I exist only as long as I am entertaining that very thought. Second, producing objective knowledge of the kind that only unshakeable foundations grant impinges on still something else: the knower's ability to prove the existence of God.

12. My example is not meant to exclude the fact that there might have been the same exact prejudice on the part of narrow-minded Westerners convinced that the Wall was the boundary between good and evil, justice and injustice.

13. See Sigmund Freud, *Beyond the Pleasure Principle,* trans. and ed. James Strachey, with an intro. by Gregory Zilboorg (Norton, 1961).

14. Heidegger elaborated on the notion of event (*Ereignis*) throughout his career. It appears in relation to death as an example of an event that does not let us appropriate it. See Martin Heidegger, *Being and Time,* trans. Joan Stambaugh (SUNY Press, 1996), part 2, section 1, 50–52. Later on, Heidegger distinguished between event and product (*Erzeugnis*; see Martin Heidegger, introduction to *"What Is Metaphysics?"* in *Pathmarks,* ed. William McNeill [Cambridge University Press, 1998], 82–96) and used the notion of event emerging from that distinction to describe the way in which genuine historical events involve a change in mentality and understanding of the world, so that they cannot be considered mere happenstances; see Martin Heidegger, *Identity and Difference,* trans. Joan Stambaugh

(Harper & Row, 1974). The notion of event pervades Heidegger's work during the last two decades of his life, where it is associated with the essence of poetry, language, and even thought. See Martin Heidegger, *Contributions to Philosophy: From Enowning*, trans. Parvis Emad and Kenneth Maly (Indiana University Press, 1999).

15. No doubt, it all depends on the standard of measurement. The attack against the World Trade Center in New York City certainly ranks among the greatest assaults against a major metropolitan area in a time of peace.

16. See David Hume, *An Enquiry Concerning Human Understanding* (Hackett, 1997), sections 2–3.

17. Both Derrida and Habermas mention Schmitt in our dialogues, who is a controversial figure because of his affiliation with the Third Reich. I expand on Habermas's reading of Schmitt in my essay on Habermas, "Reconstructing Terrorism," in particular, in the section entitled "From Classical Internation Law to a new Cosmopolitan

18. This argument brings Derrida close to Habermas, who does not discuss terrorism in relation to autoimmune processes but does affirm the systematic risk of overreaction and delegitimation that liberal democracies are exposed to in their fight against terrorism.

19. See Emile Benveniste, *Indo-European Language and Society*, ed. Jean Lallot, trans. Elisabeth Palmer (University of Miami Press, 1973).

20. Jacques Derrida, "Faith and Knowledge. The Two Sources of Religion at the Limits of Reason Alone," in *Acts of Religion*, ed. and with an intro. by Gil Anidjar (Routledge, 2002), pp. 72–73.

21. Derrida sees the survival of the connection between these two elements of the religious experience in the Catholic practice of carrying statues and marionettes in processions, usually to honor a saint. He asks, isn't the phallic, "as distinct from the penis and once detached from the body, the marionette that is erected, exhibited, fetishized and paraded in processions?" Derrida, "Faith and Knowledge," p. 83. In this way, the pagan dimension of religion, advanced by Cicero's etymological study of the word, can be assimilated into the Tertullian interpretation of it as indebtedness.

22. Derrida, "Faith and Knowledge," p. 74.

23. Derrida, "Faith and Knowledge," p. 53.

24. Derrida, "Faith and Knowledge," p. 56.

25. This expression recurs in many places, including in our dialogue. For a full treatment of it, see *Specters of Marx: The State of the Debt, the Work of Mourning, and the New International*, trans. Peggy Kamuf, with an intro. by Bernd Magnus and Stephen Cullenberg (Routledge, 1994).

26. Derrida, "Faith and Knowledge," p. 56.

27. Derrida points out that the word "community," which derives from the Latin *communitas*, also has the notion of obligation, expressed by the Latin term *munus*. "Immune" has the same derivation except that, contrary to "community,"

it means exempted or freed from obligation, originally in a fiscal sense. "This exemption," as Derrida remarks, "has been transported into the domains of constitutional and international law (parliamentary or diplomatic immunity), but it also belongs to the history of the Christian Church and to canon law; the immunity of temples also involved the inviolability of the asylum that could be found there (Voltaire indignantly attacked this "immunity of temples" as a "revolting example" of "contempt for the laws" and of "ecclesiastical ambition.""). Urban VIII created a congregation of ecclesiastical immunity: against taxes and military . . . and against police searches." Derrida, "Faith and Knowledge," p. 80.

28. Derrida, "Faith and Knowledge," p. 69.

29. Derrida, "Faith and Knowledge," p. 88.

30. Kant, *Religion within the Limits of Reason Alone*, trans. and with an intro. and notes by Theodore M. Greene and Hoyt H. Hudson (Open Court, 1934).

31. Cited in Derrida, "Faith and Knowledge," p. 49.

32. Derrida, "Faith and Knowledge," p. 50.

33. See Gianni Vattimo, "The Trace of the Trace," in Jacques Derrida and Gianni Vattimo, *Religion* (Stanford University Press, 1996).

34. The theme of hospitality took center stage in Derrida's political interventions as he confronted the subject of cosmopolitan rights as applied to immigrants, refugees, and asylum seekers. In the mid-1990s, this subject became the center of a public debate in France known as *Sans Papiers*. According to Hannah Arendt, the modern history of minorities coincides with the history of those without a state (*Heimatlosen*), without a home, those who have been deported or displaced by economic or political emergencies. As it necessarily implies either the repatriation or the naturalization of the foreigner, it represents the limitations of a hospitality that is granted either by the sovereign from whom the refugee is fleeing or by the sovereign extending refuge. In this sense, the right to asylum is a legal equivalent to the concept of tolerance

35. It is feasible to interpret the double register of the conditional and the unconditional as a version of Kant's transcendental argument. Scholars have explored this possibility, which, if accepted, considerably dispels Habermas's preoccupation that basing politics on its "beyond" is irreconcilable with democracy. See Rodolphe Gasché, *The Train in the Mirror. Derrida and the Philosophy of Reflection* (Harvard University Press, 1986); Richard Rorty, "Is Derrida a Transcendental Philosopher?" originally in *Yale Journal of Criticism* 2, n. 1 (1989): 207–217; and Giovanna Borradori, "Two Versions of Continental Holism," in *Philosophy and Social Criticism* 26, n. 4 (2000): 1–22.

36. Jacques Derrida, "Force of Law: The 'Mystical Foundation of Authority,'" in *Deconstruction and the Possibility of Justice,* ed. Drucilla Cornell, Michel Rosenfeld, and David Gray Carlson (Routledge, 1992), pp. 5–6.

37. Walter Benjamin, "Critique of Violence," in *Selected Writings*, volume 1, 1913–1926, ed. Marcus Bullock and Michael W. Jennings (Harvard University Press, 1996), pp. 236–53.

38. For the sake of simplicity, this formulation brushes over the fact that Derrida deconstructs the distinction between foundational and conserving types of violence and asserts that they are mutually enveloped, or "differentially contaminated." The foundation of all states inaugurates a new law in violence, a violence that, to affirm itself, needs to enforce and preserve itself.

39. Derrida, "Force of Law: The 'Mystical Foundation of Authority,'" p. 14.

40. See Jacques Derrida, "Declarations of Independence," trans. Tom Keenan and Tom Pepper, *New Political Science* 15 (1986): 7–15.

41. Derrida, "Force of Law: The 'Mystical Foundation of Authority,'" p. 35.

42. Derrida, "Force of Law: The 'Mystical Foundation of Authority,'" p. 16.

43. Derrida, *The Other Heading: Reflections on Today's Europe,* p. 9.

44. Derrida, *The Other Heading: Reflections on Today's Europe*, p. 39.

45 I discussed the notion of responsibility toward memory in the context of Habermas's critique of Benjamin's messianic perspective at the end of my previous essay on Habermas.

46. Derrida, *The Other Heading: Reflections on Today's Europe*, p. 29.

47. Jacques Derrida, "From Traumatism to Promise," in *Points . . . : Interviews, 1974–1994,* ed. Elisabeth Weber, trans. Peggy Kamuf et al. (Stanford University Press, 1995), p. 383.

INDEX